I WENT TO PRISON SO
YOU WON'T HAVE TO

I WENT TO PRISON SO YOU WON'T HAVE TO

A LOVE AND LAWFARE STORY IN TRUMP LAND

PETER NAVARRO
AND BONNIE BRENNER

War Room Books

Visit our website at www.skyhorsepublishing.com.
Please follow our publisher Tony Lyons on Instagram @tonylyonsisuncertain.

10 9 8 7 6 5 4 3 2

Library of Congress Cataloging-in-Publication Data is available on file.

Hardcover ISBN: 978-1-64821-201-7
eBook ISBN: 978-1-64821-202-4

Cover design by Brian Peterson
Cover photo credit: Getty Images

Printed in the United States of America

To my parents, Audrey and Harold, whose lives taught me what Love
and Devotion truly look like. To my sister, Merri—I thank you for
your relentless support and for carrying forward that same devotion
we were so fortunate to witness and inherit from Them.
And a special thanks to Dale, Clay, and Mikael, who eased my burden with
extraordinary kindness, hospitality, and grace during the toughest of times.
—*Bonnie Brenner*

To all of you in Milwaukee, whose thunderous welcome reminded
me what freedom sounds like—and whose warmth showed the world
what bravery looks like. Thank you for bringing me home.
And to Sergio Gor, Don Jr., Dave Bossie, Steve Bannon, Robert O'Brien,
Sean Hannity, Stanley Woodward, Greg Kelly, Dick Morris, Mike Flynn,
Clay Clark, Matt and Ginger Gaetz, and Chris Ruddy—who had my back
when it was against the wall.
—*Peter Navarro*

Contents

FOREWORD

The book you hold in your hands is more than just a memoir—it is a clarion call, a manifesto against weaponized injustice, and a testament to the unbreakable bonds forged in the fires of political persecution. Peter Navarro's story, shared with gripping honesty and raw emotion alongside his beloved Bonnie Brenner, is not merely a prison diary, but an epic saga about love, loyalty, and the relentless fight against an ever-encroaching Deep State.

I understand Peter's journey all too intimately, for I too have felt the cold steel of Biden's America around my wrists, and the stark reality of freedom stripped away not by justice, but by vengeance masked as law. Our paths, parallel and intertwined, reveal a haunting truth: When the ruling elite decide to silence voices that challenge their narrative, no one is safe—not even those closest to the highest office in our nation.

Peter Navarro, a scholar, patriot, and devoted public servant, was thrust behind bars not for crimes against his country, but for steadfastly honoring the Constitution and the privilege of the Presidency itself. His story speaks loudly to the dangerous precedent set by a ruthless regime willing to destroy anyone in its quest to dismantle the MAGA movement and punish the family and loved ones of those who dare oppose their radical agenda.

Behind prison walls, Peter did not break. He did not even bend. Instead, he turned his trials into triumph, his suffering into strategy. His tireless battle to implement President Trump's First Step Act from within, documented in these incendiary (and often humorous) pages, is nothing short of heroic—fighting for the forgotten men and women left behind by a corrupt system.

Navarro's powerful narrative reminds us that injustice is not abstract; it has a face, a name, a family—and often, the collateral damage lands squarely upon those who love us most. This book is as much Bonnie's story as Peter's, a poignant reminder that the Deep State's vengeance leaves no heart untouched.

At its core, Navarro's narrative is also a timeless love story. It is the story of a man and woman united not only by romance, but by purpose, resilience, and shared sacrifice. When the regime comes for American patriots, whether it's Navarro, myself, or countless others, it is our families, our beloved, who feel the pain most deeply. Bonnie's courage, grace, and unwavering loyalty under weaponized partisan fire are a testament to the strength and endurance that define the very heart of our movement.

Ultimately, Peter Navarro's journey—from incarceration to vindication—is a crucial chapter in the fight for our nation's soul. His battle is our battle. His victory, our victory. His story demands we confront the weaponization of our justice system, and fiercely defend the principles of freedom and fairness upon which America was founded.

Read this book. Share its truths. And let Peter Navarro's powerful testimony ring out clearly: we must stand resolute against weaponized injustice, ensuring that America remains not only the land of the free, but a nation where justice, truth, and freedom are never imprisoned.

—Stephen K. Bannon

HUCK POST 1:
Biden Regime Corruptus, Nashville Interruptus
June 3, 2022—Let the Lawfare Games Begin

> *Be careful, Peter. These people can hurt you.*
> —Dave Bossie, Former Chief Investigator
> House Committee on Government Reform and Oversight

Brother Dave, I wish I had been more careful.

On the morning of June 3, 2022, my fiancée and I woke up at the crack of dawn. She rose with great excitement because we were going to Nashville to meet the great Mike Huckabee. As for me, I was looking forward to appearing on Mike's TV show. Yet, I had opened my eyes with a more subtle sense of dread as the walls of Joe Biden's weaponized Department of Justice seemed to be closing in on me.

Months earlier, I had received a congressional subpoena from the United States House Select Committee to Investigate the January 6th Attack on the United States Capitol a.k.a. the "J6 Committee"—or what former president Donald Trump likes to call either the "witch hunt" or "Un-Select Committee."

Upon receipt of this subpoena, I had been commanded to testify before the committee and produce documents. However, President Trump had invoked executive privilege and instructed me not to comply; and the ultimate result was a contempt of Congress charge by the House on a strict Democrat party line vote. Now, Joe Biden's Department of Justice and his puppet attorney general, Merrick Garland, had to decide whether to indict and prosecute me. This left me in that strange limbo where I was waiting for a possible other shoe to drop.

Nonetheless, the show must go on. I had a new White House memoir called *Taking Back Trump's America* to promote, and there was no better place to do that than on the Mike Huckabee Turner Broadcasting Network show.

Plus, I love Mike. He's truly an American icon as well as one of the most sincere politicians I have ever met.

So, off I was about to go from the sanctuary of my DC swamp apartment with the aforesaid subtle dread and a fiancée who couldn't have been happier in that moment. But first, a little breakfast in the nook of my Market Square apartment, which stands commandingly a full ten floors above Pennsylvania Avenue with one of the most gorgeous views in Washington, DC, of the Capitol, Washington Monument, Lincoln Memorial, and peeker view of the White House grounds in full panorama.

Frankly, this luxury condo at more than five grand a month was out of my fixed income retiree price range. But I had rented the gem for what I promised myself would be a short time as a bucket-list reward for four years of sixteen-hour working days seven days a week in the Trump White House.

Now, here's the funny thing about that breakfast nook. Sitting there with my fiancée on bar stools, I could see right across Pennsylvania Avenue to the south to two of the bureaucracies that would eventually wind up trying to put both me *and* Donald Trump in prison—the National Archives and the Department of Justice.

And get this: I could also see across 7th Avenue to the west, literally across the street and about a fifty-yard field goal from my balcony—did I mention I was a field goal kicker in high school?—the very same agency that had slapped me with a subpoena a couple weeks earlier and, little did I know right then, was about to put me in leg irons.

I'm talking of course about the FBI—the Federal Bureau of Investigation, or, as we like to say in Trump Land, the Federal Bureau of Intimidation.

Yes, you can't really make that up. I could see from my Market Square apartment the very same three government agencies that would work overtime to deprive me of my liberty and drain me financially.

After breakfast, my Sweet Pixie and I grabbed our carry-on bags for the quick two-day trip, walked out the door, and grabbed an Uber for the short trip out to Reagan National Airport. As we got on the move, my mood brightened as my fiancée looked absolutely gorgeous that morning, and I felt blessed to be with her.

We met just after I had left the White House in the hallway of my old apartment building at the Lansberg just across the street from my new digs at Market Square. She was moving into the apartment next door to my old one as I was moving out, and my first thought upon seeing that smiling pixie face was *Damn, why am I moving out of this place?* This is a dream come true.

Of course my second thought, only slightly tongue-in-cheek, was that if a petite and beautiful blonde-haired, blue-eyed, sweet little thing with a lithe body and the best legs in Washington, DC, moves into the apartment next door to a senior White House official, she damn well might be a honeypot spy sent by the Chinese or the Russians to seduce me and then extract whatever secrets I may have had from my White House days.

Go ahead and laugh. But during the first week I was in the White House, that's exactly the kind of training I got: Don't trust anybody on the outside, and there are no such things as coincidences. And I knew damn well it certainly wouldn't be the first time that something like that happened—just ask the hapless congressman Eric Swalwell.

At any rate, I had a running joke about our first meeting that I would tell our friends whenever I got a chance to do so—and always get a little punch in the arm from my fiancée. I'd say I finally figured out she wasn't a Chinese spy when it took months before we actually shared a bed together. Yet another lesson that good things are worth waiting for.

As soon as we arrived at the airport, my dread returned. As we entered the departure level and headed towards the security checkpoint, I walked warily along, keeping my eyes peeled for any trouble in the form of FBI agents ahead. I felt in my bones something like an indictment and arrest was coming. I just didn't know if it would be that day.

Two days earlier, I had sent a long email letter to Patricia Aloi, the Department of Justice apparatchik who had sent me a threatening letter about the case. My prompt response sought a *modus vivendi*—a way around any possible arrest that would allow me to comply with the congressional subpoena without violating either the Constitution or my oath of office.

And here was the key point I made in my pleading to Aloi: After receiving the congressional subpoena, I had consistently and repeatedly said the same thing, first to the J6 Committee and then to the DOJ. The president had invoked executive privilege, and by law it was not my privilege to waive.

Most importantly, I also stated to the J6 Committee attorneys that I would be happy to testify if President Trump waived the privilege. To that end, I had repeatedly asked the J6 committee to contact the president and his attorneys to seek a waiver of the privilege. But they never did.

In my modus vivendi letter to Aloi, I asked her and the DOJ to do the very same thing and reiterated that my hands were tied because of my duty to this country, to the Constitution, and to my oath of office.

Tellingly, I also requested Aloi to contact an attorney, Adam Katz. While I had not put him on formal retainer yet, Adam had kindly offered to help mediate the situation with the Department of Justice, and I strongly encouraged Aloi to make the contact, if for no other reason than to arrange my surrender if the DOJ did indeed intend to arrest me. Such a voluntary surrender was the *normal* procedure for white-collar crimes such as the one that I was alleged to have committed—a simple voluntary and peaceful surrender without guns.

I should note here from the very outset that I did not view my failure to comply with the J6 subpoena to be a "crime" at all. The Department of Justice itself had a clear policy against compelling the testimony of a senior White House official and alter ego of the president that it had maintained *for more than 50 years*.

Since no senior White House official had ever been charged with contempt of Congress in the history of our Republic, I believed I was on pretty solid ground that the DOJ would indeed not prosecute. But, this was of course the Biden regime and an out-of-control Democrat party which was doing everything it could to stop Donald Trump and his advisers from ever sitting in the Oval Office again. So, as one of Trump's closest aides as well as a friend, of course I was in jeopardy.

As my fiancée and I walked through the airport, nothing, however, seemed amiss. I didn't see anybody following us. When we got to the security checkpoint and they saw my identification, I thought they might take me away, but all went very smoothly there as well. No second looks from the guard. No nothing.

At the gate, I finally relaxed. We still had almost an hour before boarding—both my fiancée and I like to get to airports early in case of contingencies. So we spent much of that time talking about what we might do in Nashville—music, restaurants, Grand Ole Opry visit, museums, too much fun. And as we bantered, we played a spirited game of backgammon on my iPad—I'm a little better strategically, but she often beats me because of a rare talent to throw double sixes.

And here, I can truly say that that hour with my fiancée as we waited to get on the Nashville Huckabee Express was one of the happiest moments of my life. The sun was streaming through the window, we were both feeling the excitement of the trip, and I truly did think it might be a way for both of us to leave my troubles behind, at least for a few days.

That happy moment would of course turn into six of the worst hours I have ever spent in my life. After the ticket agent at the gate scanned our tickets, we entered the gangway between the boarding area and the aircraft door and began walking.

As I looked up from my fiancée's beautiful eyes and smiling face, I looked towards that aircraft door and saw none other than lead FBI agent Walter Giardina with his partner, both strapped with handguns.

As they began walking towards me, I stopped, turned to my fiancée, held her gently in my arms and told her, "Be strong now." While I had prepared her for this possibility, I could feel the shudder of fear that went through her; and for a brief moment, as I felt my deep love for her, I felt like I was holding a wounded bird.

I thought to myself: *Do whatever the puck you want to me, but you have no right to terrorize this woman with this kind of bullshit.*

Then the thought quickly passed as she steeled herself; and together, we faced Joe Biden's music as three more FBI agents swarmed in behind us to block any escape back into the airport—like I would be foolish or cowardly enough to run from these Good Nazis.

They were not particularly gentle with me. When I asked Giardina to call my attorney several times, he simply confiscated my phone and told me no. Simultaneously, the three FBI agents who had ambushed us from behind took my fiancée and perp-walked her back out into the airport and out to the entrance to the airport to find her way home.

Thank god, nobody recognized her. Thank god, one of her bosses didn't see her from a waiting lounge as they were getting ready to get on a plane.

And did I mention yet the absurdity of this? As I told you, the FBI is literally *across the street* from me. Yet rather than simply come knock on my door as they had done a few days earlier to deliver a subpoena, they let my fiancée and I travel all the way to the airport so they could conduct their show raid and look tough on CNN—CNN had the damn news before the handcuffs even got on me.

These Good Nazis would do the same thing months later to President Trump at Mar-a-Lago. The only difference would be instead of handguns, the FBI agents—there would be many more than the ones that grabbed me—would have automatic rifles. This is what your tax dollars go to fund.

As for me, I was about to meet the ghost of John Hinckley.

HUCK POST 2:

Handcuffs, Leg Irons, and the Ghost of John Hinckley

June 3, 2022—My First Day of Jail, 655 Days Before Huck Goes to Prison

We cannot let our respect for the FBI blind us from the fact the FBI has sometimes come up short of our expectations.
—Orrin Hatch

It is an interesting thing to suddenly lose one's freedom. It would be very interesting on this particular day.

The first thing the FBI does when they grab you is pull your arms behind you and put you in handcuffs. No matter how gently they might try to do it, it's still going to take a pretty good pull on your shoulder sockets. And in this case, they weren't particularly gentle.

Of course, I no doubt appeared to these five armed FBI agents to be a very desperate and dangerous hombre. After all, I was seventy-four years old, I weigh 145 pounds soaking wet and top out at a gargantuan 5'7".

Once handcuffed, they walked me out the back door of the gangway and down some portable steps onto the tarmac where they had a tiny car waiting to transport me first back to the FBI—remember it's across the street from my apartment—and then eventually to the courthouse where I was destined for a little bit of dungeon duty that day.

At the time, Walt Giardina seemed to actually be a kind of pleasant fellow when not armed to the teeth. He presented as the quintessential "Good Nazi" just "doing his duty" without the courage to stand up to the FBI and DOJ.

I would subsequently learn, however, from internal DOJ and FBI documents that Giardina was every bit a bad FBI seed who would willingly and willfully abuse power to advance partisan interests—think James Comey, Peter Strzok, Lisa Page, for example here. Giardina belongs right with them.

Such behavior is in all likelihood an enduring vestige of an organizational culture of fear and intimidation that dates back to the days of J. Edgar Hoover. Let's remember that when Hoover wasn't cross-dressing and putting on lipstick for his own private cameras, he was abusing the FBI to spy on American icons like Martin Luther King and John and Bobby Kennedy and to gather dirt on as many congressmen as possible to make sure he would never get fired from his job.

The fact of the Lord Acton matter here is that power has always corrupted, and the absolute power that the FBI wields has always corrupted that anything-but-heroic agency absolutely. But enough of that soapbox.

Once I got to the FBI, I got my first taste of a truly evil FBI prick. Big bald dude with bulging biceps who told me to keep my mouth shut and do exactly what I was told. *Whatever*, thought I.

At least this dumb brute gave me my first of what would be three good laughs of my FBI day. It was indeed at least semi-hilarious, as said brute couldn't work his machine well enough to actually take my fingerprints. He had to do it about six times and then begged for help from a female agent with a smaller gun and no biceps at all—I notice stuff like that. It was indeed comic.

My second laugh of the day would quickly follow as Walt and his partner, who I nicknamed Clouseau, put me back in their Keystone Cops car and off we went to the District Court a few blocks away on Constitution Avenue where I would be arraigned.

Here, it is well worth noting again that it would have been the simplest thing in the world for me to walk the few blocks down that morning from my apartment and simply report to the District Court and thereby avoid all the guns, terrorism of my fiancée, and CNN theatrics at the Reagan airport. But of course, that would miss the Biden regime's weaponized point—perp walk and punish a Trump official to boost the reputation of the Biden regime in the eyes of the adoring left wing of this country.

At any rate, the laugh came when these two FBI clowns couldn't figure out just how to get into the District Court building. They had to circle the building a couple of times while they made some frantic phone calls.

Finally, they found the magic engine at the back of the building which opens up into a big freight elevator that swallows up your car and takes you down to the basement and its dungeon. Ah yes, let the humiliating strip search begin.

First, it was off with my tie and belt so I wouldn't hang myself in the cell. Don't worry, I certainly wasn't that desperate yet. Second, there was the bend over and strip search. Hardly necessary unless you wanted to intimidate the prisoner, but hey, I was just along for their rough ride.

Third, and this is where the fun really began, they put me in a pair of fifteen-pound leg irons. Yes, the sight of that triggered a John McEnroe moment in me—"You cannot be serious?"

Of course, they assured me that this was just "procedure" that everybody got, so how could they treat me any differently?

Fair enough. Why should I, as a former White House official and senior advisor to the president, who had saved hundreds of thousands of lives and created hundreds of thousands of jobs and who had now been charged with a misdemeanor, be treated any better than the usual felonious parade of rapists, thieves, murderers, drug addicts, burglars, pimps, and hookers they usually get to process in the court's dungeon?

Hey, I get that. I've always been a man of the people. But all I could wonder at the time is whether this was what they were going to do to Donald Trump if they ever got their hands and handcuffs on him.

At any rate, my last comic moment of the day would come when they walked me out of the strip search area towards my cell. Here I am in leg irons, having been told to follow this big 6'2" guard with a long and brisk stride down a long and dimly lit hallway; at best, all I could do is shuffle off to Buffalo to the cell awaiting me at a snail's pace.

At any rate, when I finally catch up with the guy after almost pulling a hamstring—nice enough fellow who I thanked for his service sincerely, by the way—he leads me into what would be my jail cell for the next several hours.

For whatever reason, he then goes out of his way to tell me that this was the same jail cell that John Hinckley sat in after he shot Ronald Reagan.

For the life of me, I couldn't find the moral equivalence there—me, a senior White House advisor who had failed to comply with a congressional subpoena out of duty to my country and my oath of office versus a deranged dude with a hard-on for Jodie Foster who thought trying to take out one of the best presidents in modern history would get him laid. I literally laughed out loud to the silence that now engulfed me.

As I sat there, I got my first taste of prison life. Cold draft—the air, not beer kind. Hard bench without padding. A crapper without a seat or toilet paper. Dim light and not a window in sight. No food at your fingertips—I was famished by this time, as I had planned to eat lunch on the plane. The total absence of any real colors of the rainbow. Just a drab, dismal world without clocks, where you are free—and I use the term as ironically and cynically as possible—to contemplate your navel or the cosmos.

Thought I: *If it doesn't kill you or bore you to death, it makes you stronger.*

Well F these Bidenites and jackboots, I thought, *I choose stronger. So take your best shot.* And that's exactly what they did.

It would take more than six hundred days. But eventually the bastards did indeed put me in a federal prison.

PIXIE POST 1:
Prologue
March 15, 2024—Four Days Before Huck Enters Prison

Pixie here, and when my Ever Huck came out of his office for breakfast that morning, I knew immediately something was wrong. Instead of a beautiful warm "Sweet Pixie" hello, my lover was quiet, bordering on somber.

As my Ever Huck approached, he said nothing. When he reached me, he just took me gently into his arms and simply whispered, "Our time has come."

I knew what he meant. We had been preparing for this day for months now. And now it was here.

The love of my life who had taken so very long to find whispered in my ear he would be reporting to a prison in Miami in just a few days and would be leaving me for what would be the longest four months of my life.

I thought back on the irony and symmetry of the moment. This month was the three-year anniversary of that beautiful and exciting morning we had met in March of 2021.

My Huck was moving out of the apartment in Washington, DC, next to mine as I was moving in. Even in a pair of gym shorts and raggedy T-shirt—that was my first glimpse of the true Huckleberry Finn he is—I recognized him as one of Trump's top lieutenants.

My Huck had been a favorite of both me and my sister Merri during the Trump administration. Whenever she or I saw him on Fox or CNN or Newsmax, we would call and tell the other—"Navarro's on."

Merri and I loved the direct way he talked to the American people and we loved his fierceness. Yet, it would be that fierceness I had seen on TV that would hold me back in the first year of our relationship from loving him the way I do now.

Frankly, his fierceness scared me. But it should not have.

Over time, I would come to know my Huck as the gentle, sweet soul he so often is, at least when he's not defending a president or trying to save the world. Yet, on that day that I met him, I never imagined we would be so deeply in love three years later and that he would be saying goodbye on his way to prison.

I did not cry that day. I had already shed enough tears. For I had been with my Ever Huck through all of the thick and thin of his legal battles.

I had been by his side at the Reagan National Airport that day, boarding a plane for a beautiful trip to Nashville when they took us down at gunpoint and put him in handcuffs in front of me and later in leg irons in a basement jail. The FBI had done that for no good reason other than that they could.

Now, as Huck held me ever so tightly this somber morning, all I said to him were three words. They weren't "I love you." That was a given.

What I said to my Ever Huck was, "We got this." As it would turn out, we did.

HUCK POST 3:
Three Books in One

*Prison time is like a book with blank pages. You're the one who
decides whether to write something or leave it empty.*
—Alexei Navalny (1976–2024)

*First time that I saw you, you took my breath away.
Might not get to Heaven but I walked with an angel that day*
—"Joy of My Life," Chris Stapleton

This book is Volume One in my memoirs about my love and lawfare journey through the American justice and prison systems.[1] It focuses primarily on the 120 days I spent in prison using the construct of three interrelated and interwoven stories.

The **first story** is about what it's like to go to prison. What do you eat? How do you sleep? Where do you while and work away your time? What are the inmates like? How did the warden and guards treat you? What kind of rape, shiv, medical care, and other dangers may lurk? What and who sustained you and helped you through the experience?

This first story is written from the perspective of a former senior White House advisor who quite unexpectedly finds himself in prison simply for protecting George Washington's doctrine of executive privilege and defending the constitutional separation of powers. As you will see, I was the only inmate in the prison found guilty of a simple *misdemeanor*. All of the more than two hundred other inmates were felons; and that speaks volumes in and of itself about the partisan politics that put me behind bars.

As a sidenote, I was also the third oldest inmate in the joint—you'll

---

1 Volume Two will function as both the prequel and sequel to the prison story. This Volume, which will only be published after my appeal is finally resolved in the higher courts, will focus on the time periods both before my entry into a Miami federal prison during my arrest, trial, and conviction and after I am out of that prison fighting my case on appeal up the ladder to what should be the U.S. Supreme Court. While Volume One is a book for the masses and ages, Volume Two will appeal more to those interested in the legal ins and outs of my landmark Constitutional case, as well as the lawfare politics surrounding it. So stay tuned for that.

meet distinguished Vietnam vet Del Gowing, the patriarch of the place who should have been out almost a decade ago, as well as a mini-Bernie-Madoff type.

And of course, I was one of the very few inmates who could legitimately claim to be innocent of the crime I was convicted of, and certainly the only inmate who served in the White House.

It was an interesting experience to say the least. I am happy to share it with you. I hope it never happens to you unless, of course, you committed a crime for which you deserve a just punishment.

Spoiler alert: I didn't get a MAGA tattoo in prison or any other kind of tattoo. Just COVID too many times because of the sardine conditions.

The **second story** in this book is about a five-billion-dollar waste of taxpayer money and the massive Bureau of Prisons scandal I uncovered.

In a nutshell, the Bureau of Prisons and its sprawling "prison industrial complex" is refusing to fully implement both the 2008 Second Chance Act and Donald Trump's 2018 First Step Act. This ironic breaking of federal law by the bureaucrats assigned to punish people who do indeed break the law is keeping more than sixty thousand primarily nonviolent, first-time offenders in prison for up to two years longer than the law dictates.

As you will see in much more detail, the price tag of these delays adds up to $5 billion. These costs start with the *direct* costs of unnecessary incarceration at a price tag of $60K a year per inmate. They include the indirect costs associated with inmates not working and paying taxes and their families drawing down on welfare benefits like food stamps and housing subsidies because their breadwinner is in the slammer—never mind the human misery suffered by the inmates and their families.

The **third story** is my favorite and I hope it is yours. This is the love story between Huck and Pixie as they do time together, he in prison and she doing the time with him on the outside.

Pixie is my nickname for the love of my life, Bonnie. While Bonnie is a beautiful name, if you ever have the joy of meeting my Sweet Pixie, you'll know exactly why, from her sprightly glow, her nickname fits like a glass slipper.

As for who the heck is Huck, that's Pixie's nickname for me. I'm the guy who doesn't always comb his hair, prefers a shirt sleeve to a napkin, loves the open ocean, and generally prefers the road less traveled.

Even now at the tender age of seventy-five, I still don't quite want to be "sivilized." If you know that literary reference of Mark Twain, you'll know why Pixie calls me Huck.

These three prison stories are woven together through two types of "postcards" and five types of documents. Most of the postcards are "Huck Posts" from me, the principal author, Peter Navarro.

But many of the postcards are "Pixie Posts," offering a look through the prison looking glass from the perspective of my Sweet Pixie.

As for the five types of documents, the principal Huck Post narrative is told through my daily journal. I would keep this *pour memoir* journal during the 120 days I would spend behind bars.

I would keep this journal with the same kind of discipline and attention to detail featured in my first White House memoir, *In Trump Time*—but without the advantage of my voice dictation software or even a word processor.

As for my Sweet Pixie, she kept a similar, although less extensive, diary. It serves as the fodder for her Pixie Posts.

The second type of document comes from the various articles I would write and the interviews I would grant during my prison stay. It took me more than a month to figure out how to broadcast my voice outside my prison walls, chained in as I was. But the pen is indeed mightier than the sword, and these communications would turn out to be very important in my efforts to out the Bureau of Prisons scandal I would unearth.

The sometimes-lyrical elements of some of our email correspondence represent my third source of inspiration—and are a source of information for you, dear reader.

Finally, there are these two important bookends: The transcript of the press conference I held the day I went into prison on March 19, 2024, which appears early in the book. This speech straight from the head and heart provides a very useful, and I hope moving, summary of the legal and constitutional issues that I was fighting—and continue to fight on appeal as *United States v. Peter Navarro* heads to the Supreme Court. In effect, it lays the predicate, as they say in the law, for what will follow.

To end the book, I will reprise my speech delivered on the stage at the Republican National Convention in Milwaukee the night of the day I was released from prison on July 17, 2024. That night I was greeted with thunderous applause by an appreciative audience, and at the end of the speech, my Sweet Pixie came on stage with me and stole the show as I gave her what would come to be famously called "the kiss" and "the twirl."

Of course, there is an Epilogue with all the surprising twists you might imagine in Trump Land.

At any rate, I think you will find the first story about what it is like in prison to be fascinating. I will take you behind bars and behind the scenes like few can.

I hope the second story will make your blood boil and motivate you into the kind of political action necessary to put an end to the particular prison scandal I uncovered during my incarceration. Despite my best efforts, both the Bureau of Prisons and the U.S. Congress refused to act to end this scandal, but I will continue to hammer both until justice and fiscal responsibility is done.

As for the third story, it is a love story that can only happen through the courage and wisdom of a fine and tough Republican woman—are you listening, Mark Cuban?

Tough and fine my Sweet Pixie is, and so much more. She is the "angel" and "joy of my life" I was forced apart from by partisan lawfare jackals for four long months.

At least now, as Chris Stapleton has sung it and Pixie and Huck have danced to it, I am blessed to walk with this angel every day.

And to steal another lyric from another song that my Sweet Pixie and I love to twirl to, "I can't wait for the rest of my life."

Can you guess the song?

—Peter Navarro
Palm Beach Florida
December, 2024

HUCK POST 4:
A Chilling Order to Report to Sunny Miami

March 1, 2024
Peter K. Navarro
3200 South Ocean Blvd
Unit D501
Palm Beach, FL 33480
Re: Notice of Designation and Date to Report

Dear Mr. Navarro:

As ordered by the Court, you are hereby instructed to report to FCI Miami Satellite Camp, located at 15801 SW 137th Avenue, Miami, FL., 33177, (305) 259-2100, on Tuesday, 3/19/24, no later than 2 p.m.

Please do not take personal items such as clothes, toothpaste, razor, soap, etc. because they will be provided by the institution. Additional personal items may be purchased through the institution's commissary. To obtain additional pertinent information about the institution, please go to www.bop.gov and search the above facility for the custody and care instructions.

Should you have any questions or concerns, please contact me or the institution.

Sincerely,
Sondra A. Rhodes, Supervising United States Probation Officer

The email came like a gut punch as I was checking my Proton Mail account before breakfast. Even though I had my stomach muscles tensed—hell, everything in my body was tense—the email took my breath away. At least for a moment. This was getting realer by the day—I had to self-surrender to a prison in Miami within a matter of days.

The funny part, and I wouldn't get the joke until a few days after I got to prison, was that all of the two hundred or so inmates and the fifty or so staff knew I was coming to the Miami prison *weeks* before I did.

In fact, they had been told a big "political guy" would arrive soon; it wasn't hard to figure out from the news what my name was, and they all were given orders to start helping to clean up the prison's act. For those several weeks before I arrived, it was full Potemkin-village, lipstick-on-a-pig speed ahead with a Miami prison makeover.

From sunup to sundown, the inmates steam cleaned the roofs, fixed at least some of the plumbing, repaired and painted the walls, replaced broken light bulbs, scrubbed the sidewalks, got at least some of the ugly black mold off the shower tiles. They even killed some of the roaches—but the rats in the kitchen just laughed at them.

And speaking of the kitchen, and this would work to my great advantage, the prison's food started getting a whole lot better too—to the point where the guys would actually thank me for it after I arrived.

The joke, of course, was, "If this food is better now, just how much worse could it have been before the Trump guy got here?"

What puzzled me about the email was the location I had been ordered to report to. Miami? Huh?

I had figured they would put me somewhere around Washington, DC, probably in Maryland, given my DC Court conviction. Then, I realized my Miami locale—one of the toughest and worst run in the system—was because my official residence was in nearby Palm Beach.

After breakfast, I told my Sweet Pixie the bad news. All she said was, "We've got this. Let's get you packed." My kind of girl. The best kind of sweetheart.

HUCK POST 5:
Third Time Is My Pixie Charm
March 10, 2024—Nine Days Before My Incarceration

Wanna catch up some time?
—Huck's opening line to Pixie

Late in life, I met my "third time's a charm" Sweet Pixie, and the only really hard thing about my doing time in defense of the Constitution will be spending some of the few remaining months of my life apart from my Sweet Pixie.

You might think it's only four months I'll be gone, but the average lifespan for an American male is seventy-six. I'm just about seventy-five as I write this. That means unless I beat that national average of seventy-six, I will spend four months and the last 25 percent of my expected life behind bars, away from the woman I love so deeply.

Yet, even if I last another five or ten or even twenty years, it's unlikely those years will be the kind of quality years I might have had if I had not lost this Pixie time in prison. Prison is no country for old men; it will take its physical toll and there's nothing I can do about it.

That said, I'm certainly not going to whine or cry at this juncture about what Nancy Pelosi, Bennie Thompson, Joe Biden, Merrick Garland, and cadres of Democrat lawfare scoundrels and jackals have done both to me and our broader system of what today passes as injustice. Yet, I do want to let these scoundrels know this:

Once you shoot at political targets like me and Steve Bannon and Donald Trump and Jeff Clark and John Eastman and Mark Meadows and Stephen Miller and Dan Scavino and Rudy Giuliani and Walt Nauta and Christina Bobb, it's the loved ones who also will take the hit. And that is why all those with names like Bragg and Willis and Smith must ultimately be held accountable.

In my case, it will be my Sweet Pixie who will spend time with me in this barrel. I know she will never complain, and she will always have my back. I know this because she's tougher than any of those lawfare jackals responsible for putting me in prison—the long list also includes names like Raskin, Schiff, and every Democrat congressman in the 2022 House: Graves, Crabbe, and Aloi in the Biden Department of Justice; Mehta, Pillard, and Millett in the DC Federal Courts; and the Republican turncoats and scum otherwise known as Liz Cheney and Adam Kinzinger.

As I write this heading into prison, I know that Pixie and I will be back dancing in 120 days to the songs of Michael Bublé, Ronnie Milsap, Ray Charles, Chris Stapleton, and Etta James.

I know we'll be back walking the beach to Benny's, watching the pelicans fly, and waiting for the sea turtles. And as our little secret, I know I'll be drinking Pixie's sweet coffee soon.

I can't wait. I just hope as I head into prison, Heaven can wait and that I truly will see my Sweet Pixie on the other side.

That uncertainty, sadness, and pending separation is why they call it prison.

HUCK POST 6:
When a Camp Is Not a Camp
March 15, 2024—Four Days Before My Incarceration

The day I got the news I had to report to prison had indeed been jarring. The only silver lining seemed to be that I was reporting to a facility in warm weather not far from my home.

Of course, after just a little research, I was quickly disabused of any notion that I might truly land at some cushy Club Fed. To get the real picture, you have to start with the fifty shades of American prisons.

Even though I had technically been sent to a "minimum-security prison"—a "camp" in the lexicon of the Bureau of Prisons—Miami FCI is not really a *minimum-security* prison. Nor is it by any stretch of the imagination a "camp."

Rather, Miami is a hybrid of a minimum and low-security prison, while the adjunct "low-security" prison in Miami (about one hundred yards from the "camp") operates much more as a *medium-security* prison.

As to why these definitions matter, it's partly about the company I was going to be keeping. Yes, there would be no shortage of relatively benign white-collar criminals and scam artists. But at Miami FCI, there would also be no shortage of more hardened criminals who had worked their way down through good behavior over time to a minimum-security prison.

As to what the definition of the different kinds of prisons matter, it is also about the facility itself as well as the procedures followed.

The biggest tell in the alleged "camp" con game would be the high fences I would find strewn with razor wire. Bureau of Prison camps aren't supposed to have such barriers. However, in Miami, urban legend has it that a rogue warden put the barriers up using inmate labor—another no-no—and so the Miami camp, to help inmates make a smoother transition to society, quickly became much more of an animal cage.

Another symptom of this non-camp Miami camp is its lack of employment opportunities off the prison site. In days gone by, inmates had been able to work at venues like the adjacent Miami Zoo, the Everglades National

Park, and the Coast Guard. Now, however, job opportunities along with any offsite training opportunities are all but nonexistent.

Did I mention that some inmates can work across the street for a Federal Prison Industries government corporation known as UNICOR? In Miami, the UNICOR facility boxes up military uniforms for a whopping salary of 25 cents to 50 cents an hour.

Irony alert: For all the years I have criticized Communist China for its slave labor camps and all the prison-made crap that winds up in Walmart, I never thought I'd be in an American prison that does the same damn thing.

Finally, in Miami, there are the prison guards and procedures (lockups, shakedowns, et al.) that are straight out of a higher security prison, not a camp. It's an organizational culture completely contrary to giving inmates at minimum-security prisons more freedoms as a gradual transition to a half-way house and then out in the world to be our neighbors.

That's why they call this particular Miami "camp" a true prison. This was no "Club Fed"—I was in for some very hard times.

HUCK POST 7:
Shipping Out
March 17, 2024—Two Days Before My Incarceration

It's D-Day. Departure day. The day I will fly out from Washington, DC, without my Sweet Pixie, down to my two homes in Florida—my regular residence and what will be my new home on March 19 in Miami at a federal prison.

The trip starts out poorly. Lookie-loos clog the roads leading to Reagan Airport for the cherry blossoms blooming early, and a fifteen-minute ride turns into a tense forty-five-minute stop and go, with me all the while having to worry about missing the most important flight of my life.

The gods of irony then have a big laugh on me. Once at the airport that I busted my ass to get to, I discover my flight has been delayed. A 3 p.m. flight turns into a 6:30 p.m. departure. That's the difference between a serene walk at sunset on the beach and a relaxed dinner versus a late-night eggs-and-toast arrival.

I put the delay to good use. In the airport, I set up my laptop and finished the two big tasks needed for my intake into the prison on Tuesday. This is first and foremost a contact list of no more than thirty people I will be able to phone or email.

I also must fill out a prison exit form to immediately qualify for what everybody has been telling me—falsely and tragically, as it will turn out—will be a thirty-day reduction in my four-month sentence to ninety days under President Trump's 2018 First Step Act.

Here, because of a loophole in that law, I actually will not be eligible for such an early release. I won't know this for more than a month; and when I find out why—stay tuned for that post—the reality will be one of the heaviest blows I will feel behind bars.

HUCK POST 8:
Getting My Affairs in Order
March 18, 2024—The Day Before Incarceration

*We will stop your benefits if you are convicted of a criminal offense
and are confined for more than 30 continuous days.*
—Social Security Administration

Sure wish somebody had told me about that *before* I went into the slammer.
Losing my Social Security for four months would cost me about $15,000,
and to mix metaphors, that curveball threw a big wrench into all of the
planning I had done for my finances in the frantic days before I reported to
my Miami prison. And so much for that "free room and board" crap.

Truth be told here, one of the biggest family challenges when you go
to prison is figuring out how to get all your bills paid. Just because you are
about to get free room and board at taxpayers' expense doesn't mean your
mortgage, utilities, and insurance bills suddenly go away.

Ergo, I had to automate all my regular expenses with a bill pay program
at the same time that I had to make sure that my Sweet Pixie had sufficient
funds to do whatever might be needed both for her needs and for any needs
that might arise on my end.

Because of my Social Security cutoff and other unexpected expenses, I
would grossly underestimate how much cash to set aside for Pixie—there
were unexpected expenses indeed! This led to a scramble in prison to get my
sweet love additional funds.

This scramble involved giving Stanley Woodward, my attorney, my
actual power of attorney and trying to put Pixie on my Wells Fargo account
so she could also write checks. Sadly, the minions at Wells Fargo were dicks
about the whole thing and I had to do a workaround, all from prison. (I'm
canceling my Wells Fargo account as soon as I get out.)

Then, there was my beloved Substack I had to tend to. With tens of
thousands of subscribers—check it out at www.peternavarro.substack.
com—these subscribers were paying good money, and I wanted to make
sure they got their money's worth.

The solution was to have one of my former aides at the White House, Joanna Miller Wischer, run the site in my absence, rotating guest columnists in with great content. A *big* thanks here to Mike Flynn, Clay Clark, Robert O'Brien, Adam Malon, Greg Autry, and more for their contributions.

I also asked Joanna to run my social media accounts—Twitter, Truth Social, and GETTR—using these social media accounts to post my Substack articles and an occasional post from me.

I had to deal with little details, too, like putting an automatic reply on my email: "Hey, I'm in prison, don't bother me." Okay, my auto reply was a lot more polite.

Still another task was to compile a list of names, phone numbers, and emails that I could bring into prison with me to construct my email, phone, and visitors lists. It would be on more than one occasion where I regretted not including someone on that list!

There was even littler stuff like unplugging the battery in my car so it wouldn't go dead while I was "upriver." It was all so surreal—a world of tasks undertaken at the speed of light before my surrender.

The funny part of it was—and it would feel very funny and strange—once I got into prison, I walked around with empty pockets. No house keys to forget. No cell phone to constantly check—hey, that felt like a very good thing. No car keys to lose. No wallet or money. Just a free man in prison.

HUCK POST 9:
A Bad News Double Tap
March 18, 2024—Eve of My Incarceration

They say bad news comes in bunches. "They," whoever they are, are right this day.

The first piece of bad news starts with an angry phone call from Pixie. She's pissed, not at me but at a so-called "prison consultant" I had talked with about what to expect behind bars.

The very first thing I had told Sam when we had talked on the phone was that all our conversations must be considered privileged, and he shouldn't discuss me with anyone, particularly the press.

Twenty-four hours later, Yosemite Sam is blabbing to some conniving CNN reporter about how I'm going to be kicking back in an "elderly" air-conditioned Club Fed dorm with amenities just short of the Ritz Carlton. While that had been true years ago when said consultant had himself served time in the Miami facility, that was then, but it sure as hell wasn't now.

It was the second part of the article that pissed both me and Pixie off, allegedly quoting the consultant saying I was "nervous." What the puck?

Nervous was at the bottom of my emotion list. More like I was just pissed at the absurdity of the situation. And the last thing any Trump guy wants to look like either to my old Boss, the American people, or several hundred inmates is a scared pussy.

I immediately phoned Sam, read him the riot act, and made damn sure that would be the last reporter he would ever talk to while representing me. I also told him to text—not call—the reporter and demand she retract the "nervous" quote, as he had not said it. Typical CNN bullshit.

It was in this agitated frame of mind—one I now rarely succumb to after four years of battle testing in the Trump White House—that I received a text from one of my lawyers, Stan Brand, indicating that Supreme Court Chief Justice John Roberts had denied my last Hail Mary appeal for release pending appeal—a favorable ruling would have spared me prison time until my full appeal was heard.

Aargh!!

After reading the one-page Roberts decision and discussing it with Stan—he was baffled—I sent out the following statement:

Justice Roberts took care to note that his reason for denial was "distinct from [my] pending appeal on the merits." That appeal on the merits will continue, and if I fail in that appeal—after nonetheless serving my full prison term—the constitutional separation of powers will be irreparably damaged and the doctrine of executive privilege dating back to George Washington will cease to function as an important safeguard for effective presidential decision-making. There is much at stake here and it is worth the fight.

Note that I left out the "puck I just can't get a break" part and called Pixie, who took the news well. God bless her. Come the next dawn, it was off to prison I would go.

BTW, the other "consultant" I called upon for advice was far more helpful. This was Paul Manafort, former 2016 Trump campaign manager and a political prisoner in his own right—read his book by the same name, *Political Prisoner*. You'll enjoy it.

Paul Manafort had left the 2016 Trump campaign by the time I showed up, but his close association with Trump Land had made him a target for an FBI/Department of Justice sting, with these agencies still controlled by Democrat president Barack Obama at the time. The weaponized Department of Justice and FBI had come down hard on Paul hoping to turn him into "state's evidence" against Trump so as to block Trump's election.

And the lawfare bastards had thrown everything they had at Paul— solitary confinement, threats of keeping him in prison for the rest of his life, confiscation of his assets, and financial destruction. Yet, Paul stayed strong. He didn't crack, both because of his principles and because there was really nothing bad he could say about Trump—Paul Manafort wasn't about to make anything up.

During several phone calls with Paul, he described what for him sounded like the trials of Job, and he thereby prepared me for a "worst case" which fortunately never came. Yet, the best thing Paul did for me is to describe the importance of quickly developing a daily work and exercise routine in prison to center your mind and protect your health and body.

Paul's advice went a long way towards making my prison stay palatable, and I thank Paul both for his advice and graciousness. If I ever decide to write a *Surviving Prison for Dummies* book, I will dedicate it to Paul Manafort. I did it good. He did it better.

HUCK POST 10:
I'm Off to a Lawfare Gulag
March 19, 2024—Day 1

> *I'd rather die standing than live on my knees.*
> —Emiliano Zapata

> *Live free or die.*
> —General John Stark

> *I'll see you on the other side.*
> —Peter Navarro

I woke up early and alone in my Florida paradise apartment. This was the day I would report to my new home for the next four months, a Miami prison.

I had left my Sweet Pixie behind at her flat in Washington, DC. We both knew it would be needless and empty pain for her to ride the last few miles with me. The drive back to our Palm Beach condo would be even sadder.

My lead attorney, Stanley Woodward, arrived late that morning. He would orchestrate my surrender.

It was windy as hell on the lakefront, and as I stood out on the lake trail waiting for Stanley, I just tried to take in the last few moments of pure freedom.

At the end of this post is the transcript of the press conference that I would hold a few hours later in a mini-mall parking lot across the street from the prison. This press event was broadcast on live TV on the cable news diaspora. Only Fox News refused to cover it—they acted like Never-Trump Murdock asshats until the end.

I include the transcript of this press conference because it provides a concise summary of the legal issues and political dynamics and crosscurrents underpinning *United States v. Peter Navarro*. At that press conference, I took Dylan Thomas's advice to "not go quietly into that good night" very much to heart.

From the transcript of the press conference, you can see that I clearly would rather stand up for God, country, and the Constitution and go to prison than grovel on my knees in a woke, broke, and broken America.

Transcript: Dr. Peter Navarro Speech Before Entering Prison March 19, 2024

[*Dr. Navarro steps up to a bank of microphones from various news organizations.*]

We've got to stop meeting like this. [*Dr. Navarro smiles, some laughter is heard*]

All right, here's what I'm going to do. I'm going to make a brief statement, I'll take a few pertinent and relevant questions, and then I'll be going over there. [*Points toward FCI Miami*]

So, the little story here is Navarro's going to prison today. You guys will certainly focus on that little story, but what I suggest to you as journalists is that there's two really bigger stories that you might want to report on and even do some research on, because these are big issues. This is not about me.

One of the big stories is about what is really an unprecedented assault on the constitutional separation of powers and the doctrine of executive privilege as a critical tool dating back to George Washington of effective presidential decision-making. And when I walk into that prison today, the justice system, such as it is, will have dealt a crippling blow to the constitutional separation of powers and executive privilege.

The second and related story has to do with the emergence of lawfare and the partisan weaponization of our justice system, which we have seen come to this country with a vengeance since the coming of Donald John Trump as President. And that [weaponized justice] keeps getting worse.

So let me walk you through those two stories; and again, I'm hoping as journalists you will do some background, some research. I'm asking you to fact-check everything I say today and write the bigger stories here, which I think are the important ones.

So let's talk about some facts here. I am the first senior White

House advisor in the history of our republic that has ever been charged with this alleged crime. And I say "alleged" because for hundreds of years, [what I was convicted of] has not been a crime. And for fifty years the Department of Justice has maintained the principle of absolute testimonial immunity [for senior White House advisors]. And it was only with my case that somehow that has changed.

And here's what your homework is, because the big constitutional separation of powers question is this: Can Congress compel a senior White House advisor, what they call an alter ego of a president, to testify before Congress?

Executive privilege goes back to George Washington and his remarks to the Congress regarding the Jay Treaty. [Washington] said very simply and clearly, succinctly, elegantly, right to the Congress, he said: "I cannot command you, as members of Congress, to come to me. You cannot command me to come to you. And the reason is the constitutional separation of powers."

And as legal doctrines have evolved, the Supreme Court has been very adamant about the sanctity of executive privilege, [and] that the privilege has extended to what's called alter egos of the president, which is what I am as one of [President Trump's] highest advisors.

And the principle here related to effective presidential decision-making is simply that if a president does not have the ability between and among his advisors to get confidential information in the sanctity of the Oval Office, he will make poor decisions which will harm the republic.

That's what this is about. That's what this is all about. And as this case has worked through the legal process, there are a number of big issues that we will be going through on the appeal that Mr. Woodward, in the back there, will lead with Stan Brand, two of the finest scholars imaginable in this area.

The biggest issue is: Can Congress compel someone like me to testify? The answer has been no ever since George Washington said that to [Congress regarding] the Jay Treaty.

But there are other equally important issues that arose in my case that the Supreme Court needs to address. These include:

- What constitutes executive privilege?
- Is the privilege presumptive?
- If not presumptive, what does a formal invocation [of the privilege] look like?

In my case, I had an evidentiary hearing for the first time in history. I presented a mountain of direct testimony and circumstantial evidence related to emails, correspondence, phone calls, and visits with the President and his top aides. And at the end of that day, the judge made the novel choice to say privilege had not been invoked, and it was absurd. It was probably the most absurd element of this case. So the appeals court and then the Supreme Court will ponder that issue, and it's a really important issue.

A third issue has to do with the fact—and this should chill you—if you're ever in my position, and you have to go to trial, it should chill you to know that your judge . . . has the discretion to strip you of any defense before you ever get to a jury.

How can that be? That can't be the law, and the way that happened in this case was the misapplication of an antiquated, misapplied precedent of the lower court, known as "Licavoli," that had no bearing on anything related to cases involving executive privilege. It was absurd.

The last issue is something called the *rule of lenity*. Again, put yourself in my shoes. The law, up to the point where I was convicted, said one thing, which is to say, I was doing my duty to this country, the Constitution, and my oath of office, according to the Department of Justice, according to the Supreme Court. [But Democrats in charge of the DOJ] flipped that.

The rule of lenity says, if they flip that, I'm not guilty. Okay? Try the next person who knows that the law has been changed, but you can't do that [to me].

So these are the big constitutional issues that we will fight, first at the appeals court, and then to the Supreme Court.

Now let me turn to the partisan nature of this. Fact-check me on this, folks. Fact-check me.

Every person who has taken me on this road to that prison is a friggin' Democrat and Trump-hater. Let me walk you through it.

It starts with House Speaker Nancy Pelosi, who forms the J6 Committee and blows away all the rules with an improperly constituted, unduly authorized, unlawful committee. She puts on [the J6 Committee] seven Democrats. Every single one—fact-check it—every single of those [congressmen] went after Donald Trump through two impeachments and the Russia hoax, and all they want to do is stop Trump.

And the two Republicans on [the J6 Committee] were not Republicans at all. Liz Cheney hates Donald Trump because Trump told the truth about her daddy. Her daddy [Vice President Dick Cheney] killed people with the Iraq and Afghanistan wars, and everybody in this country knows that.

Nancy Pelosi and the J6 Committee, they subpoenaed me. The Congress itself, when they voted my contempt charge, [it was] a strict [220–203] party line vote.

If the House had been held by Republicans instead of Democrats, I wouldn't be standing here.

And then we get the Department of Justice. Boy, is that a misnomer now. There were two prosecutors in the case. One of them, Patricia Aloi, wrote a letter to Bill Barr showing her "Never Trump" credentials. And they are the ones who, during the trial . . . consistently insisted I was acting "above the law" when they wouldn't let me explain to the jury why I was obeying the law.

Then it goes to the jury. Did I mention the jury? Look, I love anybody who serves on a jury, okay? I do not criticize the jury itself as individuals.

But would you as a Republican and a member of the Trump administration want to sit before twelve people drawn from a voter registration pool in which 95 percent . . . of the people voted for Joe Biden? That's astonishing.

So I get in front of that jury [after] the judge had already stripped me of the defenses, and I'm facing that jury. And by the way, the judge who stripped me of the defenses—fact-check me on this—before he got appointed to the bench by Barack Obama, he was what's called a "bundler."

You know what a bundler is? He bundled checks to give to the campaign of candidate Obama. And, coincidentally, he winds up on the bench. [*Makes pointing motions in a line, as if showing a chain*] Democrat, Democrat, Democrat, Democrat.

The final issue is: I go to the appeals court to get a simple release pending my appeal, which is the normal course. And it was given immediately to Stephen Bannon.

No, no, no. The judge fights me on that. [We appeal,] and think about this. Mr. Woodward files that appeal, and initially on the appeals panel, there are two Republicans and one Democrat. [They say,] "We've got your appeal."

Time passes, a short period of time, and we get the ruling back. It's "appeal denied," but we see that now there are three Obama-appointed Democrat judges on the three-judge panel.

How did that bait-and-switch happen? That's supposed to be a random draw. You know what the odds of that are? Less than 20 percent.

So Democrat, Democrat, Democrat. From start to finish. This is the partisan weaponization of our judicial system. Please write these big stories.

Now, the last thing I want to say is "that's prison." [*Points toward FCI Miami.*] That's where they take your freedom. But as hard as it will be on me, and as hard as it will be on anybody who is in there, it's harder on their families. And this is who those Democrats have hurt. This is who the Democrats have hurt.

I will walk proudly in there and do my time, but what they do to people—and, by the way, fact-check this—I will be the only person, only person in that prison who has been convicted of a misdemeanor. A misdemeanor. Everybody else is in there is in for felonies.

I will gather strength from this: Donald John Trump is the nominee for the Republican presidential campaign. While I'm away for the next four months, my new book *The New MAGA*

Deal, the unofficial guidebook to the Trump platform, will go to the printers.

[The book] is being published by Don Jr.'s publishing house, Winning Team Strategies, and it will be ready on the eve of the Republican National Convention.

The New MAGA Deal will be an important tool to show the people of America what MAGA principles are about. It's about 100 policies in the first 100 days of the new Trump administration to make us more prosperous and safer and secure, to deal with that southern border, to deal with China, Russia, Iran, and North Korea.

And I am just tired of the Democrats saying that Donald Trump and his followers and supporters are extremists. This was the man . . . make no mistake about this, [who] for four years [had] peace, prosperity, security, and price stability.

What do we have now? Inflation, an out-of-control southern border, war clouds growing in the Taiwan Strait. War in Gaza, in Ukraine. That's Joe Biden.

All right, I'm going to stop there. I'll take a few questions, and then I'm going to make my journey across the street. I'll start with you, ma'am. [*Points*]

Questioner: Thank you. Do you wish you had shown up for testimony and asserted privilege in person? You're talking about that now, you're arguing that now, but should you have shown up in Congress to make that argument?

Peter Navarro: My mission . . . is to defend the constitutional separation of powers and executive privilege, and I knew from day one of getting that J6 subpoena, based on my experiences at the White House, from reading the Office of Legal Counsel memos at the Department of Justice, that absolute testimonial immunity was in place. [Senior White House officials] McGahn, Dearborn, Conway, Porter. I can give you a whole long string of senior White House advisors who did exactly what I did and were never prosecuted. And if I had gone to Congress and played the piecemeal game with them, I would have done damage to the separation of powers, and I would not have been doing my duty.

I would not have been obeying my oath of office. Next question. Yes, sir. [*Points*]

Questioner: Are you nervous, and have you spoken to Donald Trump?

Peter Navarro: I am not nervous. . . . I'm going to claim executive privilege [*winks*] on the Donald Trump conversations. I've had the greatest amount of support from Donald Trump and his team. . . . Look, if they can put me in prison, they can put you in prison. Make no mistake about that. And make no mistake about this: They are coming after Donald Trump with the same tactics, tools, and strategies they used to put me over there today. [*Points toward FCI Miami*] Okay?

Think about this: I was stripped of all defenses before a jury trial. That's going to happen to Donald Trump. Democrats will judge him just like they did me in all the jurisdictions he's in. Fani Willis in Atlanta, the guy in Manhattan, Bragg, and of course Jack Smith at the Department of In-Justice, as we like to call it on my side of the fence.

So, I'm pissed. That's what I'm feeling right now. And I'm also afraid of only one thing: I'm afraid for this country. Because this, what they're doing, should have a chilling effect on every American, regardless of their party. If they can come for me, they can come for you. What else you got? Two more. Yes, ma'am. [*Points*] Yes, ma'am.

[*Questioner asks question, presumably in Spanish or about speaking Spanish*]

Peter Navarro: Se habla español un poquito. So no, I can't speak to the camera.

Questioner: Should anybody on the January 6th Committee be jailed for their suppression of evidence?

Peter Navarro: Look, [the] J6 Committee did not investigate, in my judgment, the most important aspects of how that riot occurred.

As I wrote in my book, *In Trump Time*, in the chapter about J6, the last three people on God's good Earth who wanted violence that day on Capitol Hill were Stephen K. Bannon,

President Trump himself, and me. And the reason is that the violence that occurred that day deprived this country of having a review of the votes under the perfectly legal 1887 Electoral Count Act. Okay?

What I think needs to happen, and I hope the Republicans— are you listening Loudermilk? Are you listening, folks up there? Jim Jordan, my brother who I used to ride with on Air Force One, you need to remember that that J6 Committee has some unfinished business.

There were more FBI informants up on Capitol Hill that day, possibly instigating that crowd, that the FBI itself could not keep track of. There were stories about that.

Why did Nancy Pelosi not provide more Capitol Hill police? Why did Mark Esper, the Secretary of Defense, have the National Guard so far away?

And as for the destruction of evidence, sir, look, the things they are doing, you know, Hillary Clinton cleansing her 30,000 emails. . . . There are so many things these Democrats have done that would actually justify prison.

You juxtapose that with me, [and] all I've done is my duty. All I have done is my duty to this country, the Constitution, my Commander-in-Chief, and to my oath of office. All right, one more. [*Points*]

Questioner: Do you want a pardon, either from President Joe Biden or Trump?

Peter Navarro: No. No, this is going to the Supreme Court. My mission . . . in this, and I will have served my time by the time that mission is completed, is to get this case in front of the Supreme Court, and I hope that they will put politics aside and look at . . . what they call a case of first impressions. Okay?

There are so many novel legal issues in this case that require the settlement, again another legal term, of [the settlement of] good law on the subject. Settling good law. It's crying out for the Supreme Court to do this.

But, the tragedy here is that because I have not been released pending appeal, I will have already done my time before that [appeal is heard and justice] is done. But that's the price of living in Joe Biden's America right now.

God bless you all. I'll see you on the other side.

[*Dr. Navarro walks away from the bank of microphones, toward FCI Miami, with cameras following him.*]

HUCK POST 11:
A Moral LOL Equivalence
March 20, 2024—Day 2

So after lunch, I get surrounded by three young Puerto Ricans out in the rec area, and I'm thinking, *What could go wrong here?*

But there's no danger. They just start laughing and joking with me, a true curiosity at the prison, about being a "Trump hombre."

After no shortage of banter, one of them, Luis, tells me that I'm "okay" with him—a high compliment in prison speak.

"*Por qué*," say I. Why?

Luis says because I'm not a snitch.

I ask him how does he know that, and he says because I didn't rat out on Trump.

Ah. The fine moral equivalence as seen through prison eyes of a fellow criminal who won't snitch or "rat out" on his accomplices and a senior White House advisor who refuses to testify before Congress on Constitutional separation of powers grounds.

I have to smile at him and that. It's just too deliciously funny. But if that moral equivalence keeps me a little safer here behind bars, I'll take it.

HUCK POST 12:
Driving Miss Pixie and a Razor-Wired Moon
March 20, 2024—Day 2

Logistics is a bitch, especially when you are in a prison cell with limited phone and email access. But where there is a will there is a way, and I decided it would be this day that I would finally solve my problem of how to get Sweet Pixie back and forth the seventy or so miles from our Palm Beach home to the Miami prison's Visitor's Center—she was coming for her first visit this weekend!

My first logistical problem was that Miss Pixie doesn't drive—Manhattan girl born and bred with a penchant for taxis. So if Miss Pixie came to visit both Saturday and Sunday for four months and went back and forth each day, that's about $800 in Uber fees—or nearly ten grand for the time I'll be behind bars.

But really, an Uber wouldn't even work because one of the rules of the Visitor's Center is that you can't bring any personal belongings with you—no wallet, no cash, no food, no cell phone, no nothing.

Remember here: To get an Uber, you have to have a cell phone and the Uber app. Of course, there are no lockers to park such stuff in while you visit. It's prison fool . . .

So if you take an Uber, you'd not only have to pay for the transport but you'd have to pay for waiting time, which would more than double the already steep cost. And who knows if the guy would still be there with your cell phone and wallet and other stuff. Ouch.

So then I thought about having Miss Pixie come up and stay overnight at a nearby motel where she could park her belongings and maybe walk back and forth to the joint. But I quickly realized that would depress the hell out of her in an already hellish situation—and might be dangerous, as the prison neighborhood wasn't exactly Bal Harbour.

Then a light bulb went off: The beautiful Trump Doral was just twenty minutes from the prison. Maybe she could stay there to ease her pain and get a driver to drop her off and pick her up. That would at least be cheaper, and it would be a whole lot more comfortable for the love of my life.

Enter once again Saint Clay, as in Clay Clark, my evangelical buddy who had been so helpful in raising money for my legal defense fund. He was a close friend of Eric Trump, who managed the Doral property, and Clay and Eric, along with General Mike Flynn, had hosted several pro-Trump events at which I had spoken.

So when I let Clay know of Pixie's plight that day, he volunteered to reach out to Eric to see if we could get a reduced "family" rate and some TLC.

It all fell beautifully into place, with not just a discount room rate but also a driver named Dale who would tend to Pixie's every need—including a much needed rendezvous with Barry Manilow at a critical emotional time. (Stay tuned for that.)

Thanks Clay and Eric Trump! Thanks Dale and the on-site manager Mikael who treated my princess like a queen at a delicate time.

I would now be seeing my Sweet Pixie again in just a few more days in the best of bad circumstances.

HUCK POST 13:
Trust No One in Prison
March 21, 2024—Day 3

Of the roughly two hundred inmates in my prison, most were either kind and simply cordial to me. Only two tried to mess me up. But it would have been a big mess up if either had pulled it off.

In this first case, on Day Four, I was approached as I was leaving the walking track by a guy who introduced himself as Mike. This was not unusual—guys introduced themselves all the time, as I was a curiosity, not just as the "new guy" but as the "Trump guy."

Yet, Mike stood out as a particularly personable fellow as well as a fellow traveler in the exercise activities I like to engage in. Like me, he gravitated to the track and the ball courts and what passed for weights.

Here, I can safely say that at least up to this point in my life, I had never met a better bullshit artist than Mike, and the guy's pedigree in this as a top-performer pharmaceutical sales rep was impeccable. As you might now guess, Mike was in prison for illegally pedaling prescription narcotics.

At any rate, later in that same day, Mike invited me over to his dorm that night with an offer of some of the arroz con pollo that the large Puerto Rican contingent whipped up most every night; and while nothing at all seemed gay about the invite, it just didn't smell right.

Turns out it would smell just like CNN. Mike's alleged ulterior motive was to snap a few photos of me in my prison garb and sell them to CNN—boasting to some of the other guys in his dorm he'd get a hundred grand. And that's what saved my ass—the guy boasting ahead of time of his planned sting on me.

It wasn't long before I had more than one guy warn me off over the rest of the day. Most of these, like Ritchie, simply had my back. Yet, these inmates were smart enough to know that if CNN published any "Navarro in prison photos," the camp would be locked down for weeks while a relentless search would root out any contraband cell phones, and inmates would have to subsist on bologna sandwiches while confined inside.

It was a close call that helped me quickly sort out some of the comrade wheat from the treacherous chaff. While I would be even more on my guard for the rest of my confinement and would like to say I learned my lesson not to trust anyone in prison, the second scam artist nearly got me with what would have been an even bigger fiasco.

HUCK POST 14:
The Kindness of Strangers and Prisoners
March 22, 2024—Day 4

> *The coldest winter I ever spent was a summer in San Francisco.*
> —Mark Twain

Like Twain, the coldest winter I would ever spend would be my summer in a Miami prison. But first let me tell you about my most pleasant surprise. That surprise was the camaraderie and support among the prisoners.

Here, I can honestly say after four years in the White House and three years working my way through the federal court system, I would rather go into battle with any ten guys from my prison dorm than with any ten guys from the White House or any ten judges from the District of Columbia Federal Courts.

From Day One, my dormmates, about forty in all, were helpful in finding me running and walking shoes to supplement my one pair of virtually unwearable work boots. They got me the shorts, sweatpants, and sweatshirts I would need to supplement my basic prison uniform so I could get some exercise and sleep without freezing.

My fellow inmate also got me a decent mattress and pillow—contraband in America's prisons—and especially some extra blankets to further ward off the cold. That was indeed the most unpleasant surprise. Here I am in Miami, Florida, at the epicenter of the sunshine capital of America, and I'm freezing my ass off day and night every time I step into the dorm.

Seems that a lightning bolt had struck the building at one point and burned out the circuitry for the mammoth air conditioner. To get the beast running again, the engineer—another inmate, not exactly with the best training—had simply bypassed the thermostat. So now, the air conditioning unit ran 24/7 on full blast.

During the day, that would keep the temperature down into the low 60s. At night, however, it might even get into the low 50s. So every night, it was a three-dog, five layer, multiple blankets night; and it *still* didn't feel like quite enough.

Now you may be thinking that my fellow prisoners were good to me simply because I was seen as some kind of celebrity, but that wasn't the case at all. Every new inmate (unless they were a snitch or "ChoMo," a child molester) was afforded the same courtesies; and the deal was, when you left, you just donated all your stuff to the common pool for the next guys.

It was a "pay it forward" kind of prison, if you will. And the courtesies that were extended were both large and small. Sometimes such a courtesy might even boil down to a simple gesture or shake of the head.

For example, for some stupid reason, it was against regulations to bring plastic containers with you to the chow line that would allow you to take leftovers back to the dorm. "Better you throw away whatever you didn't eat" was the underlying principle. However, because that was such a stupid waste of food, the only guard that really enforced the rule was a nasty piece of work of a woman named Williams.

So it was that on "Fish Friday"—*Viernes de Pescado* to at least half the mess hall—a couple of guys in line saw me with my plastic bin, pointed at it, and flashed me the "no" sign. When I went inside the mess hall, sure enough, Big Nurse Williams (if you get the *Cuckoo Nest* reference) was indeed on duty. I had been spared a tongue lashing by my fellow inmates. That's why they call it prison.

HUCK POST 15:
Potemkin Prison
March 23, 2024—Day 5

One of the biggest laughs I got during an otherwise grim first week in prison came from the repeated tales of inmates wryly thanking me for all of the improvements that were quickly made to the facility in the two weeks prior to my arrival. As I briefly mentioned earlier, the red tin roofs on all the buildings were high-pressure steam cleaned to take years of blackened crud and sludge off their surfaces. That way any news helicopters would see a bright shiny facility which was anything but bright and shiny beneath these roofs.

The tattered fence coverings facing the main road running past the prison were replaced. That new pretty face would both present well and keep out prying camera eyes.

Burned-out lights were replaced in the dorms. This got mixed reviews, however, from the inmates, as it was a feast-or-famine switch—from dark, dark interiors to interrogation-room-style Klieg lights. *I confess! I confess!*

Of course, paint was splashed everywhere while the kitchen got particular TLC. And get this, they finally fixed the humongous dishwasher. It was a bitch to wash by hand the brown plastic trays used for every meal. So the Puerto Rican crew on dishwater detail was particularly grateful for my arrival.

As for the food, they stopped serving ground beef that was past the due date almost every day and varied the menu instead with shredded chicken, chicken, chicken, cooked Sahara style, with every possible ounce of oil and nutrients boiled out of it.

It was a laugh in and of itself when guys would tell me the food had gotten a whole lot better. It was a laugh because the food just sucked. Dried out meat and not a vegetable in sight except for peas or carrots out of a can. And here I was in the middle of the citrus capital of the world and nary an orange in sight—I would find out weeks later exactly why, so stay tuned.

Anyway, my compliments *and* my condolences to the inmate chefs. They do a heck of a job with what they are given to work with, but what they are given ain't much.

BTW. The breakfasts were almost always the worst, despite the admonition of nutritionists that breakfast should be the best meal of the day. Invariably, breakfast would not meet even the bare minimum of the calorie requirement. It topped out at about 400 calories maximum each morning, plus it was usually a mega-dose of sugar in the form of various cake breads, skim rather than 2 percent or whole milk, and cardboard bran cereal which, in the absence of any other fiber in the prison diet, at least kept the pipeline moving.

The only healthy element in that breakfast was an occasional small, and I mean small, apple. Of course, as a taxpayer, I don't want our prisons to compete with even Holiday Inns for amenity levels. Yet there's no reason why a prison should have to wait for a VIP inmate to clean up its act.

Paint and light bulbs are cheap, and there's plenty of inmate labor to maintain upkeep. There's also plenty of money in the budget for decent meals if that money is handled properly. That, however, was not the case, as some of the high-end food frequently left the facility in the trunks of the guards and administrators. But that's why they call it prison.

Praise the Lord that my Sweet Pixie is coming to visit today!

PIXIE POST 2:
My Huck Smells Guiltily Good
March 23, 2024—Day 5

Pixie here, and after I first met my Ever Huck three years ago and we started to date, before he picked me up I would be so nervous to go out with a Trump guy. So I would do my yoga breathing exercises to calm my nerves. Now, in the car with my driver Dale heading to the prison for the first time, I'm feeling that nervousness all over again.

Cálmate, cálmate, my Ever Huck would say to me in Spanish whenever I got anxious. Relax, relax. I shall try that now with my yoga breathing before I arrive at the prison.

At the prison, it is definitely an out-of-body experience. Whether or not the prisoners in there that I saw in the Visitor Center were guilty or innocent, I felt so very sad for humanity that one could put themselves in a position like this.

To see grown men in the hands of police, living every day basically with no freedom and in a "hands up, don't move" type of scenario potentially at every minute of any day. To lose all their God-given rights and their dignity by sacrificing their freedom and letting themselves be trapped like animals in a cage. It was one of the saddest days in my life.

As I'm signing in at the front desk of the Visitor's Center, I see a very handsome man in all army green with his collar up and in a totally ironed shirt and pants coming towards me as the prison guard calls out, "Mrs. Navarro, Mr. Navarro is here."

I hardly recognize my Ever Huck. After a double take, these words are good and comforting to me, and I hope and dream of walking down the aisle with that handsome man.

During our visit, we talk nonstop face to face in front of about thirty other prisoners and their loved ones from 11:15 to 2:30. I'm astonished how my Huck's shirt is so ironed to perfection—he's usually a wrinkled clothes model.

I'm also amazed at how he has never smelled as good as he does here today because he never wears cologne.

He tells me with an impish grin that a fellow inmate lent him a bottle of "Guilty"—he laughed as he said it because that's the name of the cologne they sell in the commissary.

"You can't make that up," says my Huck. And you surely can't.

But this cheap prison commissary cologne is the greatest cologne I have ever smelled—because he's wearing it, and I finally get to see him and hold him and press my face to his neck.

Later, when we stood up to stretch our legs and take a hug moment, the guard came over to us and ordered us to sit down—you are allowed only one hug at the beginning of the visit and one at the end.

Can I get a break here? No way, no where, nothing in sight.

As we walk to the exit, the most important thing right now I want to ask him is whether he would have done things any differently, whether he would have testified. During our exit hug, he draws me close and whispers in my ear, "Never." He has no doubt in his mind about this, despite the misery it is causing us.

I feel good about his commitment to America. That even in prison he still stands constant no matter what, and then I know the suffering I now endure is all worth the stand he has taken, not just for Donald Trump, but for the country.

I know, too, that he will be as true to me as his country, and who would not want to live with a man like this?

So, onward and upward we go, because as we promised each other over a month ago: *We got this.*

HUCK POST 16:
Howling Wolf
March 25, 2024—Day 7

I'm flat on my back thinking about my Sweet Pixie and doing my stretching lying out in the rec yard underneath the skies of a just set sun.

I see the full moon rising now through the razor wire fence holding me in—biggest damn moon I've ever seen.

It's beauty and the beast of incarceration.

I laugh out loud.

That's why they call it prison.

PIXIE POST 3:
The Pandora Prison Blues
March 25, 2024—Day 7

Pixie here, and it's a full moon tonight. Huck will see it from the prison, and I will watch it out on the beach in Palm Beach—*la luna llena* the only common thing we will be able to share after a seven-and-a-half-minute call tonight.

Our situation isn't getting easier. I can't listen any more to all of our beautiful love and dancing songs on Pandora, as any music just reminds me of my Ever Huck.

That I am not that strong just tears my heart. I try to be a soldier, but like I tell Peter's close confidants, I am not as strong as he.

HUCK POST 17:
Just Pick It Up at Walgreens
March 26, 2024—Day 8

So, I get a "call out" on my seventh day in prison to report to the dentist for my intake evaluation—never mind that if you want even a cleaning, it's more than a year wait, and I'll be long gone.

So I dutifully go for my 8:30 appointment and am pleasantly surprised at the thoroughness and professionalism of the dentist. While my teeth are in pretty good shape, he warns me that the sun is taking its toll on my lower lip and facial skin.

So what do I do, Doc? He tells me to get some Blistex for the lips and some sunblock with at least 70 SPF.

When I tell him the prison commissary doesn't carry Blistex and only stocks SPF 50, he says I can get it at any Walgreens or CVS.

Yea, Doc, but how do I do that? I'm in prison.

He just shrugs.

I just laugh.

This is truly a theater of the absurd.

HUCK POST 18:
No Mirrors, No Keys, No Clocks, No Problem

March 27, 2024—Day 9

Old habits die hard. Every time I needed to comb my hair, I'd go into the bathroom thinking I would do it looking in the mirror. But there are no mirrors in prison.

I'm not sure why there are no mirrors. Perhaps it's part of a prison strategy to turn human beings into faceless numbers.

No guard ever asked me for my name, only my PAC or prison ID number. 04370-510 by the way. Forget that, and you're screwed in prison.

Regardless, I didn't see my reflection in a real mirror the whole time I was in prison. Here, some inmates had tiny, distorted ones to shave with, but I didn't bother. For the entire time of my incarceration, it was oddly liberating not to see one's reflection.

The same was only slightly less true for clocks. Aside from one in the dorm, I didn't see a single clock anywhere else on the grounds, which raises that age-old Zen "if a tree falls in an empty woods does anyone hear it" question: Are you really doing time in prison if you never know what time it is?

Drumroll please. That's at least a little funny.

The last habit that would die hard in prison was that of checking that I had my keys before I left the dorm. There are no keys in prison except, of course, for the ones the guards carry on massive chains the size of blackjacks for the four to five doors with huge locks that shut you in for the four-count a day and then again for the night.

Note: you're locked in that dorm qua cell for at least half of your life every day.

It was an eerie feeling, always checking for the keys you didn't have and didn't need in prison. In some sense, it was a weird freedom. Except, of course, when you were locked in by the guards or locked out by your own stupidity.

That stupidity happened to me only once and it was in my first week as a rookie inmate. I thought the count was at 4 p.m. but didn't know they went into lockdown at 3:30. So I left the dorm to walk over to the other side of the compound at about 3:20 to check my email, thinking I had plenty of time. Yet, when I got back, I was locked out and stuck on the outside.

I had to bang on the back door until one of the guys inside saw me. He laughed his ass off for a bit and then told me to come around to the main closed entrance. Then, he summoned the guard to let me in.

If the guard hadn't also been the chaplain that day, I might have wound up in the hole or the SHU (Special Housing Unit). But the kind lady let me in with grace.

When I went through the doors to the waiting area where there was a crowd of inmates, I raised my fist in victory and shouted, "Rookie!"

Everybody laughed and some ice was broken. Even the famous guy could do some dumb things. It was hilarious, all in all.

BTW, did I mention that for the first two weeks I had to comb my hair with a fork because the commissary was closed and I couldn't buy a comb or brush? Actually, a plastic fork works pretty well. But that's why they call it prison.

HUCK POST 19:
The Art of the Prison Dump and Flush
March 28, 2024—Day 10

Flush twice. It's a long way to the kitchen.
—Anon

So it's 5:30 a.m., before the lights come on in the dorm, and it's that calm before the daily stir of activity, and I'm sitting on the can doing my business thinking about Roe v. Wade and the art of the prison flush.

In a dorm with close to fifty people and only four toilets, it's always a crapshoot to get a free stall (nice pun intended), but I got lucky this morning.

As I'm sitting there thinking—God only knows why—how to explain to a swing voter why the overturning of Roe v. Wade shouldn't determine your choice in the 2024 election, a guy sits down in the next stall and starts the ritual flushing.

Prison etiquette demands that if you are going to toot your horn (if you catch my drift) and deposit something malodorous in the porcelain, you need to immediately flush to spare your mates and fellow inmates the displeasure of your company.

At any rate, as the guy in the next stall starts a series of flushes, I think about how the abortion issue—that's what it is, abortion, not "choice"—might cost us the 2024 presidential election.

It certainly wounded Republican efforts in the 2022 congressional elections—still waiting for that Red Wave. This time around, the sweet nubile coeds of Madison, Wisconsin, and Ann Arbor, Michigan, and college campuses in the battleground states are going to be whipped yet again into a social issue frenzy.

Obama beat Romney with the social issue stick in 2012. Biden leveraged it in 2020, and here we go again. Rationally, you'd think most voters would put a good job with a decent wage, lower risk of being a crime victim, and peace at home ahead of ripping a budding baby from a womb. But not in America today. It's the political conundrum of our times, and I have no answer.

As for the "dump and flush," I didn't have a name for it until weeks later when Zach would school me on the terminology. It's a technique every inmate must master to avoid getting the crap knocked out of them after they take a crap. Thank Zach for naming this postcard.

PIXIE POST 4:
No Bunny for Easter
March 28, 2024—Day 10

Pixie here, and it's Day 10. Yes, I count the days. And I won't be able to see my innocent man until Day 12. And Day 13 will be Easter Sunday.

For the first time in my life, the sound of the word "Easter" is so sad to me. Not sad in a religious way, as it is a sacred marvel of an event. But sad because for the first time since we met, I won't be able to give my Huck his chocolate Easter bunny.

I know it sounds silly, and of course it is. But it was a special ritual for us and just one more thing, one more sweet playful element of being with Huck, that they are taking away from us.

I lived in NYC most of my life, and I always remember criminals who mugged old ladies or even did bodily harm, but they would get bail. They would go free. Why not my Huck?

I end my day with a call from him. He is in good spirits—because they cannot break us—and because he is on the bravest mission that anyone could ever be on.

HUCK POST 20:
Funny Signs and Fantasy Menus
March 28, 2024—Day 10

If there is one movie you'd never want to watch before you head off to prison, it would be *Deliverance*. If you've seen that sadistic hillbilly sodomite "bromance," you'll know why. If you haven't, I'll spare you the details.

But having seen the movie, along with all the bulletins about rape prevention splattered all over the walls of the prison that I had entered, I had to laugh my ass off the first time I noticed this sign posted prominently across the four individual shower stalls available to us:

ONE INMATE AT A TIME

If you don't laugh every day in prison at some absurdity, you surely will cry.

Of course, one of the biggest laughs I would get every day, in fact three times a day, was every time I went to the mess hall for breakfast, lunch, or dinner. That's because equally prominently displayed, in this case behind the inmates ladling out our chow, was a scrolling neon menu high up on the wall.

The sign was funny because it would announce the most tantalizing and tasty meals that we would *never, ever* be served. Fried chicken, fresh vegetables, slices of pie, even beets and salad. It went on and on with its scrolling fancy menus for Monday and Tuesday and Wednesday and a future that was a longtime thing of the past, when the Miami facility was a true minimum-security prison sans fences, the guards were friendly, and the food was palatable.

At any rate, a man can dream, and that menu sure made you dream every day. Maybe the day before I leave, I'll unplug the sign and stop the torture. Or maybe if I did that, they'd give me four more months. That's why they call it prison.

HUCK POST 21:
Sins of Youth Come Back to Haunt
March 29, 2024—Day 11

They say to "expect the unexpected." I hate "they," whoever they may be.

In this case, I'm out in the lobby area—where the various offices are for the Unit Manager, Case Managers, and prison secretary—trying to warm up from my freezing dormitory, and my counselor sees me and calls me into his office.

He says he's been trying to get me into a halfway house before my sentence is finished, which would get me out of the Miami prison as much as thirty days early. But there's a snag.

"Do tell," I say.

He says I may have an outstanding warrant for an arrest from back in 1970 when I was a student at Tufts in Boston. This didn't exactly compute for me, as I have a top level security clearance from the FBI.

Yet, back in that college day, I was indeed arrested. It was a totally bogus beef—wrong time, wrong place—and the case had been quickly dismissed with a promise from my lawyer that it would be off my record.

Yet, still, there was an outstanding warrant. Talk about a bolt from the Boston Blue.

And here was the unexpected kicker: If I couldn't prove the case had been dismissed—that was likely impossible because the case record had long ago perished—there was no way I would be released to a halfway house.

This problem would haunt me for weeks and I never did get it resolved. But it wouldn't matter. The Bureau of Prisons would screw me out of any chance of getting to a halfway house anyway, and do so for political reasons. But you'll read about that in a later post.

HUCK POST 22:
Christ—and Forks—Have Risen
March 30, 2024—Day 12

Prison dehumanizes you in ways large and small—often needlessly so. Here's a case in point:

The day before Easter and two days before Passover, the chaplain marches onto the unit, summons four of the Jews in the unit, and then marches them back to her office so she can read one of them, a particularly devout Jew, the riot act in front of the others.

Seems like the inmate, call him Saul, had dared to request a proper three-hour seder to observe the high holiday, and the female chaplain, a Nigerian immigrant with an alleged anti-Semitism bent, decreed the seder would be limited to one hour. Saul, of course, had no recourse as the regs said "up to three hours."

With a long prison term yet to go for Saul, my sense was that it was his faith that was the only thing holding him together. By denying Saul and his flock a full seder, the chaplain had shaken Saul, if not his faith.

BTW, I watched on Easter morning as one of the guards refused to let another inmate out into the hallway where the microwave was kept. The inmate, who looked like a defensive tackle on the Los Angeles Rams and called himself "15," wanted to heat up his Ramadan meal *before* the sun rose.

During Ramadan, Muslims fast in the daylight hours. So 15 was either going to starve all that day or break his faith. It was all he could do not to turn the guard into pulp. Dehumanizing is as dehumanizing does.

And speaking more of dehumanizing, the Easter from Hell and to Hell with Ramadan Sunday would also feature a shouting match between the lady guard on duty and some inmates who were troubled by her refusal to unlock the doors on time—she was an hour late keeping us in our cages.

After her shouting match, she went back to her command center and turned all the lights on in the dorms—it was still only around 8 a.m., and on Sundays they are supposed to keep the lights off until 10 a.m. to let folks relax and sleep. Needless, tormenting BS of course, just because she could. That was far too often the mindset of vengeful guards.

At least Easter morning would end with a very good laugh at breakfast. For weeks, I had never seen any forks handed out as utensils, only spoons. Today, however, the fork had risen. I grabbed one eagerly and put it on my tray as I said, "Praise the Lord."

Then, I discovered as I handed my tray to the server for food, the main course was grits, watery, watery, grits. Try eating that with a fork. It was truly too funny. The one day I needed a spoon, I got forked.

The cosmic joke is on you Navarro. That's why they call it prison.

HUCK POST 23:
A Visit to Visitor's Hell
March 31, 2024—Day 13

A big part of losing one's freedom is the reduced physical, emotional, and spiritual contact with one's family. Upon lockup, you are limited to about five hundred minutes of phone calls a month—a little more than fifteen minutes a day. And it doesn't matter at all how big your family or circle of friends are. You still have to abide by your limits.

In my case, I chose to allocate every single minute of my phone time to my Sweet Pixie, but I can see how the phone call limits could strain relationships.

Of course, the other ways of reaching out include letters, email, and personal visits, and here again restrictions come into play that may dehumanize or humiliate both an inmate and family members or friends.

In our case, Pixie made her first visit yesterday and during the second weekend I was there. It would be a proverbial cattle call—visitors could only come on weekends.

Although understandably necessary, Sweet Pix had had to stand in a long line in the hot sun and then had been searched by a guard (who got uncomfortably close to places he needn't have had his hands) for weapons and contraband.

This sadistic guard named Ajemon was absolutely the *worst* part of the visit and would be a recurring nightmare. He was a big bruiser of man who wore a mask, not to protect himself from COVID, but to hide a face that would scare a Stephen King novel; and he had been transferred from the prison across the street allegedly because he had let a prisoner die in solitary confinement—the prisoner had screamed for help for hours while Ajemon was either asleep or indifferent before choking on his own vomit.

For whatever reason, the warden didn't want to fire Ajemon despite the fact he was universally loathed by the other guards and inmates alike. For whatever reason, the prison's top brass decided to put him in a public-facing position that was the worst-suited for this guy's sadistic tendencies.

During the visit, while we could hug and chastely kiss, we had to sit rather than stand in chairs across from one another and at one point got chewed out by Ajemon for simply stretching our legs.

I remember clearly the Monday morning after Pixie's first visit, sitting at breakfast and talking with a newcomer inmate whose wife and six-month-old baby had also just visited for the first time. Ajemon the Terror had barked at her from the moment she had walked in and terrified her as well—she with a young newborn in her arms.

I also personally saw Ajemon force an elderly woman to stand on one leg and then bend the other up so he could wand her shoe for possible weapons or contraband. Of course, she nearly fell down. Another elderly woman was rejected for wearing heels a quarter of an inch over the limit and was forced to go out in a heavy rain to change. One of my inmate buddies couldn't use an extra chair for one of his visitors. And so it went.

At a later visit, I even saw Ajemon make a double-amputee grandfather take both his protheses off to make sure there was nothing stowed in them. That's why they call it prison.

It was all so humiliating and dehumanizing. It was also ultimately so damaging to the families trying to deal with the grief of having a loved one inside.

One of the emptiest moments Pixie and I would both feel my whole time in prison was every Sunday afternoon at the end of visiting hours when I had to watch my Sweet Pixie walk out the door and skip away into the big bad world to fend for herself while I cooled my jets in prison. We felt that for the first time this unhappiest of Easters. We both hid how much it hurt, but it damn well hurt. That's why they call it prison.

HUCK POST 24:
Contaminated Water and Crime School
April Fool's Day, 2024—Day 14

Two weeks into my sentence, I resolved I would drink more water. So, after an afternoon run on the way into getting locked in for the count, I stopped at the outside water fountain and guzzled twelve gulps. As soon as I'm done, the guy we call "Smuggler" (because that's what he's in for) says, "Don't be drinking that water."

"Why?" say I.

"Cause it's contaminated, that's what they told us."

"Thank you sir for that keen sense of timing," say I.

"Say what?" says Smuggler.

"Exactly," say I.

But really. The whole culture of a prison is designed to leverage your criminal instinct. Ration your phone minutes, so you smuggle in a cell phone. Put you on a starvation diet, and pretty soon, you're looking to buy bootleg food. Ban containers for the cafeteria so they can throw away food rather than let you take it back to the dorm, and now you're wearing bulky clothes and a jacket to hide said contraband bins or bags. And so it goes.

HUCK POST 25:
Pettiness Which Plays So Rough
April 2, 2024—Day 15

> *There will be no retaliation. I promise you that.*
> —Captain Verdejo, Camp Administrator

Every time a newbie comes in to lead a bureaucracy, he or she tries to change things. It rarely works, especially in a prison.

So it was that on my fifteenth day in the joint, the new FCI administrator and third in line to the warden held impromptu town halls in each of the four dorms and let us all know that he was instituting daily inspections.

Going forward, there must be nothing left on (or underneath) the beds or chairs, and everything must fit in one's locker. Otherwise, it will be treated as "excess property" and will be confiscated.

Never mind that the lockers are way too small to accommodate both the clothing, towels, and food one buys from the commissary to survive the paltry offerings from the chow hall. We shall henceforth follow the rules.

After this law was laid down, the administrator, an affable fellow who expressed genuine interest in our welfare, asked if anyone had any questions.

Unlike everyone else in the room who might get shipped out to another prison or given "diesel therapy" tomorrow if they questioned anything today, I thought, *What the puck can they do to me?* and offered two suggestions.

Offering the preface that we all understood that learning to follow the rules was an important part of our path to a successful reentry into society, I further offered that wouldn't it be nice if there was reciprocity. Here, I suggested that having the mess hall open on time for breakfast, lunch, and dinner rather than at random, and often absurdly late times, might be a good signal of a rules-based regime.

I further suggested that opening the doors to the dorms, the computer facilities, and the rec area right at 6 a.m. might be useful as well, particularly if you want folks to get to work on time.

Finally, I gently suggested that it might be nice for inmates to offer these kinds of suggestions without fear of retaliation. In response, the administrator offered that these were excellent suggestions and assured that he would work on them—and, of course, you should never worry about retaliation. His door will always be open.

The next morning there was a pouring rain. As a few hungry inmates stood under the portico trying to stay dry as they waited for the mess hall to open, inside the inmate workers were told to keep the doors shut for another twenty minutes after breakfast was ready. They were further instructed to leave off the jam and sugar packets normally provided and told that this was being done because some asshole inmate had complained about the mess hall not being open on time.

When the door was finally opened at 6:20, the twenty or so inmates waiting came in, ate, and were promptly ushered out and the breakfast line was quickly closed. It all took less than 15 minutes.

As I left the hall, I watched as more inmates came to breakfast only to find the door locked. Chow had never been called in the dorms as it normally was, so nobody really knew the mess hall was open.

"Puck you" from the guard in charge received. As Bob Dylan once said, "Pettiness which plays so rough." No retaliation to see here.

HUCK POST 26:
Of "ChoMos" and Snitches
April 2, 2024—Day 15

The worst thing you can be in prison besides a "ChoMo"—a child molester or sex offender—is a snitch. Snitches are dangerous because if they've done it once, e.g., by turning state's evidence against a friend or colleague to get a lighter sentence, they will certainly do it again inside the prison walls. So the last thing any prisoner wants is a snitch in their cell or dorm looking to trade information in exchange for some benefit.

So it is that inmates themselves regularly use the database PACER—Public Access to Court Electronic Records—to screen all new inmates for danger signs. In fact, such searching is highly sophisticated and organized among the inmate population for both safety and security.

The way snitches are sniffed out is by looking for either a 5K1.1 or a Rule 35(b) (or both) in an inmate's "jacket."

A Rule 5K1.1 motion refers to a provision in the Federal Sentencing Guidelines that allows a court to impose a sentence below the guideline range if the defendant has provided "substantial assistance" to the government, often in the form of cooperation, such as testifying against a co-defendant or colleague.

In contrast, Rule 35(b) permits a court to reduce a defendant's sentence if they provide "substantial assistance" to the government *after sentencing*.

Here's the point: Any incoming inmate that has a 5K1.1 or Rule 35(b) in his jacket will be avoided like the plague. A case in point is an inmate who walked into the prison with a thousand-yard stare and immediately took a bead on me.

I did my homework with the help of the guys. The guy was the CEO of a company in for a short bid, and all of the other guys he had snitched on were at other higher security prisons on five- and ten-year bids.

My first take of him before my research was that he was a snitch and someone with more than a few screws loose. If I ever wanted to cast a prison movie, he'd be perfect as an extra.

Suave, I'll call him, was in his sixties and straight out of an Esalen

Institute retreat. Wavy GQ hair, a lean yoga body, but a shuffle that indicated some severe pain issues and likely a painkiller problem.

Over the course of his first week, he would come at me at least five different times. The first couple of times, he would chat me up trying (way too hard) to befriend. He obviously knew who I was—did I mention he had a copy of one of my books with him?

Two breaking points came in quick succession. The first: one of my good buddies and I were sitting at one of the very small tables in the mess hall, and Suave comes over with his food tray and sits on the bench beside me less than a foot away.

WTF. This is prison. You simply don't do stuff like that—it looks weird at best and gay at worst. I just got up without a word and walked away.

The *next day* I come into my dorm and find Suave angling to move to the bunk beds beside me. Del, a wheelchair-bound eighty-year-old, had the lower bunk, and the top was left unoccupied in deference to Del's wheelchair condition. Now, this asshole Suave was insisting he get the bunk. WTF again.

Yes, the last thing I needed was a stalker, a snitch, or somebody whacked out on antidepressants (a hot rumor about the guy) living one bunk away. And nobody else wanted him anywhere near the dorm.

So our dorm leader, General, had the guy sent over to the Puerto Rican side to make Suave's life miserable. His first night on the PR side, they woke him up at three in the morning and serenaded him with Happy Birthday in Spanish. It was hilarious. That's why they call it prison.

HUCK POST 27:
Institutionalized on Commissary Day
April 3, 2024—Day 16

> *This shit's gas station food.*
> —Inmate 92 returning from the commissary

Yes, indeed. You know you've been institutionalized when the most exciting thing of the week is the weekly commissary call.

Oh what a joy it is to fill out your order the night before. Missing your protein? You can get bags full of tuna or chicken or salami or pork that does indeed taste like it came out of a bag.

Need a shave? It's cheap plastic razors by the bucketful.

And if you're a sugar freak, it's next to impossible to get any kind of snack food that *won't* spike your blood sugar.

As for me, the most precious foods were peanut butter, peanut butter, and peanut butter. Ate it by the spoonful along with oatmeal and Raisin Bran and some low sugar power bars.

As for the commissary experience itself, you grab your laundry bag to hold your haul of the day, haul ass over to the commissary store, wait for an hour or more, and then frantically load your bag as the clerk throws your shit at you like a machine gun and fellow inmates glare at you if you're too frigging slow.

At least now I know what it was like to be a citizen of the Soviet Union circa 1960 visiting a Soviet store. Did I mention that half the stuff you want is usually out of stock? That's why they call it prison.

HUCK POST 28:
Hope Floats
April 4, 2024—Day 17

After ten days of either sitting on, or cogitating about, my request to release me pending an appeal of my bigger case, Supreme Court Justice Neil Gorsuch announces he will pass the motion on to the full court. To my surprise, my lawyer, Stanley Woodward, is bummed—he thought Gorsuch might just make the decision on his own.

I saw the move as the best possible outcome—although I was disappointed I'd have to wait several more weeks before SCOTUS met on April 26 to discuss the case. As I would write to Woodward, Gorsuch really faced two choices.

The first was whether to grant the motion and release or not. If it was a "not," he would be agreeing with Justice Roberts and therefore would simply deny the motion.

If, however, he was in favor of release, he had to choose between doing it solo and offending Roberts or passing it to the full court—and perhaps lobbying for a "yes" with colleagues.

Since collegiality is important at SCOTUS, Gorsuch was unlikely to want to offend Roberts, so passing the decision on to the full court was both the most likely and hopeful of options.

Of course, I was setting myself up for an emotional fall, but by this time, I had learned Buddha's lesson that desire is suffering—and hope is a sucker's bet. So I welcomed Gorsuch's move but refused to get my hopes up, even though the decision was made on the day a crescent moon—my good omen moon—would pop into the sky over Miami. Stay tuned.

PIXIE POST 5:
Nietzsche in Manhattan
April 4, 2024—Day 17

Pixie here. My Ever Huck and I are talking on the phone after dinner, using our full fifteen-minute prison allotment. We keep talking because he senses my sadness even though I am putting on a brave face.

"What doesn't break us makes us stronger," my Huck reassures me. He says it's a Nietzsche thing, and I tell him he's a Harvard thing and I'm just a humble Georgetown girl. But I do feel that incredible strength only because it's Navarro showing me the light.

What doesn't kill us makes us stronger, and we ain't dying from this, no way no how!

I tell my Huck I will see him in two days. He quips back, "See you soon not zoom, my Sweet Pixie!" It's one of our favorite funny farewells. I smile as I hang up the phone.

HUCK POST 29:
Ray-Ray
April 4, 2024—Day 17

Imagine running a successful construction company laying down asphalt roads for various Puerto Rican cities and municipalities, and a mayor calls you up and offers you lucrative contracts if you simply kick back a part of the profits.

Now imagine further that this mayor had already been caught in a corruption scheme, and to lessen his charges and jail time, all he had to do is tape record himself offering contracts to folks in exchange for kickbacks.

That's exactly how Ray-Ray wound up in a prison in Miami for thirty months of his life. And what's interesting about that sentence is the prosecution asked for only twenty-four months, but Ray-Ray drew a "hanging judge" who took another six months of the young man's life.

It just seems wrong—particularly if you got to know Ray-Ray, a smart, polite, hard-working entrepreneur with a family back in the P.R. he won't see (much) for what will seem a very long time—so far he's only four months into his thirty-month bid. But that's why they call it prison.

I wish Ray-Ray the best. He's got a long way to go.

HUCK POST 30:
Again, I'm the Mark at Mehta's Con Game
April 5, 2024—Day 18

As you may recall, my sentence was for four months. However, for the first few weeks after I arrived at my prison, everyone was telling me that under Donald Trump's 2018 First Step Act, I'd be out a month early because you get ten days off your sentence for every thirty days if you simply participate in programming and training and keep your nose clean.

So, silly me. I took that thirty days off my sentence idea to the bank and settled into a mental state where I could do ninety days easy peasy rather than 120. God bless Donald John Trump, the First Step Act, and even a little bit of me—I had played a small role in getting the FSA to the finish line with Congress.

On my eighteenth day in, however, my case manager, Coeltze, calls me in to give me my release date, and it's four months, not three. So I say what about the thirty-day reduction for FSA credits, and I'm stunned when he says I'm not eligible.

I'm stunned because of the reason—what is in fact a gaping loophole in the FSA law. I will not get my thirty days off because my judge, Judge Amit Mehta, did not impose any probation period after my sentence is finished.

So let me translate that for you. Because my alleged crime, a misdemeanor, was so minor that I was given no probation, I will get punished for the minor misdemeanor nature of that crime by being denied FSA reduction and thirty days of earlier freedom. Meanwhile, all the felons and everybody else in the prison whose sentence includes probation—which is to say everybody else—will get time off while I won't.

The obvious question is whether my nemesis Judge Amit Mehta knew he was screwing me out of an early release when he gave me no probation.

Of course, he knew. How could he not know. He's the cleverest of jackals. He proved that at trial.

But such punishment for no probation was not the intention of the law. I was indeed there in the White House when it passed. Yet, there the Bureau of Prisons policy was.

From a personal perspective, this was indeed a learning experience. I *never* should have believed the FSA credits until I saw them, and when they were taken away before I even had my hands on them, it was a harsh blow inside the joint when life already was tough enough. But that's why they call it prison.

[*Author's Note: As I read and edit this, I see here that this incident would be the beginning of my investigation into the broader issue of the failure of the Bureau of Prisons to properly enforce the FSA. It was just eighteen days in when I began to find my mission for the rest of my sentence. I knew I wouldn't be able to help myself, but I damn well would fix this mess for others.*]

HUCK POST 31:
Snuggle Bunny to Smuggle Bunny
April 6, 2024—Day 19

> *I had become an expert in turning out young girls,*
> *tricking them into my game.*
> —Iceberg Slim

A moment of praise now for the joy and miracle of earplugs in prison. It took me almost a month to discover their utility.

It was a month of tossing and turning at night as my sweet dreams were intermittently interrupted by the sounds of anything but silence.

A cacophony of snoring. No shortage of farts.

Then there was Mad Dog's digital timer randomly firing at 3, 4, or 5 in the morning.

Boris back from his latest chemo with his death-rattling cough.

The loudest toilet flushes in the western world.

The mega-squeak of dorm doors opening as insomniacs and the guards doing the midnight, 2 a.m., and 5 a.m. counts shuffled in and out all evening.

My Sweet Pixie would save me from all of this, but only after I had to turn my once Snuggle Bunny into a Smuggle Bunny. I did it as quickly as a pimp turns an innocent angel into a Crack Ho.

On one of our Saturday morning visits, she brought two pairs of my precious Mack's thin earplugs—the ones I usually use for swimming.

She stuffed them in her bra in case the Evil Ajemon made her empty her pockets. Once inside the joint, it was a simple trip to the ladies room and, upon her return to our seating, she slipped the precious cargo into my hot little hands.

Contraband bliss. And yes, I had turned the most honest woman I have ever known into a Smuggler Ho. That's why they call it prison.

HUCK POST 32:
Of Time and Punishment
April 6, 2024—Day 19

Prison not only takes from you the time which you spend within its razor-wired walls. Prison invariably takes time from you *after* your release by both shortening your lifespan and reducing the years of a quality life.

Indeed, it is only the rarest individuals who come out of prison physically stronger and healthier. At the center of this problem is not just the stress of the experience—although there is no shortage of that. It is the nutrition—or lack thereof—together with the lack of adequate medical treatment.

On the nutrition front, without question, the biggest challenge I faced in my relatively short stay was getting the calories, vitamins, fiber, and especially protein that I needed to maintain strength and muscle mass.

Here, it is true that we were fed three meals a day, and that's better than tens of millions of people living on the rest of the planet. Yet, it was a diet heavy on carbs and devoid of fresh fruits or vegetables—except for the occasional tiny apple. Also missing in action was any fresh meat, poultry, or fish.

In fact, prison "cuisine" reminded me of the famous Gore Vidal diet. When Vidal wanted to lose weight, he only went to bad restaurants. He could have tried prison food instead—yes, many inmates lost weight. And if they didn't, it was because they were curled up in a ball on their bunk any time they could, eating donuts, cookies, and ice cream from the commissary.

As for the longer term health-care implications, the high carb, high sugar, high cholesterol diet especially elevates the risk of heart attack and diabetes. Yet, the ultimate risk for many inmates is the risk associated with the inability to get prescription medication on a timely basis.

I was blessed at age seventy-four not to require any medicines. In contrast, many inmates were dependent on a wide variety of prescription drugs readily available on the outside but as rare as black swans inside the big house.

In the most heartbreaking case, a man in the early stage of MS simply couldn't get the medicine he needed to slow the advance of a disease that kills. This was nothing short of murder in my book—the man had five years left in his sentence, long enough to cause irreversible damage. In several other cases, inmates were stymied in their quest for insulin and other diabetes treatments. Yes, indeed, that's why they call it prison.

PIXIE POST 6:
Our Third Prison Date
April 7, 2024—Day 20

Pixie here, and Dale as usual arrived a few minutes early to pick me up for the prison journey. He is my wheelman for today's 8 a.m. Sunday visitation.

I know it will be a joyous day with my Ever Huck. Yesterday we sang together and danced when we knew people (and the terrible guard Ajemon) were not watching.

And we had some pretty moments looking at a beautiful yellow-blossomed tree right outside of the window where we usually sit near the windows in the visitors area.

And we watched a pussycat navigate the top of the fence between the razor wire like Baryshnikov. And this sweet daring cat reminded of us of our sweet gentle Lucy Girl back home.

We have learned how to stay out of sight of Ajemon the Terrible behind a pillar so we can touch like a first date—well maybe a third date. See how I'm learning how to break rules in prison—because the rules are sometimes so stupid and they should be broken.

Yes, today must be fun (as fun as we can have)—we must learn to make it fun—because this week, my Stoic Huck learned that he—we—may have to be here for ALL four long months, so we might as well make the best of it!

My soldier that he is, I'm in for him and with him forever.

HUCK POST 33:
My Kingdom for an Orange
April 7, 2024—Day 20

When I was a kid, the stereotype of a prison meal was bread and water. That was part of the punishment.

It certainly wasn't that bad where I was housed. As I have noted, every inmate I met thanked me for the improvement of the meals the prison administrators ordered as a Potemkin maneuver just days before I got to the prison—that, along with some painting and cleanup and little stuff like replacing burned-out light bulbs, was also done. So I didn't get the completely real deal these guys had been getting.

Still, there was no putting lipstick on this pig—and I'm certainly not asking anyone to shed any tears for convicted criminals living in Spartan conditions.

Yet, I do think every prison should at least meet the minimum guidelines required by law, particularly for nutrition; and if I had one thing I could change on the menu in Miami that was just too damn funny, it would be this: In the epicenter of the American citrus industry, how about serving a fresh orange once in a while—the cheapest, healthiest damn thing you can buy outside of prison in Florida. [*Author's Note: I will explain in a later post why this is so, and you are likely to laugh your ass off.*]

More broadly, organizations ranging from the American Heart Association, Centers for Disease Control, and National Institutes of Health to the United States Department of Agriculture and World Health Organization all tell you to eat plenty of fruits and vegetables, and there is precious little of either. In fact, the only "vegetable," such as it was, that I would typically see was corn right out of a can. As for fruit, we did get a baby apple a day, but that was it, other than some syrupy shit that might have been fruit cocktail.

Not surprisingly, virtually every inmate quickly gets constipated when they arrive. And one of the hottest sellers at the commissary is Raisin Bran, if you get my drift.

This observation fits right in with the broader "for profit" nature of the prison business. In this "prison industrial complex" model, prisons and the private companies that run many of them like to hold on to inmates as long as possible because funds are allocated on a per head basis. As a result, there is tremendous inertia when processing inmate requests for release.

If I were a total cynic about it (I am), I could easily imagine that one purpose of the kitchen not meeting inmates' caloric and protein needs is to drive sales to the commissary.

At the commissary, you can buy much higher quality protein—chicken, pork, salmon, mackerel—bags mind you, nothing fresh.

You can also buy soups. I would turn into a Ramen noodle freak by the end of my bid, have a big bowl as my bedtime snack. Yet, I never saw soup served in the cafeteria.

Nor did I ever see any real sugar in the mess hall, just artificial sweeteners otherwise known as the oncologist's full employment act. BTW, the lack of real sugar in the prison is yet another enigma, since Belle Glade, a main sugar producer, is, like the orange groves, just a few miles from the prison.

And how about this still unsolved puzzle: Why do they serve only skim milk in prison and never low-fat or whole milk? They couldn't possibly be worried about cholesterol given the other crap they serve. Or maybe they are—so maybe that's why fried or scrambled eggs were as rare in my prison as innocent men.

Did I also mention as part of the commissary business model that the prices are high? Yeah, Navarro, you did.

Hey, I'm just telling you again for emphasis. It's a Tennessee Ernie Ford world in prison—sixteen tons, another day older, and I owe my soul to the company store.

HUCK POST 34:
Blood on the Walls
April 8, 2024—Day 21

This postcard is dedicated to all you hockey fans.

It took three weeks until I saw my first fight, and it wasn't pretty. The consensus asshole of the dorm started mouthing off again after getting high on bootleg liquor and pills, and somebody just picked him up by his scrawny neck and bounced him off the concrete wall a time or two.

The most interesting aspect of the spectacle was its aftermath. One of the inmate-doctors checked him for a concussion—negative.

Another inmate quickly got out a mop and a bucket to clean up the blood.

And the blowup was carefully hidden from the guards.

If the fight were discovered, it would lead to interrogations and a lockdown and nobody wanted that. So it was all handled internally.

Like it never happened. Did it?

HUCK POST 35:
Sacrilege on a Sacred Sunday
April 9, 2024—Day 22

> *The beatings will continue until morale improves.*
> —Captain Bligh, HMS Bounty

The most sacred of times at a federal prison are those times when you are allowed visits from your friends and family members, particularly your wife, girlfriend, or, in my case, my fiancée.

At my Miami prison, every single visitor, young and old alike, was harassed by the guard in charge of monitoring such visits—typically, the notorious Ajemon the Terrible, as the inmates called him.

After watching this spectacle for several weeks—and being on the end of several Ajemon verbal assaults—it became my White Whale of an Ahab goal to have this sadistic SOB transferred to more appropriate duties.

The problem with Ajemon started with his simultaneously weird and imposing appearance. At 6'3" and built like a linebacker, he always wore a black pointed mask that made him look a crow—mind you, this was years after the end of COVID and the mask rarely covered his nose.

The mask was stupid, it made him look stupid, and it may well be he was really more stupid than sadistic—although the blend of those two traits can be a very deadly combination.

I was hardly the only or first inmate who wanted to see "Ajemon the Terrible" gone. Dozens of inmates had already filed so-called "cop outs," the complaint forms of the prison, detailing Ajemon's long list of abuses.

With the women, Ajemon would get uncomfortably close with his wanding for any contraband. With the children, he'd harangue them for moving around too much. With teens, he refused them entry if they didn't have a federal ID—even though prison regs didn't require it.

On top of all this, one of the biggest problems with Ajemon was the glacial pace in which he processed visitors. Other guards performing the very same function got visitors in in real time with little or no lines. With

Ajemon, it could take up to forty-five minutes to an hour and thereby eat away about a full third of one's visiting time.

Despite all these abuses having been carefully documented by outraged inmates in complaint after complaint—at the very real risk of retaliation from the higher ups and Ajemon himself—*nothing* had been done to transfer him.

I was hoping, however, that the weekend of April 8 and 9 might be Ajemon's Waterloo, thanks to several monumental puckups.

F-Up Numero Uno occurred on Saturday when Ajemon was ordered to do an emergency count among the visitors after the four dorm pods came up one inmate short. For over a half an hour, he had all of us inmates standing in a line, pulled abruptly away from our families because he had twenty inmates but only seventeen inmate IDs; and he had erased all the data he had entered into the computer.

Finally, Fredericks, the duty officer, came in—to a standing ovation from both the inmates and visitors to clear the cluster puck up. Fredericks quickly discovered Ajemon had accidentally covered up the three missing IDs with some papers.

While Ajemon and Fredericks then got the count right, they had to abort our Sunday visit a full half hour early. So with the delays and the early closure, we got to spend only about half of the allotted three hours with our loved ones.

Incredibly, Ajemon would double down on this stupidity the next day when we had to do a count which should have lasted five minutes. However, Ajemon couldn't even get that right—it was more wasted time and a *late* count.

Of course, all of this went into the formal complaint I filed the next day with the new guy, Verdejo, who was promising big changes but hadn't yet delivered a single one. Perhaps that first one might be to replace Ajemon. Oh Navarro, you are so naïve sometimes. That's why they call it prison.

HUCK POST 36:
A Morning of Anguish and Tranquility
April 10, 2024—Day 23

In prison, you quickly figure out the very best ways to pass your time in an otherwise bad situation. And by the middle of the third week, I figured out that I could find tranquility every morning walking around the prison track as the sun rose on the countdown from 120 days to freedom.

This particular morning, as the sun rose in a red glow while I walked the track and a crescent moon moved closer to setting, I contemplated the heartbreak I had just heard from one of the guys at breakfast twenty minutes earlier. Said inmate had gotten his hopes up for an earlier release under the First Step Act (FSA), but just the day before, he had been told by his case manager he wasn't eligible.

This kind of news at FCI Miami was as common as the clap in Bangkok. For whatever reason, FCI Miami had a very well-earned reputation for hanging on to inmates as long as possible, and they did it through a three-card monte game with the credit you were supposed to earn each month for early release.

Of course, other ways to slow an inmate's release included things as simple as sitting on paperwork to more complex gambits like closing halfway houses so prisoners could not be moved because of lack of halfway house space.

As for compassionate release, no matter how close you may be to a coffin, forget about it. And forget about any furloughs for births, deaths, weddings, or any other family markers.

At any rate, the latest inmate casualty of the "we got ya so we're gonna keep you" was one of the nicest and smartest guys I've ever met. He had been over the moon about the prospect of getting out in less than a month. Yet now, his case manager—a newbie to her job—told him he'd be around for another two months. Said Newbie Case Manager couldn't even give him a straight answer as to why.

Instead, all she said was if he wanted to complain, he'd have to file not one but two forms to send up the chain—knowing full well the BP8½ and BP9 forms would sit in inboxes for months and long past the time the inmate would be released.

I remember well the days leading up to passage of the 2018 First Step Act (FSA). Around the White House, it was generally considered Jared Kushner's baby, and some of the law-and-order types within the West Wing scornfully looked down on Jared's effort, as they feared it might make the Boss look "soft on crime."

But Jared was dogged. When Jared was in college, his own father had been imprisoned; and that imprisonment had wreaked havoc with his family. Jared still bore those scars, and he was intent on the FSA's passage.

In fact, it would turn out to be legislation with significant political benefits—the black and brown minorities that disproportionately occupy America's prisons would welcome the Trump opportunity to get out of prison, and their families would vote accordingly.

Economically, it also made great sense to move at least first-time and nonviolent offenders out of a prison system plagued by over-sentencing. This could be sold to the American people as a compassionate conservative act that would turn inmates from being a burden on the federal budget back into taxpaying workers and contributors to society.

So the FSA got passed with Jared's help. But with Trump gone, the Bureau of Prisons and Biden administration did everything not to implement it fully and properly.

One of the first things I'm going to find out when I get out of this prison is whether prisons like FCI Miami get funding based in real time on the amount of inmates they house. That's the only explanation (other than sadism) that might explain it; and if that's true, its perverse incentive is radically at odds with both proper use of taxpayer funds and basic humanity. [*Author's Note: I would learn much more about this, which I will share in later postcards.*]

As I walked the track, I couldn't help but again think of the Buddha's admonition that "desire is suffering" and the Thai credo of "sanuk"—living in the moment.

The moment you desire something as simple as an earlier release in this sunny Kafka Motel, and that hope is then crushed yet again by the prison bureaucracy, anguish and suffering becomes the order of the day. That's why they call it prison.

HUCK POST 37:
A Training School for Liars
April 11, 2024—Day 24

Here's a riddle for you. Two inmates of identical age are charged with the identical nonviolent crimes and each is sentenced to a five-year term in a minimum-security prison. One is a clean-living, sober, and drug-free man; the other is a pill-popping alcoholic. Which individual is likely to get out first on a reduced sentence?

The answer is a poster child for the kind of perverse incentives that pervade our broken and broken down justice system—and create more dilemmas for prisoners. That's because the answer in this case is the man with a substance abuse problem.

Here's the perverse incentive twist. Any nonviolent, first-time offender with an alcohol or drug problem becomes eligible for the Residential Drug Abuse Program (RDAP). This is a nine-month, five-hundred hour drug and alcohol education program that comes with the most precious of prison prizes—a full twelve-month sentence reduction upon completion.

And here's the perverse incentive, "teach me how to lie" punch line: No such comparable RDAP credits are available to the teetotaling, sober inmates.

Ergo, this moral dilemma: If a sober inmate wants to get back twelve months earlier to his family, he has every incentive to lie about having a drug or alcohol problem to begin with.

Did I also mention that RDAP is offered at only *some* of the camps (like Pensacola) and that these are some of the best facilities in the entire BOP minimum-security system. That's just one more incentive to lie.

I should say here that by the time a new inmate arrives at his prison, he has likely already been conditioned to lie by the system in order to minimize his prison sentence. Sadly, almost *every* inmate I did time with arrived at the Miami prison courtesy of a *coerced plea deal*.

In this plea deal game, prosecutors will stack up multiple charges to the ceiling and threaten a defendant (and sometimes members of the defendant's family) with staggeringly long sentences. If, however, the defendant pleads out, that long sentence—twenty or thirty years in some cases—will be "reduced" to "only" five or ten years.

And here's the kicker: To take a plea deal and thereby get a lighter sentence, defendants are often forced to plead to a whole menu of charges, some of which the defendant was not even remotely guilty of! As the coup de grâce, such a plea deal also forecloses any appeal options.

To put this all another way, at the very start of your prison journey, you are forced to lie to save your own skin. And once you are in, you have every incentive to tell administrators you are a drug addict or alcoholic so you can get into an RDAP program and get out twelve months earlier than you otherwise would. That's why they call it prison.

HUCK POST 38:
An Epidemic of Over-Sentencing
April 12, 2024—Day 25

Mandatory minimums ensure that a sentence reflects the seriousness
of the offense, averts the prospect of lenient sentences, and promotes
certainty and predictability in sentencing.
—U.S. Sentencing Commission (1991)

That was then.

The use of mandatory minimum sentences is an ongoing human
rights violation in America. These one-size-fits-all sentencing statutes
. . . often backfire, giving drug addicts and small-time offenders
enormous sentences.
—American Bar Association (2009)

This is now.

If Miami FCI is typical of the rest of the minimum-security prison system, that system is wasting a shit ton of taxpayer money while significantly increasing the probability of recidivism among a prison population that is heavily weighted towards nonviolent first time offenders. Simultaneously, this is both absurd and insane.

The epidemic of over-sentencing, which I found myself in the midst of, will indeed be one of my lasting—and most poignant—prison memories.

Walk with me now for a few minutes as we enter my dorm wing housing, hosting forty-four souls when I arrived. As we enter the first corridor of twenty-two beds, there's Mad Dog on my left in a wheelchair, and on a diagonal to my right, Brother Del also in a wheelchair.

At sixty-six, some twenty years removed from a crack addiction and winding, up in the wrong place at the wrong time, Mad Dog should have been released on compassionate release years ago. Ditto for Del Gowing, a distinguished Vietnam vet in his eighties, whose more than twenty-year odyssey has transformed him from a healthy, strapping Irishman and prominent attorney to the wheelchair-bound gentleman he is. He has long paid for his white collar crime and should have been home over a decade ago.

Then there's Izzy, likewise in his golden years and another Vietnam vet wasting away ironing the camp uniforms to make a few bucks at commissary.

Following down the line there's Elliot, the private equity guy, and the doctors Jose and Jesus—all given punishingly massive sentences for crimes that would have far more easily been handled in civil litigation.

Indeed, none of these three should even be here to begin with. Add Mad Dog, Del, and Izzy, that's at least six of twenty-two inmates on my side of the dorm pod that should be home and off the taxpayer dole.

Of course, on the other side of my dorm pod, there's Boris with a severe cancer who leaves the unit periodically for extensive chemotherapy. He has been repeatedly denied compassionate release for home confinement for unfathomable reasons.

As another example of over-sentencing, there's Wally who is doing a ten-year stretch for a relatively minor infraction that likewise could have been handled civilly. He's lost his lady love as the time has passed him and his relationship by. At sixty-four, he has little to look forward to on the outside, in large part because of the years he has spent behind bars. And he should have been out over a year ago by the letter of the law.

Then, in the younger dorms, you have a lot of the nonviolent drug offenders who got caught up as a first offender in the bane of too many prisoners: the "mandatory minimum sentence." It breaks my heart to see these younger men, many with wives and young children, forced to grind through what will be eight- to ten-year prison sentences that will ruin their families and earnings potential.

Don't get me wrong here. I'm not going "soft on crime." I believe folks should be punished for their crimes, and that punishment has an important deterrence value. But how many months or years does a man need behind bars to get the "walk the straight and narrow line" message, particularly as a first nonviolent offender?

It sure the hell isn't ten years. It probably isn't even three to five years. Because it doesn't take long to get the message from a prison cell. I know. I've been there now, and I've seen the thousand-yard stares not just in the eyes of the inmates but in the eyes of their family members.

And the broader point here is that for every extra month that an inmate spends in prison beyond what might be needed for deterrence of future crimes, that's wasted taxpayer money and forgone tax revenues from inmates who would be working if free. These extra months through over-sentencing also raise the probability of recidivism because of the corrosive effects on family ties and earnings potential.

I wish it weren't so. But that's why they call it prison.

[*Author's Note: You can see with posts like these that with each passing day, I'm getting deeper and deeper into these issues and will eventually turn a "smart on crime" prison reform into the most integral part of my mission in prison.*]

HUCK POST 39:
Nature Versus Nurture
April 13, 2024—Day 26

One of the most interesting guys I met offered a classic case of nature vs. nurture. His name was Ricky, and he was a big strong young man of about thirty who freely talked about having been a crypto bandit on the outside.

When I asked him what he was in for, he just matter-of-factly said, "I stole people's bitcoin." To do that, you have to be damn near a rocket scientist, and, in the course of our first discussion one day, I learned how a few twists and turns in life can lead you to a prison rather than, in Ricky's case, either a starting center fielder for the New York Yankees or a CEO of a Silicon Valley cybersecurity startup.

The difference in Ricky's case was about two points on his ACT test to get into college. If he'd been my kid, I could've got him those two points and then some simply by enrolling him in a class many high school kids regularly take to boost their SAT and ACT scores.

But Ricky didn't have that kind of parental guidance and nurturing, so he didn't get the college scholarship to play baseball that he would have had. In his case, when that door closed—his family couldn't afford college—the cyber bandit porthole that opened would lead straight to prison

Later, in the early evening of this same day as I'm walking the track, I stop and watch the softball game when I see Ricky come to bat. As I told you, the softball field is inside the perimeter of the expansive track, which is a third of a mile around.

I stop because I wanted to see if Ricky was bullshitting me about his baseball prowess. As I watch, I see the bases are loaded.

Sure enough, after taking a few sinker balls, Ricky unloads on a juicy one down the middle and sends the ball first over the softball field fence, and then, as it keeps going, right out of the razor-wire fence guarding the yard. No bullshit from Ricky there.

An inning later, after I'm around the track three times for a mile, I see the funniest damn thing I've ever seen on a baseball field. (That's aside, of course, from Tony Fauci's infamous and hilarious first pitch at a Washington Nationals game that took off at a 45-degree angle and hit a cameraman.)

Anyway, Ricky's at shortstop; and a big, overweight guy named Carl—I called him the Jolly Giant—hits a hot grounder to Ricky and starts lumbering toward first. Just for the fun of it, rather than gun the ball over to the first baseman, Ricky sprints and beats the guy to first base for the out. Yep. He wasn't bullshitting about his lightning speed either.

[*Author's Note: Stay tuned for more about how Ricky would be yet another inmate kept in the slammer long past his due date.*]

PIXIE POST 7:
Vending Machine Haute Cuisine
April 13, 2024—Day 26

Pixie here, and this lovely Saturday morning, Dale picks me up once again at the Doral. We make our first and immediate pit stop at Starbuck's—dark roast Grande black as pitch, none of that froufrou, Macchiato, Frappuccino, California prissy stuff. I'm a Manhattan girl—whiskey and coffee straight up. Although my whiskey days are in the rearview mirror.

Just near the prison, we stop again, this time at Publix—which is the greatest pit stop before heading to the prison gates. I get to use a *clean* restroom, plus I have to grab some food to scarf down—in case the vending machines don't work—so my stomach doesn't suffer too much during the four hours I am with my Huck. (Tums for the tummy is my latest prison accessory.)

To use the vending machines, I can bring up to fifteen one dollar bills into the Visitor Center. If the machines are fully stocked and working—which is rarely the case—Huck and I can go so very Huck style by sharing and nibbling on a burger together. Huck says it tastes so good compared to the prison food—the best proof he offers me that the prison food truly is really terrible.

Of course, when there's no real food left, we must resort to potato chips or candy bars, and it is really hard on Huck because in order to see me on the weekends, he has to skip the lunch meal at the mess hall. And he hates eating "sugar shit," which is what he calls it.

The only good thing that Ajemon the Terrible ever does is use his brute force to "fix" the vending machines when a sandwich or a burger gets stuck coming out of the chute. Ajemon just grabs the machine and shakes it like he has an inmate in his clutches, and out pops the food. It would be funny if he weren't so terrible.

HUCK POST 40:
Broken Windows, Broken Rules
April 14, 2024—Day 27

Do as I say, not as I do.
—Anon

The only consistent thing here is inconsistency.
—Inmate Jobim

If there is any cliché that best epitomizes the behavior of far too many prison guards, it is the old "do as I say" cliché. And I get why it happens.

Prison guard duty is dangerous, the pay is not commensurate with the risks, and it's easy to get a bad dose of low-grade PTSD as the years wear on in drab environments with convicts you dare not turn your back on, always out to hustle or outwit you.

That said, it's well past time, particularly for minimum-security prisons, for wardens and other administrators to revamp an organizational culture that does anything but prepare inmates for the outside. Here, any such organizational culture overhaul must begin with a variation of the broken window theory—unless you immediately fix vandalized broken windows and punish the vandals, you invite more and bigger crimes (thanks to Professor James Q. Wilson for the broken window theory and to former New York mayor, Rudy Giuliani, for popularizing its use!)

In this case, one of the first broken windows to fix as part of an organizational culture overhaul at a prison like the one in Miami is for the prison guards to set a good example in following the rules. And it should start with the most simple stuff like the prison schedule itself, where the only consistency is inconsistency.

For example, beginning at 6 a.m., the guard is supposed to open the doors of the dorms as well as the computer room for inmate email and the rec facilities so that inmates might get some exercise before the workday starts and get to work on time. However, the opening times each day varied by guards and by as much as an hour or more.

Ditto for the meals. Breakfast is supposed to be at 6:00, lunch at 11:00, and dinner at 5:00. Yet again, the times varied wildly, and the guard was more often late than early.

More than once, I saw an early breakfast where the guys, who were used to breakfast being late, showed up a few minutes past the scheduled time and breakfast was already over.

And of course there was the ubiquitous and almighty "count" five times a day to make sure no one had escaped—or taken a little trip outside to stock up on contraband.

The count on weekdays is supposed to be at 4 p.m. and 10 p.m. when you must stand in silence by your bed, and at midnight, 3 a.m., and 5 a.m., when you are expected to be in bed.

Rarely, if ever, was the count on time, and the worst variations came when the 10 p.m. count stretched up to as late as 11 p.m. when everyone is dead tired and long past ready to sleep.

Of course, as you read this, you are probably thinking I'm trying to make some mountains out of molehills. But if the guards are trying to teach how to live by and obey rules to prepare you for remaining free on the outside—as they should be doing—it sure doesn't set a good example when they break every little rule in the book on a daily basis. But that's why they call it prison.

HUCK POST 41:
A Stacked Appeals Court Redux
April 15, 2024—Day 28

Today, I have my first formal legal call with my lead attorney, Stanley Woodward, after almost three weeks in prison. We talk about the status of the appeal of my case to what first will be the District of Columbia rotten-to-its-partisan-core Appeals Court and eventually to the Supreme Court.

Absent strong encouragement and multiple exhortations from me, Stanley and his team will still produce a very good appeal. But Stanley will do it the same way Japanese automakers manufacture cars, through a "just in time" schedule.

As the guy who coined the phrase "In Trump Time," which is to say "as soon as possible," Stanley's approach drives me nuts. There's simply too much at stake for even a comma to be out of place, so, with Stanley's blessing, I get his commitment to have the team get cracking on the appeal, with the goal of having weekly Friday phone meetings at 1 p.m. from prison, with an outline of the appeal due next Friday.

That taken care of, I also discuss with Stanley the possibility of firing a shot across the DC Court of Appeals bow regarding the three-panel appeals judge we have been drawing. The broader question is whether these panels are being fairly drawn up at random, as everyone assumes them to be, *or* whether they are purposely being stacked with Obama judges and Trump haters to screw us.

Stanley is resistant to any such a shot being fired. He doesn't want to rock the DC Circuit boat because he's playing the long game and will have other clients with appeals he doesn't want exposed to prejudice.

I, on the other hand, want to sink that weaponized U-boat because it will be impossible to get a fair appeals panel for this next round under the current rules and previous results unless we raise Holy Hell.

Why do I think this? Because I've already drawn three appeals panels—two in my civil suit and one in my criminal case—while Steve Bannon has drawn several more. In most cases, our panels have been *all Democrat* despite a two to one ratio of Democrats on the courts. Probabilistically, there's well below a 20 percent chance of that happening if the draw is random.

Even more to the point and far more alarming, one or both of two particularly woke and Trump-hating Obama-appointed judges—Cornelia Pillard and Patricia Millett—have appeared on every single panel that Steve and I have had. The odds of that are just a little better than getting struck by lightning, or Joy Reid switching to the Republican Party.

It's a stacked deck, and that's just not the way the justice system is supposed to work in America.

At any rate, my discussion with Stanley ends in a stalemate for now. As my old boss Donald Trump loves to say, "Let's see what happens."

[*Author's Note: Pillard and Millett played a key role in my having to go to prison before my appeal wasn't even heard. As outrage goes, it was an 11 on a scale of 1–10.*]

HUCK POST 42:
A Training School for Criminals
April 16, 2024—Day 29

One of the most important goals of imprisonment, particularly for first-time offenders, should be to minimize the chance an inmate will "recidivate," that is, be a repeat offender. Yet, the justice and penal systems are structured in far too many ways, large and small, to breed or encourage criminal behavior.

The biggest stuff we've already talked about, like over-sentencing and destroying the ability of a released inmate to earn a decent living and support a family. But a la the "broken window theory," the small stuff can be equally corrosive.

For example, once you realize the mess hall can't possibly meet your nutritional needs and keep you healthy, you begin to search out the black market for food and find ways to get "seconds" at the mess hall, which is forbidden.

Next, you bring an illegal plastic container to take with you what you can't eat—but that's against the rules too. So immediately, to survive, you start to break rules.

Then there are the minute limits on phone calls—about five hundred minutes a month to parcel out among your loved ones, your lawyer, and everyone in between. That's only about sixteen minutes a day.

Plus, half of the few wall phones may not work, as it was in my unit. So there are often long lines to make a call. On top of that, you can't hear your conversations well because of inmates talking in the halls and bad acoustics, and everyone—including the guards monitoring your calls—can listen in while you express your love and tender thoughts to your girl. So what do you do?

You try to get a contraband cell phone and a good place to hide it. Because if they find it, you'll likely wind up on the next bus out in leg irons headed for God knows where and your only guarantee will be that it's worse than where you're coming from.

That's because cell phones represent one of the worst kinds of contraband you can smuggle in besides dope.

But you want a cell phone because you want to talk to your loved ones. Because not talking to your girlfriend, wife, or family is worse than anything they can throw at you. And that's why they call it prison.

PIXIE POST 8:
Our First Prison Anniversary
April 17, 2024—Day 30

Pixie here, and it's one month now in prison for my soldier—three more to go. By now, I call the Trump Doral Hotel my second home because it truly does feel like a home.

This beautiful hotel is always so full of people to distract me. And Mikael and Dale and the crew always take such good care of me.

Thank you so much Eric Trump and Clay Clark for making this possible. Thank you Mikael and Dale for making it wonderful salve for my sadness.

Off I will go in a few days, back to the Golden City of Doral and to see my Ever Huck! Yay!!!

HUCK POST 43:
Prison for Price Gougers
April 17, 2024—Day 30

> *The Appeal's investigation reveals that incarcerated people in many states are charged significantly more for essential items than those outside prison even though they typically earn pennies an hour—or no wages at all. The Appeal found prison prices up to five times higher than in the community and markups as high as 600 percent. This financial burden, which can cost hundreds of dollars per month, is often passed onto prisoners' loved ones. In just one example, Indiana prisons charged about $33 for an 8-inch fan, even though a similar item sells online for about $23 at Lowe's. Incarcerated people in the state, who are often confined to dangerously hot prisons in the summer, can earn as little as 30 cents an hour, meaning it could take more than 100 hours of work to afford the fan.*
> —*The Appeal* newspaper, April 17, 2024

It took almost a month. But a steady prison diet of calorie-deficient, protein-lite, no-sign-of-any-fresh-fruit-or-vegetables meals finally began to take its toll. The top signs were lower energy, loss of strength, and a tendency towards lethargy.

The biggest problem was breakfast. Like the *Groundhog Day* movie, the sun rose on cereal, skim milk, and corn sugar syrup with a dash of canned peaches or pears—only a small apple would break up the monotony.

Okay, I'm whining a bit here, but the reason I'm telling you this is to tell you about the bigger problem of price-gouging in the prison system. This problem starts in Florida with two monopolies—one runs the food services, the other runs the commissary. To the extent the food services side can restrict the diet of the inmates, that boosts demand for supplemental food at the commissary.

Part of the food restrictions is a combination of laziness and maliciousness on the part of some of the guards that wind up in charge. Literally tons of food gets thrown away every month because it simply is not provided before it rots or becomes bug infested.

A poster child for this is the boxes of bananas that will sit ready for distribution as they ripen from green to delicious yellow to mottled brown. Chris, an inmate who helped run the kitchen, told me that he routinely asked the guards if he could serve the fruit in the delicious yellow phase but was regularly turned down for no reason at all.

Was this maliciousness? Maybe more like sadism if you got to know this particular son-of-a-bitch guard.

Of course, another problem that leads to shortages of usable food in the prison mess is the fresh meat, usually beef or chicken, that winds up in boxes in the trunk of a guard's SUV for a weekend barbeque. Sometimes, the inmates in the kitchen are even asked to prepare and season it for the grill. The thinking here seems to be: *they don't pay us enough, so this is ours.*

Regardless, the bigger thieves are those who profit from the commissary. Malnourished inmates flock to it once a week for the privilege of buying food at prices 30 percent, 40 percent, 50 percent or higher than you'd find even in a discount big boxer like Walmart or Target.

For example, during my prison stay, I became a self-described "ramen noodle freak," having a bowl every night before dinner. Little did I know I was in a lot of very bad good company inside the joint and across the prison system. During my research, I found this priceless quote from the same *Appeal* article leading off this postcard:

> The Appeal *examined the price of a single packet of ramen on commissary lists in more than 40 states and found prisoners were routinely charged significantly more for ramen than they would be in the community.*
>
> *One package of ramen goes for about 35 cents at Target, but many commissaries charged over 40 cents per package, according to documents obtained by* The Appeal. *Prices for identical products also differed greatly from state to state. Maruchan-brand ramen noodles cost 57 cents in Missouri prisons, for instance, but $1.06 in Florida prisons—about three times more expensive than at Target.*

BTW, my worst commissary rip-off came when I tried to buy a new pair of $60 Under Armour running shoes. The cashier said all they had were some Skechers. So I said, what the hell, why not? Without asking the price!

So I wound up with a wrong-sized nothing of a shoe that cost me $81—about 25 percent of my total monthly commissary allotment. I discovered the same damn shoe sold on Amazon for $34.

And by the way, a lot of the shoes that are sold at premium prices are "irregulars" with weird stitching, wrong sizing, etc., that typically sell for half the regular retail price.

Of course, the poorer inmates who can't afford these prices get screwed. They have to sell themselves as handymen and servants to those within the prison with means, doing their laundry, making them meals, and so it goes.

As an economist, this pisses me off. From a crime-fighting perspective—this kind of bullshit only raises the risk of recidivism—it's just stupid. But that's why they call it prison.

HUCK POST 44:
Enter Stage Right, The Prison Gestapo
April 18, 2024—Day 31

As I was finishing my midday workout between work assignments, I noticed that the usually deserted pavilion was jammed with inmates. A quick question revealed that the dreaded Special Investigative Squad (SIS) gestapo had arrived from across the street at the low-security prison.

The SIS shit was about to hit the inmate contraband fan. It was a classic case of cops and robbers. The inmates had an elaborate system to hide valued items like cell phones, cell phones, and cell phones from the guards, and SIS spent a ton of taxpayer money trying to find them.

It was just stupid. It would have been far better to simply let inmates buy cell phones and minutes from the commissary to supplement their limited landline prison phone time of about five hundred minutes a month—not nearly enough for a family man.

All the prison would have needed to do is put throttles on the phones to prevent some of the fun and games inmates used cell phones for—arranging dope deals, coordinating gang activity, etc.

You weren't going to stop the cell phone traffic. You might as well make some money from it.

At any rate, as soon as I saw the SIS, I hustled over to the email room to get out this missive to Sweet Pixie as a heads-up. It's a copy of an email I sent to my Pixie through the prison "CORRLINKS" system.

The prison gendarmes not only read everything you send and receive. They have been known to edit outgoing emails in ways that would curl the ACLU's hair. You'll start seeing more of my email correspondence with Pixie as these postcards continue.

Note who the email is from. That's yours truly as reduced and reductio ad absurdum to my prison inmate number: 04370510.

FROM: 04370510
TO: Brenner, Bonnie
SUBJECT: Re: Miercoles
DATE: 04/18/2024 8:00:07 PM

My love my love my love Sweet Pixie,

Bad day here at the ranch for the inmates. The dreaded Special Investigative Squad AKA SIS AKA Prison Gestapo came in with dogs and all of the inmates are out in the yard while they search everybody's lockers and the dorms.

BRACE YOURSELF: Sometimes if they find some contraband from a FEW people, they lock EVERYONE down and we don't have access to phones or email. I hope this doesn't happen tonight, particularly since you are feeling blue, but if you DON'T hear from me tonight and maybe tomorrow and longer, I'll be locked inside the dorm and fed balony sandwiches until the prison police decide we've been punished enough.

I HOPE this doesn't happen and you will hear me at 5:30 but like a good girl scout, be prepared. That is indeed why they call it prison.

On a happier note, I conked out for an hour after we talked in a cheeseburger coma and then had a good run when they drove us out into the yard like cattle.

I love you so much. This is so wrong and stupid. It is what it is. We will have the last word and laugh I promise you.

Love you more,
Huck

HUCK POST 45:
The Showers Don't Work 'Cause the Vandals Smashed the Handles
April 19, 2024—Day 32

*They're mad because they're not real cops. They couldn't pass the
tests for the police or FBI so here they are. Everything they find
you can buy at a convenience store.*
—Inmate Zach

I loved Inmate Zach for his purity as an archetype. Big powerful dude with
gold teeth who ran fanatical daily workout sessions for the inmates—burpees
until death—and who had a work ethic that would make a Sherpa proud.

Zach ran the prison laundry by day and dispensed prison wisdom by
night—he's the one who described the "dump and flush" and a guy the
prison counselors relied on to ease inmates into the flow of prison.

At any rate, after what would turn out to be the Special Investigative
Services (SIS) jackpot raid, Zach made the quip above, and it's as true as his
sentence was long.

It was not a matter of *if* but *when* the dreaded SIS stormtroopers would
come to smash things up and then maybe lock us down. I had been warned
about that possibility for weeks—and the day had finally come yesterday,
Day 31 of my lovely prison sabbatical.

As I had come off the track after a three-mile bout with swarms of
gnats, I noticed a large crowd of inmates clustered at the pavilion at the
entrance to the rec fields—it's an area where inmates watch TV, play chess,
shoot pool, or just hang out and shoot the shit.

Normally, on a hot Florida afternoon, most inmates not at work are
huddled inside the dorms. But not today. *What's going on?* thought I.

Turns out the SIS was busy tossing the dorms—and I mean *toss*—looking for contraband. The three big prizes they sought out—available in every
convenience store from Bombay to Birmingham, hence Zach's quote—were
cigarettes and vapes, along with cell phones.

I get that the prison gendarmes want to prevent contraband. But there are two things I don't get.

Why not allow inmates to have cell phones, particularly at a minimum-security prison, as well as vaping cigs or regular cigs—yeah, that shit can kill you and it's not my bag, but it is legal on the street.

It's the second thing I would not understand about this particular raid that should bug you, too, particularly if you are a taxpayer. This was the considerable vandalism inflicted by the SIS. Come with me now as I explain.

They finally let us back into our dorms at about eight at night—after a pat down and wand search of each of us—and the chaos that awaited us was beyond the pale. These punks in prison guard garb had gone on a rampage that made the hooligan aftermath of a British soccer match look tame.

My own locker was knocked sideways and most of its contents were strewn all over the floor. My "mattress," such as it was, had been also tossed on the floor. There was all sorts of trash and tape strewn throughout the dorm. It was a clear message to "the Trump guy," because no one else's locker had gotten such treatment, but, thought I, *Just what the puck is the message here?*

As for the vandalism, the biggest damage was to the bathrooms and utility rooms. Of the five working showers for almost fifty people in my dorm, two of the showers were disabled, with tiles smashed and valves crippled. On the opposite side of the hall, the other dorm in our pod, already down to a few toilets and urinals, had one urinal completely ripped out and another toilet smashed.

There were also holes in the wall everywhere that would have to be patched. All in all, it looked to be at least $10,000 in damage, but the repairs, which would have to be done by the inmates, would take weeks or months until replacement fixtures, tile, and mortar arrived.

If there were a method to this madness, I'd perhaps understand. But the whole thrust of these kinds of raids was to punish everyone for the smuggling of a few bad actors and let taxpayers pick up an even bigger bill than the $40–50k per head tax we all pay as taxpayers to fund prisons.

And yes, the SIS did find some contraband, as they always do. But the smash and burn tactics they used will certainly not deter a repeat of this same cat-and-mouse, hounds-and-hares eternal battle between good and evil—after what the SIS did, the lines are clearly blurred.

The last thing to note about this sad, sorry incident is about the one guy, "Palmy," they hauled away to the dreaded Special Housing Unit or SHU, the solitary confinement type of cell to punish the rulebreakers. Along with Zach, Palmy was one of the hardest-working inmates in the prison. When Palmy wasn't singlehandedly scrubbing and mopping the entire bathroom area clean, he was outside machine-washing the sidewalks.

Unfortunately, the kid also had larceny in his soul. He went from dealing on the street to dealing in the dorms, and none of the older and wiser inmates—or threat of the SHU—could stop the kid.

Palmy would get caught with over forty cell phones hidden not so well just underneath his bunk. It was stupid and careless. He'd never get back to the minimum-security side, and he had just added another year to his sentence because they would strip him of the time-off credits he had earned.

There are a thousand stories like this in the naked prison. But the biggest part of this story was the rampaging vandalism and intimidation I had just borne witness to.

HUCK POST 46:
SIS Lemons into Warden's Lemonade
April 20, 2024—Day 33

Early in the morning several days after the Special Investigative Squad (SIS) sacking of our prison, and particularly my dorm, the only person that may have been more pissed than the inmates was Administrator Verdejo. He was the new cop on the block who was trying to rebuild the organizational culture of the worst prison in the system and thereby get this rudderless vessel back on track, and this was, in his eyes, clearly a setback.

As I walked around and surveyed the damage, he quietly waved me over to get my take on the event and see if I wanted to take it up to the top brass, meaning the warden himself.

This was a possible gift from the gods—the heavy-handed SIS overreach might literally open the warden's door. After I walked him through all the extensive damage to make sure he had it all on film, he told me to be on standby.

So, I got into my prison uniform and treaded water the rest of the morning to see if he'd call me to the meet. When nothing happened, I went to lunch; and after a call to my beloved Pixie at noon, I said F it, and went out for my midday workout.

Sure enough, on my last lap of a three-mile roll, Elliot lumbers out to the track and tells me to get my sweaty ass over to Verdejo's forthwith. So in I went for a quick change of clothes, and with sweat still dripping off my brow, I found myself sitting in a private room with Verdejo and Grant Huett, the warden himself.

I told them the God's honest truth. The vandalism of the SIS raid had completely undercut their authority—particularly Verdejo's—and they needed to go big or risk losing any support they might have from the inmates. As for the going-big optics, I put out the top reforms I had been working through with a group of inmate activists sick of the way things were being run (into the ground).

One obvious option was a crackdown on SIS involving an investigation. Incredibly, the two lieutenants running the raid had allegedly been put on administrator leave for a scam they had been running involving the sale of cell phones to inmates. For God knows what reason, they were restored to the ranks and even promoted.

A second low-hanging fruit was to solve the "Ajemon Problem" in the visitor's center. I assured them, if they permanently replaced Ajemon, it would score big points with the inmates. Still a third possibility was to shift focus to getting the inmates released at earlier dates in conformance with the First Step Act. This would involve shifting the way FSA credits were counted. Plus, such a step would help ease the fiscal burden the facility was operating in.

Other topics we touched on were the crying need for more programs to prepare inmates for the outside, getting pills on time, and improving nutrition.

One of the most interesting points of discussion was about how to build programs that would allow outside employment—the nearby zoo and only slightly further away Everglades were two possibilities. As good as each job might be in preparing inmates for the outside, the warden was candid about the fact that if anything went wrong, it was his ass.

Point taken. *Ah*, thought I, *there's a risk-averse rhyme for every reason everything moves so slow. But that's why they call it a bureaucracy.*

All in all, it was a good meet. I took my best shot.

Let's revisit it in a week or two to see if it was a waste of my time.

HUCK POST 47:
Who Moved My Queso?
April 21, 2024—Day 34

Everyone knows that not all change is good or even necessary.
But in a world that is constantly changing, it is to our advantage
to learn how to adapt and enjoy something better.
—Spencer Johnson, *Who Moved My Cheese?*

Today, I got a "bunky"—someone to fill the top bunk of the creaky steel bed frame I spent about half of my time in or around. It was the evil Gandu's doing—the prison secretary who fancied herself an administrator who liked to screw around with Cookie, the real administrator, and who like to screw me. Something about Trump Derangement Syndrome.

At any rate, it was Gandu who stuck me with my new bunky on Cookie's day off, when Cooke had issued an edict not to give me a bunky—too damn dangerous, and he had a point.

Truth be told, it was a bit of a small luxury to have a solo bunk in a space built for two. It meant extra locker space for all the stuff I was accumulating—bags full of mail coming in too quickly to read, extra sweatshirts and sweatpants to wear in the freezing nights, provisions from the commissary to supplant the starvation diet, and room beneath the bunk for the shoes, boots, and sandals needed for exercise, work, and showers.

So when the new bunky came—and moved my queso, if you know the reference—it was yet another reminder that I was indeed in prison, as I had to move half my stuff and now share an already cramped space that suddenly got far more tight.

The fellow was nice enough. A young Puerto Rican nearing thirty, already five years into a fifteen-year bid for drug smuggling with a gun.

Three kids and a wife in San Juan. Entrepreneurial, too—he had built up his own paragliding tourism business into a unique, successful enterprise.

But like far too many of the Puerto Rican young men I would break bread and shoot hoops with, he had picked up some drug trade work and was now paying a very heavy price.

I get it—he was moving "a lot of weight," as they say in the trade, and was packing to protect himself in his dangerous occupation. They caught him with a couple of kilos of cocaine and an arsenal of rifles and handguns.

But this young man—little more than a boy when he got busted—will spend his own golden years of twenty-five to almost forty at American taxpayer expense that will approach $1 million.

There's got to be a better way. But that's why they call it prison.

HUCK POST 48:
Skate to Where the Bunk Is Going to Be
April 22, 2024—Day 35

Skate to where the puck is going to be. Not to where it is.
—Wayne Gretsky

This day was absolutely delicious. Because every once in a while when you're in the asylum, you can put one over on Big Nurse. If you've never read *One Flew Over the Cuckoo's Nest*, you won't know the Ken Kesey I'm talking about—but that battle of wills between an inmate played to the hilt by Jack Nicholson and Louise Fletcher's Academy Award-winning Big Nurse was epic.

As for the analog here, after the evil Ms. Gandu—the prison secretary who thought she was the warden—stuck me with a young, rambunctious upper bunkmate on Cooke's day off—it was time to take evasive action.

So after Cooke came back to work the next day and moved the guy out, I gently suggested we take a countermeasure. Why not just dismantle the top bunk and move it either into mothballs or somewhere else? When Mr. Cooke said I shouldn't have to worry about Gandu, I said that he underestimated her treachery—I know a Trump hater when I see one, and she was one of the very few in the whole prison, inmate *or* guard. So Cooke says okay, and I ask Chez Ray to do it.

Chez Ray, by the way, is the guy one bunk over who, for a modest fee, cooks extra dinner every night for whoever can afford said fee. And Ray would be happy to do other contract work, such as fixing it so I'd never ever get a bunky again.

It was touch and go for a few days, but finally on Monday morning, Chez Ray rolls in with his tools cart and off goes the top bunk, not just on my bunk but on Ray's—he didn't want a "bunky" any more than I did.

Sure enough, that afternoon, Big Nurse Gandu brings in a new recruit fresh off the bus to terrorize me with, but when she enters the dorm and sees only my lower bunk, she knows she's been outfoxed. Yes, it felt good to win that one—a little payback for what I had found out to be her role in helping to trash my locker during the SIS raid.

HUCK POST 49:

Guns for Ukraine, No Butter for the Bureau of Prisons

April 23, 2024—Day 36

*After months of intense congressional debate, Congress passed and
the president signed into law a $61 billion aid package for Ukraine.
The legislation gives the president nearly everything he wanted,
which is surprising given the drama in the Republican House caucus.
The new legislation brings the total U.S. commitment to $175 billion
since the beginning of the invasion.*
—Center for Strategic and International Studies

The news that House Speaker and Republican Mike Johnson had abandoned his promise to hardliners and instead had successfully spearheaded a $61 billion aid package to Ukraine hit very close to home, as over the last several days, I had gotten really good data on all of the stuff at the prison *not* getting done for lack of funding.

To put the Ukraine $61 billion package in a foreign guns versus domestic butter perspective, the entire annual BOP budget for the federal prison system is a mere $14 billion a year. With just a small fraction of the Ukraine aid going instead to the BOP, I could fix every broken machine and appliance in the kitchen, get every spare part necessary to repair all the prison's vehicles and generators, start up five new education programs, and ensure timely provision of all the prescription drugs that the inmates were supposed to be getting but weren't.

It should piss off *every* American taxpayer that our politicians are willing to give away money we don't have and weapons we may well soon need even as our prison system implodes, our borders are swarmed, our cities crumble, and homelessness spins out of control. That's why they call it the Swamp.

HUCK POST 50:
Moonlight Through the Pines (and Barbed Wire)
April 23, 2024—Day 36

It was a full moon last night, and via email, I promised my dearest Pixie we would share a moment as the moon rose. She would watch from the rooftop of my apartment building in Washington, DC. I would watch from the field at the prison as I stretched.

'Twas not to be. The guard that night, Rodriguez, had a sadistic habit of locking us back in the dorm early—and long before it was necessary. So instead of seeing the moon rise with my Pixie, I was back in the windowless freezing dorm.

It was little moments like those that would drive home the loss of my freedom. But I would have my full moon Pixie moment on the back end. At dawn, as I waited for the breakfast line to open, a beautiful full moon was setting through the barbed wire fence. It was a sweet, lovely moment thinking about my girl.

PIXIE POST 9:
My Stages of Prison Grief
April 23, 2024—Day 36

Pixie here, and I know they say there are five stages of grief:

- Denial (I can't believe my Huck is actually in prison)
- Anger (just so mad at the "jackal Democrats," as Huck calls them, that put him in prison)
- Bargaining (trying to make some rationale that's it's not so bad)
- Depression (down so long now, it looks like up to me)
- Acceptance (we got this)

Well, my prison grief is just a bit different.

Instead of denial, it's utter heartbreak. When I think too much about him, smelling his shirt, seeing his things in the apartment, eating dinner with him, going to sleep without his embrace, waking up in an empty and cold bed, it's just *painful*.

What about that anger? I mostly skip that. Instead, whenever I leave him at the Visitor's Center, my heart just breaks.

I could cry so hard. But I didn't let myself do that. Only when I get back to my hotel room—and only a little, because he wouldn't want me to and definitely not in front of him.

He says he cries sometime on the inside, yet sometimes, I think I see some moisture in his eyes when I visit.

But he is a man. Unlike me as a woman. I know that crying lets the sad out of me. I do it quite often now, mostly at night when the loneliness sets in, but I allow myself only a little.

As for the bargaining, I'll never say, "It's not so bad" because that would be a lie.

We'll see what else lies ahead, but I will do my very best never to get to the depression stage—and I believe he won't either, because we have each other and we are still alive.

So I'm skipping right through to the end stage as soon as I can, and "We got this." And we do and we will.

HUCK POST 51:
It's Just Routine
April 24, 2024—Day 37

I didn't serve time. I made time serve me.
—Don King

Motion is the potion.
—Gordon Lightfoot

Ask any inmate what the biggest challenge of prison is, and most will tell you it's figuring out how to pass the time. In prison, you have *nothing* but time; and if you don't figure out how to pass it, you'll quickly wind up in the fetal position depressed as hell. That's where your routines can ride to the rescue.

The prison itself provides the structure around which I would build my routine. At FCI Miami, breakfast is at 6 a.m., lunch at 11 a.m., and dinner at 5 p.m.—sort of, because while they had plenty of Mussolinis around to bust your chops, their trains never ran on time, whether it was meals, the count, pill line, or whatever.

And speaking of "the count," this is when you stand silent at your bunk and get counted to make sure you haven't escaped. Yes, that happens. One guy had gone over the wall just before I got there, and he ain't been seen since.

So as you can see, there is a fair amount of structure to begin with. But that still leaves six hours in the morning after dawn, another three hours in the afternoon, and almost four hours in the evening.

Now some of that time may be filled by a job. Most of the hard-time, longtime inmates wanted to get a job in one of the paying placements to help them both build a nest egg for their release and, in many circumstances, get the funds for the restitution they have to pay to their victims.

For others, however, jobs were in short supply, as were any training programs. So, many inmates had little to do but eat, sleep, and be counted. That's where routines would kick in; and the best-adjusted inmates seemed to be those who would get out to the recreational area once, twice, or like me, three times a day.

This rec area would never be confused with Planet Fitness, much less a high quality Equinox. In fact, the previous warden had ordered the removal of every single free weight and exercise machine from the yard on the theory that he didn't want inmates to get so strong they could overpower the guards.

This was really stupid because mine was supposed to be a minimum-security facility getting inmates ready for the transition to the outside. We had no weights, but the higher security prison two hundred yards away was fully equipped.

At any rate, the inmates got around this through ingenious methods. One was to recycle the big mayonnaise jugs from the kitchen into dumbbells filled with sand from the volleyball court no one ever used. Plus, you could use the shelter out by the softball field to do pull-ups and chin-ups. And you don't need any damn equipment to do sit-ups, burpees, et al.

As for what else was in the rec area, there was a one-third of a mile track, two racquetball courts, a full-length basketball court, a makeshift pickleball court, a softball diamond, and even—as the ultimate outlier—a bocce ball sand pit.

The funniest stuff was the "aerobic equipment." It was under the roofed pavilion where the pool table and bank of TVs were. You had two exercise bikes without workable pedals while the elliptical trainer thumped and groaned in ways that made it a nonstarter for all but the most desperate.

My challenge was to develop a set of workouts that would help me maintain my strength and mental and physical health in an environment of high stress and poor nutrition without risking injury in a facility with little health care. So over the first few weeks, I tried out some routines while I watched how other guys and groups of guys organized their workouts.

By now, I had settled into a set of routines in which I worked half the time either on my legal appeal or on finishing the second volume of this prison memoir. The other half I spent working out or stretching in three separate morning, afternoon, and evening shifts.

I always started at sunrise with a mile around the track, morning, afternoon, early evening. After breakfast midmorning, I would shoot some basketball hoops and practice my racquetball stroke hitting a ball against the wall with a racquet that Pepe, one of the inmates who was in charge of such things, had graciously provided.

Loved Pepe: Cuban health-care scammer in for a long bid who looked every bit like a silver-haired Zorro without a mask. Just a good dude who had done a bad thing.

After lunch, I would nap for a half hour and then go do my running. Three miles around the track in the summer sun and humidity. I'd follow this with push-ups and my dumbbell mayonnaise jar workout; and I'd always finish with sit-ups and at least trying to do a pull-up—no luck yet! As for the other guys, there were the handball and racquetball crowds, the weight lifters, and the runners.

Lest you think this all sounds like Club Fed, you'd laugh at the crappy exercise stuff we had to use. And you have to remember the dangers and stress every inmate lives with, along with the constant threats to one's physical health from the cramped living quarters and low quality food, and the severe threat that boredom poses to one's mental health.

Motion is indeed the best potion, and those inmates who fared the worst mentally and physically spent most of their time bored and depressed in the TV room eating Honey Buns from the commissary.

My routines—and of course my Sweet Pixie—would save me. Thanks again to Paul Manafort for encouraging it all.

HUCK POST 52:
Crime and Punishment
April 24, 2024—Day 37

There are some people who should be here, maybe forever, but there are some people who, for all sorts of reasons—bad lawyering, bureaucratic inertia, mismatched sentencing—stay here far too long.
—Doc Arman Abovyan

Everyone in prison has a story to tell, and after listening to many of them over the Samuel Beckett days of my incarceration—and by simply observing men grappling every day with the loss of their remaining youthful years—two things are clear: The current system does a piss poor job of matching punishment to the crime and an equally piss poor job of ensuring that released convicts don't come back.

The first obvious principle is that any prosecution is a gross mismatch between an experienced prosecution team and a very-low-on-a-very-steep-learning-curve defendant. In this game, prosecutors pursue a minimax strategy.

They want to minimize the cost of putting away a defendant yet still maximize the time that defendant stays in prison within that budget constraint. As I wrote in an earlier postcard, there are numerous strategies and tactics prosecutors use to execute what is essentially a "plea deal" gambit, and only those defendants with the best lawyers can effectively counter what is about to be thrown at them.

As an aside, the "best lawyer" is often not the most expensive—and good lawyers are indeed hard to find. And the worst kind of lawyer— and this may be counterintuitive—is a former prosecutor who is conditioned to the plea deal route and always seeks to appear cooperative with the other side.

In a typical plea deal gambit, a defendant will first be wildly overcharged with multiple counts to run up the potential prison time meter and thereby scare the bejesus out of even the most innocent of men. Then, the defendant will be given a stark choice: Either plea out for a lesser sentence or, if you go to trial, risk going away for much of the rest of your life.

In weighing the prospects of an acquittal, a defendant will also often deal with a "conspiracy" charge and/or a "should have known" charge—both of which are tough to beat. With a conspiracy charge, it's relatively easy for a prosecutor to weave individual pieces of evidence into what appears to be broader, far more nefarious patterns.

As for the "should have known" charge, a significant number of the people I met inside were heads of companies or high ranking officers who wound up taking the fall for the bad acts of employees under their supervision.

For example, "Rick" built a successful telemedicine company in the early stages of telemedicine and a few of his licensed physician employees falsely represented they had conducted video interviews before prescribing medicines, a violation of the law. Even Rick admits he "should have known," but simply didn't—he got ten years for that oversight. A bit much, no?

As part of the broader overcharging strategy, prosecutors may also successfully convict someone else in the target net and have the judge stiffly sentence the individual. Then, prosecutors can point to that person and say to the defendant, "See? That's what will happen to you if you don't plead out—we'll give you five years now, but you'll get fifteen if you go to trial."

It's important to mention here that once prosecutors decide to get you, all of their obligations to seek true justice go out the window. All that matters is the conviction with the harshest sentence possible.

I saw this in my own case. No matter what sound arguments we offered and no matter what the longer run consequences for the constitutional separation of powers might be, all that mattered to the prosecutors was taking their pound of, in my case, political flesh.

In the case of my inmates, I heard story after story of men who believed they were innocent, who fought and fought until their resources were exhausted and they finally took a plea.

Several inmates I encountered were doctors who had prescribed buprenorphine to heroin addicts to help with their addiction and did so because it's a better alternative than methadone. But this drug is also valued on the street as a "high," and these doctors were convicted of peddling illegal drugs, even though even Hippocrates would have approved.

The next result of this plea deal game is to leave men in prison often for far too lengthy periods of time in the prime of their lives and earnings potential while taxpayers foot the bill and the prison bureaucrats and private contractors running the prisons prosper. There has to be a better way, particularly for these men who slowly slide into old age and infirmity and present no future threat to security.

If you think after reading this that prison has turned me "soft on crime," think again—then just remember it is you, the taxpayer, footing this bill.

And I'll leave you with this: Lock up the violent, repeat offenders forever. Let go nonviolent offenders after *appropriate* punishment *and* give them a fighting chance to regain their lives on the outside. If they recidivate, throw the book at them.

HUCK POST 53:
A Lifeline Severed
April 25, 2024—Day 38

With five days still left in the month, I called my Sweet Pixie for our morning catchup call and was stunned that we were out of minutes. I literally ran over to the computer room on the other side of the prison to crank out an email letting my Sweet Pixie know—knowing that it would still be several hours before that email found its way to her.

Here again was a variation on my first rule at prison—it's tougher on the loved ones and family than the male inmates.

I'm not saying I didn't enjoy my phone calls with Sweet Pixie. Just the opposite. But the daily calls were an important part of connecting and thereby dealing with the separation.

As soon as I heard that "You have no more minutes" message, I understood *completely* why burner phones are the most prized contraband in any American prison. Which begs the question: Why don't they just sell the damn things at the commissary and make money off the venture rather than pay SIS, the special investigators, to smash walls and shower tiles to find the bootleg ones?

It's a good question. Maybe I'll get a burner phone to call Pix.

Nah. Above all, I shall be a model prisoner, because if I misstep in any way, it would be *all* over the news.

Still, you can see yet again how prison teaches inmates to break the rules. But that's why they call it prison.

PIXIE POST 11:
How Many New York Minutes in a Miami Prison Minute?
April 25, 2024—Day 38

This call is from a Federal Prison. If you'd like to accept this call, press 5.
—Message with outgoing prison calls

Pixie here, and before my Huck went into prison, we promised we'd talk three times a day—morning, noon, and night. Hearing his voice and talking about what we are doing is just very important to me. It's maybe a girlie thing. Or maybe just being human.

So it shocked me when I found out that my Huck would only be allotted five hundred minutes a month for his phone conversations. That may seem like a lot, but it's only about sixteen minutes a day for our three phone calls.

And just imagine an inmate with other family members or friends he wanted to talk to. Or if Huck needed to call someone else on business or a friend.

It's just not a lot of minutes, and my Ever Huck tells me it's the biggest reason why inmates are willing to take the high risk of smuggling cell phones into the prison—the other being the indignity of being monitored by the prison censors. (If they catch an inmate, he'll get sent to a higher security prison and lose even more freedom.)

Fortunately, the first few weeks were fine while we were acclimating. That's because my Huck came into the prison on March 19 and they gave him the full month's allotment, so we had more than five hundred minutes to burn over just twelve days, so we got used to longer phone calls.

But we knew in April we would have to be a lot more careful with our minutes.

We weren't. And today, it was official—we wouldn't be talking on the phone until the first of May, almost a full week away.

The running out of minutes had just crept up on us. The night before, Huck had checked the phone logs, and he said they showed we still had about fifteen minutes left. But I guess overnight, they did some phone accounting, and it went down to zero. So when Huck dialed me up at 8 a.m., the robo lady on the other end of the phone said no dice.

On my end, the silence in the morning was like a punch in the stomach, like the air had been taken out of me. Because the first thing that came to my mind was that something had happened to my Huck.

It's never like him not to phone me when he says he will. And this is when it really felt like I was in prison not *with* Huck but totally alone, as I couldn't pick up the phone and call My Huck to find out what had happened and if he was okay.

It wasn't until I got an email later in the day when he explained we had indeed run out of minutes that I could settle down. At least sort of settle down.

It was one of my worst days during the prison times. The rest of the week didn't get much better, because I couldn't hear his voice.

HUCK POST 54:
The Third Rail of American Politics
April 26, 2024—Day 39

[*Author's Note: You can see in this postcard how I am getting ever and ever deeper into the prison reform game as I gather more and more information and see the chessboard with my own eyes.*]

If the words "prison reform" make your eyes glaze over because you've got your own troubles and you don't need to worry about the quality of life of some scumbag convicted criminals *or* if the words "prison reform" just piss you off because it sounds like woke liberal shit, I can certainly sympathize, particularly in a world where crime appears to be absolutely batshit out of control and criminals regularly now get repeatedly released without bail only to do their bad shit again. (I bet you didn't think I could get the word "shit" in one sentence three times. But hey, I'm in prison developing new skills and a new vocabulary.)

At any rate, while I can indeed sympathize with any apathy or anger you might have about prison reform, at least give me a postcard or two to illustrate how the right reforms may well be in your self-interest.

The topline observation for citizens and politicians alike is that it is a fruitless quest to argue for prison reform on the basis of compassion or morality. Public sentiment is on the other end of that carrot while the law-and-order stick is very much in.

This is particularly true for Republican politicians who have to bear at least some share of the burden of moving the prison reform ball. The obvious political problem here is that if a Republican on Capitol Hill or in a state legislature utters the words "prison reform," his next opponent will almost assuredly brand him as a "soft on crime" pussy.

Of course, for conservative Republicans, there is an obvious way out of this "prison reform as the third rail of American politics" box; and it is to argue the case for prison reform simply as a means of reducing both our tax burden and the rate of recidivism and therefore crime rate.

So let me lay this out for you: The United States puts more people in prison on a per capita basis than any other country short of the Communist Chinese slave labor gulags. Indeed, as I write this, Federal prisons alone incarcerate 150,000 inmates, and tens of thousands more are in halfway houses or monitored home confinement while another 120,000 are on probation. That adds up to a total annual budget for the Bureau of Prisons of almost $10 billion.

Now, if you approach these numbers from a purely economic standpoint, and you take the minimum amount of food, clothing, housing, and medical care prisons must provide to inmates, then two of the best ways cut the costs of you the taxpayer are to (1) eliminate over-sentencing, and (2) lower the recidivism rate. So, how to hit those two marks will be the focus of future postcards focusing on an epidemic of over-sentencing in the justice system and the boomerang effect of crushing asset forfeiture and restitution penalties.

HUCK POST 55:
The Jubans at Passover
April 27, 2024—Day 40

I believe that we should have done everything we possibly could have done to prevent Castro from taking over in Cuba. We made a number of mistakes; we were badly advised.
—President John F. Kennedy

Everyone always has an angle in prison—you have to if you are going to survive. And one of the funniest angles involved all the non-Jews that would sign up for the special kosher meals on Jewish holidays like Passover.

I didn't figure this one out until I noticed Pepe in the kosher lineup one morning during Passover. I asked Jose what was going on and he said, "That's the Jubans."

Like Jose, Pepe was about as Jewish as a leprechaun. He had come over from Cuba as a young kid, and he was always a breath of fresh air when you saw him. He also was an expert racquetball player; and the angle this "Juban" was hitting at the mess hall was simply access to better food.

While we gentiles would eat the usual cardboard cereal for breakfast, Pepe and several of his fellow Jubans would be dining on real eggs, cheese blintzes, and matzoh lathered with that rarest of commodities—butter.

Hey, we didn't even get margarine in Prison Land.

So mazel tov, Pepe. Your Juban gain was not my loss, and more power to you.

By the way, we did irrevocably mess up Cuba, which is to say our foreign policy establishment in the 1960s all but shoved Castro into Khrushchev's disastrous bear-hug embrace.

Oh, what a different world (and hemisphere) it would be if Castro had chosen JFK instead. Just sayin'.

HUCK POST 56:
Dr. Navarro Is In
April 28, 2024—Day 41

The longer I was in prison, the more it became obvious both to me and the other inmates that I could pull off stuff with the higher-ups that the rest of the folks inside could never dream of. That power would give me the opportunity to likely save at least *two lives* while I was behind bars.

Case One was Inmate Joel—you can read about the other case in my Mother's Day postcard. At any rate, Joel had entered the Miami prison with Stage 3 kidney disease and a large mass on one kidney likely to be cancerous, and the diagnosis had progressed to Stage 4 over the last year in which the prison medical staff had repeatedly ignored Joel's pleas for help. So, Doc Abovyan asked me if I would help—he couldn't do anything without fear of retaliation from the warden and his staff.

So I said of course I'd help. So Doc ghost-wrote the memo below to the warden, and I signed it. And yes, it helped accelerate Joel's access to the care he needed.

Just another day's work in Hell for both me and Doc.

> FROM: Inmate 04370510
> TO: Warden
> SUBJECT: Joel Franco Ortiz
> DATE: 04/29/2024 07:44:50 PM
> Memo to: Warden
> From: Peter Navarro
> Re: Joel Franco Ortiz 08807-509
>
> Mr. Ortiz is in urgent need of medical care, and the failure of such care is likely to lead to Stage 5 kidney failure and the possible spread of a malignant cancer, due to a large mass.
>
> Mr. Ortiz has been in camp for roughly a year as I can ascertain. He has repeatedly requested immediate treatment for two conditions but has thus far been ignored.

Mr. Ortiz has adult polycystic kidney disease, stage 4, with 27 percent GFR function. He entered FCI Miami with stage 3, 40 percent GFR function and his condition continues to deteriorate. He is now anemic with low Vitamin D levels and suffering from hypo-parathyroidism. At stage 5, he will need kidney dialysis and a transplant.

Mr. Ortiz also has a 5.4 centimeter mass on one kidney diagnosed at Larkin Hospital in December of 2023 that is presumed cancerous until proven otherwise. He is likely a candidate for the removal of that kidney; failing that, any cancer is likely to spread and be fatal.

MY REQUESTS:

Please arrange for immediate appointments for Mr. Ortiz with both a urologist and a nephrologist with TIMELY follow through on the findings. He is likely to die on your watch if this neglect continues.

Please have someone on your staff help Mr. Ortiz with an application for compassionate release.

PLEASE DO NOT IGNORE THIS REQUEST. THE MEDICAL STAFF HAS BEEN HIGHLY UNRESPONSIVE BUT A MAN'S LIFE IS AT STAKE.

Besides trying to help inmates get better medical treatment, I would also start a project designated to force the FCI warden and administrators to follow the rules and guidelines of the FCA and SCA and thereby move inmates out for freedom at a far faster pace. Other projects would include efforts to upgrade both the kitchen and garage facilities to serve inmates and the camp better. Mother Teresa I was not. But at least I would try to make a difference.

HUCK POST 57:
The Amy Coney Barrett Blues
April 28, 2024—Day 41

The dogma lives loudly within you, and that's of concern.
—Senator Dianne Feinstein to Supreme Court
Nominee Amy Coney Barrett

I slept last night with Amy Coney Barrett—at least, with the most lasting memory of Barrett from my days in the White House.

I remember that day well. She would be introduced that day at a press conference in the Rose Garden by the Boss, and before that event, she and the Boss held court in the Oval for what would be a revolving door of fans within the West Wing and EEOB.

I wasn't one of those fans, as I saw Barrett as a one-trick, social conservative pony. I just wasn't sure she had the intellectual heft to parse complex constitutional issues in the tradition of court giants and legends like Scalia, Scalia, and Scalia, and I was damn well sure she was neither MAGA or a Trump supporter.

What unsettled me about her was the doe eyes that hid a political killer. She knew exactly what to say and what not to say about how she would be fair and objective while everyone on both sides of the aisle knew damn well that her role was to provide the swing vote that would kill Roe v. Wade.

In short, I didn't trust her with broader constitutional issues, and on this April 26th day, it felt uncomfortable to know she likely held my fate in her hands.

I would need five votes when the Supreme Court met this day to consider my last best chance to be released pending my appeal. If it went 9-0 against, her vote wouldn't matter. But if I had support of the court, it would likely be from Neil Gorsuch, who had referred my petition to the full court, the conservative warriors of Clarence Thomas and Samuel Alito, who would surely get the law right, and Brett Kavanaugh, who had already opined in a Trump case in a way that favored my appeal.

But that adds up to only four votes out of nine, and it would be up to

Barrett to break me out of prison, as Roberts had already denied me on the first try. Five to four one way or the other was my best guess, and my bet was that she'd go against my release.

That long ago day when I met her at the White House, I had had a premonition that she would play some role in my life—and it wouldn't be good. In this particular choice, this would be a test of my power of perception and Delphic powers.

As the Boss loves to say, let's see what happens today. I'm more than ready to get out of this hellhole, but I'm also more than ready to stay if I must. What really matters are the bigger issues in my case and what they mean for the nation. The only hope I will indulge in this day is the hope Barrett gets it right.

[*Author's Note: She didn't.*]

HUCK POST 58:
Et Tu Scotus, Then Hunker Down Huck
April 29, 2024—Day 42

It was the proverbial bad day at BlackRock. After a track workout in the afternoon and some upper-body strength work, I quickly ducked into the computer room to check my email before the 3:30 lockdown for count. OUCH.

Despite my admonition to myself to keep my expectations at zero—hope kills in prison—I nonetheless thought my request for release to the Supreme Court might be granted, even though 99.8 percent of such petitions are routinely denied.

Sure enough, there was an email from my lawyer, Stanley Woodward—request summarily denied. I'd like to think that SCOTUS's hands were tied by how the worthless DC Appeals Court had framed their own decision on my appeal. That's the excuse Roberts had given on the first try—he explicitly said the SCOTUS decision would have no influence on my appeal.

The worst part of it was the lack of information about whether it was a consensus 9-0 decision—not a good omen for my bigger appeal—or a split vote where the court's conservative trio, Thomas, Gorsuch, and Alito, simply could not win the day. We'll never know—votes on such petitions aren't recorded.

I immediately emailed my Sweet Pixie with the bad news—I preferred that she hear it from me than those scumbags at CNN. Here's me delivering the bad news to my Sweet Pixie via the prison email service CORRLINKS.

FROM: 04370510
TO: Brenner, Bonnie
SUBJECT: my sweets
DATE: 04/29/2024 03:19:47 PM

bad news from supreme court. Wanted you to hear from me first. nothing that we didn't expect. Love you so much.

we will work it through!!

Huck

After sending this email, I let the news sink in a little more. As I sat there in front of the computer taking the blow, Wally was rattling on about how some Columbia University student on Fox News was boasting. About what, exactly?

About how all the LGBTQ students on the Columbia campus were manning, womaning, and transgendering the ramparts in support of a Palestinian "river to sea" extermination of Israel. It was just too wokely funny.

Every one of those alphabet soup Ls and Gs and Bs and Ts and Qs would be beheaded anywhere in the Islamic Middle East. I guess they don't teach that at Columbia.

Screw it, I thought. You're stuck in prison now for the duration, and all hope is lost for an early out. So man up and finish whatever mission God and a pack of vengeful, lawfare Democrats put you in prison to start.

In fact, every day that mission was taking on more shape and momentum. But sometimes I got to just whine a little bit. Which is what I just did to you.

HUCK POST 59:
Of Diesel Therapy and Optimal Sentencing
April 30, 2024—Day 43

It's the legal system, not the justice system.
—Inmate Karl

Unless you've been inside prison and taken the time to talk with inmates, it's hard to understand the scope and scale of the injustice that pervades our legal system. This is not to say many, indeed most, of the inmates I did time with were innocent flowers. Far from it.

Yet, it is also true that far too many inmates are serving for more time than they otherwise should for all manner of reasons. You should care if for no other reason that the Bureau of Prisons and Department of Justice are wasting too many of your tax dollars on over-incarceration.

The best way to understand this is through the economist's notion of "perverse incentives." In an ideal world—or optimal world, in economics speak—the BOP and DOJ would seek to minimize taxpayer costs by imposing the lowest possible sentences that still achieve the goals of a just punishment and sufficient deterrence of future crimes.

In the real world, however, the BOP wants to maximize the time inmates spend in prison to justify and increase staffing and thereby build its fiefdom. By the same token, prosecutors want to rack up the plea deals, jury convictions, and years sentenced as performance metrics for their climb up the professional ladder.

And here's the ultimate perversity: The more years the BOP and DOJ tack on above the optimal sentencing level, the more the BOP and its private contractors profit, and the more DOJ prosecutors are rewarded for their wins, but—and here's the punchline—the more taxpayers *and* inmates lose.

What do I mean by an "optimal sentence"? From both an economic and social justice point of view, the goal should be to impose a sentence long enough to deter future criminal activity but no longer. In most cases involving nonviolent crimes committed by first offenders, a few months to a year or two should be enough to establish deterrence—at least in my experience.

Yet, in the vast majority of first-offender cases, the sentences are far too long; and such over-sentencing imposes very real costs both to the inmate and society at large.

For an inmate, the longer the sentence, the more likely his marriage or relationship will falter or fall apart. This can be highly damaging, both economically and emotionally.

In addition, an individual's earnings power is likely to diminish over time as skills erode and the marketplace changes.

A longer time in prison also makes it more difficult to keep and maintain a business—with short sentences, a wife or partner can keep an enterprise going, but over time, not so much.

There is also the "prison as a college for criminals" problem. Many of the men I met would likely be back behind bars in the years ahead because of the networking they had done with other inmates.

As for the economic costs of over-sentencing, the math is pretty straightforward. It costs about $60,000 a year to feed, clothe, house, and provide educational and medical services to an inmate. If you get ten thousand inmates in prison a year longer than necessary for punishment and deterrence, that costs taxpayers over half a billion dollars. That's real money.

Lastly, the longer an inmate stays inside and the world changes around him, the more likely he is to be alienated from society and the more likely he will have difficulty integrating back into that system.

Just how do inmates wind up serving more time than they should? It starts with the overcharging and plea deal game I described earlier. Yet, once inside prison, there are all sorts of games the BOP can play to keep inmates inside—never mind the bureaucratic inertia that likewise extends sentences.

Consider, for example, a practice known as "diesel therapy." This involves bussing inmates after they are sentenced and taken into custody to a series of detention jails *before* they ultimately wind up at the prison where they will serve their sentence.

Sometimes this diesel therapy lasts for a few days. Sometimes it can go on for a year or more. It just depends on how much the inmate has pissed off the BOP or how much the BOJ and DOJ want to pressure that inmate to do things like turn state's evidence on someone else.

Just how does "diesel therapy" extend an inmate's incarceration? Under the First Step Act, nonviolent offenders get ten days off for every month served. *But* when an inmate is in transit, no time-off credits accrue.

This little loophole in the First Step Act can cost an inmate days of earlier freedom—and sometimes a hell of a lot more. One inmate, a Russian-American, rode the diesel therapy railroad (to mix metaphors) for fully eighteen months before winding up at my prison. During that limbo, he lost the opportunity to shave fully *five months* off his sentence.

And note here, it's not just the *time* the inmates lose from over-incarceration. The longer an inmate serves, the more likely he will commit crimes and become a recidivism statistic. This happens because with every additional day in the joint, you are more likely to learn more criminal ways.

But, more importantly, the longer you are away from a wife or girlfriend, the more likely they won't be there when you come out. And there are strains on the family as well—if I had a dime for every inmate whose extended family wouldn't take them back to accommodate a "home-confinement" transition from prison, I'd have a lot of heartbreaking dimes.

The attitude here—dare I say the organizational culture of both the BOP and DOJ—is that inmates deserve *whatever* happens to them along the way from their first to last day in jail.

Here's the bottom line: No taxpayer should want any inmate to overserve his time. It's just a waste of taxpayer dollars and likely to lead to *more*, not less, crime.

Indeed, nobody wins here. The defendant loses. The defendant's friends and family lose. Taxpayers lose three times—once for the direct costs of hosting a prisoner past his "expiration date," twice for the loss in tax revenue from an idle prisoner rather than one gainfully employed, thrice for the welfare payments that arise to support an inmate's family in the absence of having a breadwinner at home.

Only the prosecutors who have claimed another victim and the Bureau of Prisons bureaucracy—which has another per capita prisoner fee to collect—win. And that's why they call it prison.

HUCK POST 60:

Why Oranges Aren't Served in Florida Prisons

May 1, 2024—Day 44

The Sunshine State's warm climate and fertile soil make it the perfect place for growing oranges, earning Florida its reputation as the nation's top citrus producer.
—Visit Florida

There is a certain freedom of speech inside prison that comes with the possibility that the person in prison speaking up once served in the White House and might well be back working for that very same president.

Because of that status I held, very early on I began to speak up for my fellow inmates without (too much) fear of retaliation.

So it was that one day at lunch when a gaggle of new prison officials came into the lunchroom and I found out that one of them, a "Mr. Lucki," was the new head of food service that I proceeded to bend his ear about the follies and foils of the starvation dirt that was being served. What I learned was not comforting.

For example, when I suggested that the occasional fresh vegetable—say, broccoli or green beans—might be a refreshing and healthy change of pace, I learned the canned vegetables were served as a matter of policy.

Similarly, when I described a breakfast of cereal and sugary fruit with an occasional piece of cake was not exactly the "eat like a king" breakfast recommended by the American Medical Association, I learned that hot breakfasts had been removed from the menu for God knows why.

And when I pondered why fresh oranges were *never* served in a prison at the epicenter of Florida orange-growing, the second explanation was even funnier than the first.

The first explanation was that canned fruit was actually cheaper than fresh fruit. To which I replied: "Of course, when most of what is in the can is cheap sugar water with barely a touch of real fruit, that makes sense. It just sucks to eat."

But it was the second explanation that was truly LOL; and follow me here. The minimum-security facility I was in was part of a broader facility which also included a much larger low-security prison.

Because the two prisons bought jointly, and because the prisoners in the other prison had a nasty habit of using any kind of fresh fruit as feedstock for their makeshift stills to produce liquor, the warden had ordered the stoppage of buying fresh fruit.

To which I said, "So we can't get fresh fruit here because you can't control bootleggers in the other prison. Have I got that right?" "Yep" was the answer. And it turns out, that explained why real sugar wasn't served either—only artificial sweeteners.

In case you never made it to Hillbilly High School, sugar and fruit serve as the primary source of fermentable sugars, which yeast converts into alcohol during fermentation. Just thought you should know.

In prison, you either laugh or cry. Today, I laughed.

HUCK POST 61:
Buddy, Can You Spare Me a Part?
May 1, 2024—Day 44

My kingdom for a horse.
—King Richard III

A missing spare part is all it takes to turn precision into paralysis.
—Anon

Other than Mitch McConnell—a cunning Never-Trump assassin who will stab you in the back as soon as he drinks bourbon with you—I've never met a gentleman from Kentucky who wasn't just that: a gentleman.

One such gentleman was a sixty-six-year-old inmate named David whose life had been absolutely destroyed by overzealous prosecutors.

Sure, David was a guilty man, at least in the sense that the small hospital he owned had overbilled for lab costs. But it's not at all clear that David's punishment really fit this crime.

Before he even had arrived at the prison, David had been on home detention for *five years*. Eventually, his case was even settled in the obligatory coerced plea bargain—they threatened him with nearly life in prison for *both* him and his innocent wife if he went to trial—David was in his late sixties.

As part of that plea deal, David had to agree to an asset forfeiture that took his hospital ownership and everything else he owned; and he was effectively a broke, if not broken, man.

I admired his toughness—an Army veteran and enlisted man who had learned to be a mechanic in the army and used his GI Bill benefits to become a CPA. A true American dream story.

Now, in prison, he effectively ran the motor pool, and as we talked, waiting for the mess hall to open on a busy Monday morning—it opened forty-five minutes late that day and too late for many of the working inmates—David described the same kind of dysfunctional "nothing works" horror show I had heard days earlier on my tour of the kitchen where, likewise, nothing worked.

At the prison garage, David had at least most of the tools he needed to repair and perform maintenance on the prison's buses, trucks, cars, and generators. The prison ran about thirty vehicles in all.

What was in *very* short supply were the spare parts needed to keep the machines moving—simple stuff like plugs to repair tires and air filters, more complex stuff like valves, spark plugs, and carburetors.

So a lot of the vehicles would sit idle waiting for parts while the broken generators were a disaster waiting to happen—if we lost power in our dorms because of a storm or, God help us, a hurricane, we'd all have to be moved into tiny cells in the low-security prison across the street.

When I asked David why they didn't have parts, he said it was a money problem. It was not that the prison didn't have any money. It's just that the funds were always being siphoned off, either to some other higher priority pet project or, in David's view, bureaucrat's pockets.

Said David, "I'm a CPA and if I had the power, I'd audit the shit out of them. I think you'd damn well be amazed by the balls these people have as they steal left and right and run this place into the ground." Yep, that's why they call it prison.

HUCK POST 62:
My Chipi Comes In
May 2, 2024—Day 45

Timing is everything. Sometimes the stars do align. Clichés are us, *but* there is a grain of truth in every cliché. Follow me here:

I'm out in the yard working through my basketball routine after being cooped up most of the morning because of a driving rain, and I hear on the loudspeaker, "Navarro, Navarro, report immediately to the CO's office."

My pulse went up a bit, as I hadn't heard by email from my Sweet Pixie that a.m. after her return from Doral after our visit, and I had visions of an accident or something.

So I sprint over to the CO's office, not even bothering to put my uniform on, and I say what's up? He tells me to report immediately to medical, and this freaks me out more: Has Pixie been injured?

So off I sprint across the yard, breaking every "must be in uniform between 7 and 4" rule in the book, and I'm immediately waved into Dr. Chipi's office.

Dr. Chipi is the pro-Trump Cuban-American who did my intake physical, and I'm relieved to know there's no emergency. She just wants to know how I'm doing.

After some pleasantries, I use the door that has just been opened to lay out not one, but four of the medical cases I was working on.

I started with the Ortiz kidney case I had sent a memo to the warden about. Just laid it all out.

Then I worked through the three compassionate releases that were needed for the two wheelchair inmates, Del and Mad Dog, and Boris, the terminally ill cancer patient.

It was a home run, as she promised to take all four cases up the chain, with a special urgency for the kidney case.

As for the timing-is-everything angle, if Dr. Chipi hadn't called me out of the blue, I would have had to try and find her or corner the ever-elusive Dr. Alarcon to deal with all of this. (Alarcon was the ultimate arbitrator of compassionate releases, and a lazier, more disinterested individual it would be difficult to meet.)

Dr. Chipi promised to update me the next day, and that was all I could ask for. I suggested she take a good-cop, bad-cop approach up the Alarcon and Warden chain.

On the good side, she might point out how the recent change in BOP compassionate release policy had led to a surge in approvals. So Miami could get on the bandwagon. On the bad-cop side, there was yours truly. She could let it be known folks would be held accountable down the road if kidney-man died because of the gross negligence of Miami FCI administrators.

Who knows if I will be able to scale the walls of bureaucratic inertia. But that's what passes for a good day in prison.

HUCK POST 63:

From Inmate to Jailhouse Lawyer and Prison Ambassador

May 2, 2024—Day 45

In the weeks following my *et tu*, SCOTUS? Moment—"You are staying in prison, you puke"—I would significantly accelerate my efforts to get inmates the hell out of the prison when federal law actually said that should happen.

This ball took a little bit to get rolling. Ever since I had arrived at the prison, inmates had been complaining that they were supposed to already have been released per the law, but that the prison itself wasn't obeying the law.

The most common reason offered for the Bureau of Prisons dragging their feet was speculation of a "head tax." To wit, because the prison got paid by the inmates, they kept them there as long as possible.

My initial reaction was that it was just inmate bullshit and paranoia. But the more I dug, the more obvious it was that the prison wasn't following either of the two major laws passed by Congress or the policy direction of the Director of the Bureau of Prisons, Colette Peters.

In a nutshell, the 2008 Second Chance Act and its 2018 reauthorization was a policy reaction to a wave of over-sentencing laws and practices that had emerged from the war on drugs and the crack epidemic. Mandatory minimum sentences and hanging judges were working in tandem to warehouse first-time and nonviolent offenders for staggering lengths of time, whole lifetimes in some cases.

The Second Chance Act specified a 15 percent reduction in an inmate's total sentence and further mandated up to six months of home confinement as a form of prerelease custody and transition to freedom.

When I was in the Trump White House, President Trump also signed the First Step Act, which would be a major initiative to both reduce total sentences and get inmates much faster into halfway houses and home confinement—again, so-called prerelease custody.

The problem was that the Bureau of Prisons, note the irony here, simply was not obeying these laws—indeed, congressional mandates—when it came to processing inmates out to halfway houses and home confinement and eventually home.

To address this problem, I first had to wrap my head around all the ways, subtle and obvious, that inmates were being screwed. This I did by first reading the legislation and then reviewing a set of cases from the inmates.

There was no shortage of such cases. Inmates were coming at me to review the printouts each of them got from their case managers. These printouts projected the dates, both for their prerelease to halfway house/home confinement and ultimate release to probation or outright freedom.

But I had to systematize the process to understand it, and this is where Elliot led the effort. Elliot, by the way, was in for a white-collar offense involving fraud related to some private equity fund dealings. His was a case that arguably should have been handled civilly with some fines. But he wound up with a long bid and was trying to make the best use of his time as the go-to teacher of economics and finance for the inmates in the few classes offered by the prison.

At any rate, over the course of several weeks, we developed a standard form that we could plug the inmate's data into. Then we could calculate when the inmates should be prereleased to halfway house and home confinement to final release—and compare that with the timelines the prisoners' case managers were coming up with.

Time after time, we found inmates were facing delays of months and sometimes years. Often, we found an inmate should already have been released months before.

This was insanity for two reasons. First, it was a massive waste of taxpayer funds; $60,000 a year for any given inmate, and cumulatively, the cost runs into the billions in the aggregate. (Much more about this later.)

Second, these bureaucratic delays were not just inhumane. The longer an inmate stays in prison, the more likely he is to recidivate. So in the aggregate, the BOP's neglect was increasing the crime rate! Insanity!

Under my direction, Elliot led the effort to develop a simple data form every inmate could fill out so he and I could estimate more accurately their prerelease to custody and final release dates. What we planned to do next in a strength-in-numbers showing was to work with the two case managers to get them to follow BOP policy. Failing that, we would go to the warden.

Anyway, that was our strategy.

[*Author's Note: Little did I know that this day would mark a major turning point in my stay at the Miami prison. I would go from being just another inmate doing his time to an embedded investigative reporter and policy analyst who would wind up uncovering a $5 billion scandal that, down the road, I would work to try and solve, both during my prison stay and afterwards. So this was a real game changer that could potentially affect over sixty thousand inmates and save taxpayers billions. It was even a game changer that had implications for the presidential election. Stay tuned for that too.*]

HUCK POST 64:
Scully Duggery
May 3, 2024—Day 46

It's always a happy day at the dorm when one of our own is going home; and May Day was supposed to be Scully's turn.

Young Scully was a very high-IQ young man who had blown a small fortune with his wife absolutely the right way. When he and his brother sold their trucking company, Scully had taken his share to travel the world with his spouse, and it was three sweet years in the prime of their lives. Great decision, in my book.

When he got back, he got into crypto trading as a broker; and he got caught in the middle of a Nigerian scam in which several elderly folks were billed using crypto transactions. The Treasury Department didn't blame him for the scam—that would have been a ten-year bid. But they slapped his wrists with a six-month sentence because he didn't have a proper license to transact in crypto—hell, nobody really did at the time. Talk about collateral damage.

At any rate, May 1 was supposed to be his release date, and it was a straight First Step Act calculation. He'd had forty days of FSA credits, so his sentence should have been finished on May 1, May Day.

Literally, as he was getting ready to walk out the door, they had pulled him back because of a computer glitch that had wiped out his FSA. Scully was as depressed as he was outraged and was looking for my help. (I could help get everybody out but me, apparently.)

Serendipitously, the next morning, the warden and Verdejo showed up for a snap inspection and Scully and I cornered them to plead his case. They promised to get him free within twenty-four hours—stay tuned.

There was no excuse for this. Absolutely the easiest case to calculate. But such Scully-doggery was par for the "that's why they call it prison" course.

I wish the kid well—he won't be back once he's out.

HUCK POST 65:
Divine Romanian Intervention
May 3, 2024—Day 46

God helps those who help themselves.

When I woke up on my forty-sixth day in captivity, I never would have guessed that a possible solution—or at least a reduction in my sentence—might come from a Romanian dirtbag. Follow me here:

As I have already vented about in a previous postcard, I should serve only three out of the four months of my sentence under the First Step Act. However, because I had no probation, by a quirk in the FSA, I'm not eligible for earned FSA credits toward release.

After several weeks of asking my lawyer to come up with a way around the absurdity—denying FSA for release to folks *without* probation punishes the "lesser criminal" in favor of those criminals *with* probation—I finally stick a paralegal on the problem.

It was going to cost a few extra thousand bucks, but time was of the essence. And boy did we hit the jackpot.

Eric found a perfect 2023 case in Oprea v. Warden in which an inmate had petitioned his district court judge to add a period of probation to his sentence so his FSA credits towards sentence reduction would kick in.

I note here that this guy was a dirtbag, and the only reason he didn't have probation is that he was going to be deported back to his nation of Romania the nanosecond his sentence was up.

Predictably, the DOJ prosecutors fought the Romanian—never give a sucker or inmate an even break. But the judge saw merit in the proposal, gave him one year probation, and with that, the guy would get out of at least his American prison a full year early.

Okay! This was a case my lawyer, Stanley Woodward, could use as a template to file an emergency motion before my old nemesis and judge in my case, Amit Mehta.

My only hesitation was that I thought if we reopened the sentencing, the sly jackal Mehta might *increase* my sentence just for the heck of it or slap me with five years probation.

I ran that by Stanley on our weekly legal call, and he frankly couldn't rule that out—he distrusted Mehta by this time as much as I did. But we decided to give it a whirl; and Stanley promised to file an emergency motion no later than COB Tuesday. Knowing Stanley, I'll take the over on that—but let's see what happens. In the meantime, if I hadn't acted in prison, that case would not have been found.

God does indeed help those who help themselves.

HUCK POST 66:
Scully Duggery Cookie Fix
May 4, 2024—Day 47

Recall here, Eric Scully should have been released on May 1, but a glitch in the computer system pulled him back into the devil's bosom of prison. And yesterday, Scully and I had made the warden and Verdejo aware of the situation, and the warden promised to make it right.

By this morning, *nothing* had been done. The warden was off for the day. So was Verdejo, who the warden promised would be around if Scully still was around and not released.

Into this breach, at my request, steps Jason Cooke, a.k.a. Cookie, the Counselor. He was kind enough to schlepp over to the low-security prison to assess the situation. He came back, and we went and dug Scully's file out of Donaldson's cabinet—Donaldson is Scully's case manager.

"Ah, so," says Cookie. He confirmed Scully's FSA credits were not up to date, and the computer was to blame. So Cookie fixes the form and faxes it off to the higher-ups, and all—including Scully right out the door—should be good to go.

Except. Being Friday, nobody was really working, so Scully had to wait over the weekend to get free—it would take until Tuesday, a full week late.

That's why, as Cookie loved to frame it, BOP stands for Backward on Purpose.

What they did to Eric was just wrong—and cost the taxpayers a few extra shekels. That's why they call it prison.

PIXIE POST 12:
Complaining Is the New Cancer
May 4, 2024—Day 47

Pixie here, and my rock and security blanket, Dale, was supposed to pick me up this morning at the Doral to start my seventh weekend visit to the prison. But when I go out this morning in front of the portico, Dale isn't there. My security comfort ride and symbol of me getting to the prison on time is a no-show.

Inside the lobby, I find out there was a miscommunication, and they had sent Dale to pick me up this morning in Palm Beach, not the hotel.

Now, my heart is palpitating—just as it always does while waiting in line to visit Peter, but now, it started two hours earlier.

Leave it to the Doral associates. They secured me a pinch hitter fifteen minutes later and off I went. When I arrive, and I'm the first in line to see my soldier; only then does my heart return to a normal pulse.

I need not have rushed. Today, as is often the case, the guard is late, and the other family members in line with me start complaining, mostly in Spanish, and it is in that moment that I wish I didn't understand Spanish perfectly from my days in South America, because they complain all the time.

Of course, there is much to complain about, far too much. But as I tell my Huck when I finally see him, I was brought up by parents who believed that no matter how bad something is, ranting and raging about it just adds more negativity and stress. You just have to ride the wave and do something about the cause of the negativity, but don't sit there and complain just to vent.

People get strokes, cancer, and heart attacks if they do this. As my Huck tells me, we must always ride that beautiful California wave even through the rip currents.

HUCK POST 67:
Zen and the Art of a Pull-Up
May 4, 2024—Day 47

Today, after visiting with my Sweet Pixie, at the ripe young age of seventy-four, I was able to do a complete pull-up for the first time in thirty years out in the yard after dinner.

Am I getting stronger in prison—or just losing so much weight that I can now do a pull-up? Inquiring Zen minds want to know.

I'm down from about 150 pounds to close to 140. If I breach 140, I'll have to jump the fence and hold up a McDonald's with a lock and a sock, the preferred weapon of many inmates.

I'm reminded here of the Gore Vidal diet. Try prison, Gore, if you really want to rush the pounds off.

[Author's Note: By the way, my pull-ups weren't the half-cheesy ones like RFK Jr. had out in his videos when he was running for prez. These were the real deal. Still thinking about challenging the MAGA man to a pull-up and push-up contest just for the hell of it. Raise a few bucks for charity.]

PIXIE POST 13:
Forever Young Wins Me a Restaurant
May 4, 2024—Day 47

Pixie here, and it's a trifecta party this weekend: a visit with my Huck, my mother Audrey's birthday, and the Run 4 the Roses, the 150th anniversary of the Kentucky Derby. We make it a game, just like we do every year.

My Huck picks two horses and I pick two horses, and whoever is the closest to winning wins the prize of a choice of restaurants for our next date. Then we agree that he'll watch the race in the computer room at the prison where there's at least one TV likely to have it on, and I'll watch from the Champions Club sports bar at the Doral, and then he'll call me right after the race and one of us gets to claim bragging rights—and rights to a rain check on the next restaurant.

Later that night, I get to brag. I didn't pick the winner—that was Mystik Dan, an historic 18 to 1 shot. But I won the bet because one of my picks, Forever Young, finished third, right ahead of Huck's fourth-place winner, Catching Freedom. Wonder why my Huck picked that one? Ha!

This is how we would pass our time in prison. At least this time with the Derby game, it was just like we would do on the outside, so it felt good and right and even normal. No tears on the pillow tonight.

HUCK POST 68:
Eight Miles High
May 5, 2024—Day 48

You can't keep the new hires. The job is dangerous, and TSA
and Border Patrol and others just pay higher.
—Guard X

I'm a criminal and I'm the only one out here in the yard tonight
that's not high. No alcohol, no drugs. And I'm the criminal.
—The Smuggler

Idle hands are the devil's workshop.
—Anon

One of my favorite guys at the prison was the Smuggler. There was no "I'm innocent" or "they railroaded me" bullshit about him. He freely admitted they grabbed him and his fleet of smuggling boats in the Virgin Islands with enough "weight" to put him away and out of business for a very long time. And he was using that time to be the prison's eight ball and chess champion—all at American taxpayer's expenses.

At any rate, it's a Sunday night at the outer pavilion, the sun has set, and dusk has turned to black. I've finished my stretching, and tonight's guard is going to let us stay out until almost 9:30 when we have to be in for the count. So it's me going mano a mano playing eight ball with the Smuggler as a parade of drunks and addicts wander in and out of the pavilion.

Smuggler is as disgusted as I am. All getting high in prison guarantees is that you'll be back in the joint shortly after you get your freedom this time around. I don't have any data here, but I'd bet a *lot* of money there is a very high correlation between alcoholism/drug addiction and recidivism.

Yeah, I get that prison isn't supposed to be Harvard—or even high school. It's prison. But everyone in a minimum-security prison is going to have an opportunity to be our neighbor on the outside. Yet, the way the system is structured, most of the inmates, particularly the lower-income ones, are going to leave the prison poorer and less equipped for the job market than when they came. If you throw in alcohol or the synthetic cannabinoid K2 or heroin on top of that, that neighbor coming out of prison will likely be the neighborhood dealer or burglar.

The other part of the drugs-and-alcohol-in-prison problem is the rampant corruption that runs through the prison-guard ranks. This is not to say all, or even most, guards are corrupt. It's simply to say there are enough bad apples to puck up everything.

The fact here is that the levels of contraband that exist in prison, particularly drugs and alcohol, simply can't exist unless some guards are either turning a blind eye or running the trade themselves. It's a slippery slope that some guards may find it fairly easy to justify—"man, the pay sucks here so I have to boost it somehow." That's why they call it prison.

HUCK POST 69:
The High Cost of Tomatoes and Onions
May 6, 2024—Day 49

> *Pettiness which plays so rough.*
> —Bob Dylan

So I'm waiting in the lunch line with an inmate, and he told me how he had spent three years over at the low-security side of the prison before landing on our side of the fence.

He, let's call him Speedy, was in on a ten-year, mandatory minimum bid for meth dealing; and he indeed had the look of a former speed freak—bad teeth and all. But sober, Speedy was a good guy, just another blue-collar guy gone astray—what else is new in a prison lunch line?

The twist in his story, however, was how he had gotten busted in the low-security prison for the heinous sin of having a single tomato and onion in his cell.

Speedy had been busted in a routine inspection, and some sadistic guard had written him up for what? Unlawful possession of fresh vegetables in a prison killing everybody with canned peas?

That single infraction had delayed Speedy's transfer over to our side—slightly less dangerous, a bit more freedom—for a full year. For a frigging fresh tomato and onion.

Just another example of how prison turns people into criminals. They feed you a diet largely devoid of tomatoes, onions, and other fresh vegetables, drive you to the black market inside the prison, and then bust you for trying to stay healthy. You can't make this up.

HUCK POST 70:
Free Scully, Scully Is Free
May 6, 2024—Day 49

It took six unnecessary days, but Scully got the word first thing in the a.m. that he's going home today.

All the work we did pushing the process on Thursday and Friday paid off. It shouldn't have been necessary, but it felt good to have helped. It doesn't happen without me and Cookie.

Just another day in prison.

I told the kid not to screw it up and wished him well.

HUCK POST 71:
Notorious PKN
May 6, 2024—Day 49

*On Monday, House Judiciary Committee member Matt Gaetz (R-FL)
was denied a request to speak with Navarro by Peters on the grounds
that he was "too notorious" to meet with a member of Congress. That, in
addition to the failure to comply with requests for information in another
case, prompted the committee to demand Peters testify in Congress.*
—Washington Examiner

*A trio of U.S. congressmen is demanding that the Bureau of Prisons
(BOP) director testify before a Congressional subcommittee after the
bureau allegedly blocked a request to interview Peter Navarro, an
economist and former Donald Trump advisor serving a four-month
prison sentence in Miami. U.S. Representatives Matt Gaetz of
Florida, Jim Jordan of Ohio, and Andy Biggs of Arizona sent a letter to
BOP Director Colette Peters, directing her to appear before the House
Judiciary Committee's Subcommittee on Crime and Federal Government
Surveillance on June 13 over the "politicization of [the] BOP."*
—Miami New Times

Hell hath no fury like a congressman scorned—and in this case, rightly so.
For more than a month, Congressman Matt Gaetz had tried to get into my
prison to interview me for his podcast and get briefed on prison conditions.
Yet despite his right to visit me, Matt had repeatedly been denied permission.

This all came to a head in a verbally violent confrontation with Bureau
of Prisons Director Colette Peters on May 6 on Capitol Hill. Incredibly,
Peters would defend her censorship on the grounds that I was one of the
most "notorious" inmates in her prison system.

Yep, little old me. Right there, above all the murderers, rapists, and
child molesters was the Notorious PKN—Peter Kent Navarro.

Could this be an opening? thought I when Gaetz demanded Peters to
Capitol Hill to testify and answer questions.

Imagine if I could submit testimony that day—or perhaps even get a furlough from prison and testify in the flesh. It would be a great opportunity to blow the lid off the BOP's refusal to implement the FSA.

BOP director Peters would have to either assert she was implementing the FSA faithfully according to the statute—a lie to Congress and a felony—or admit her failure. Either way, a *big win*. Stay tuned. Let's see how this develops.

I vowed to contact Gaetz's office and see if we can develop a strategy.

HUCK POST 72:
No Pills at the Pill Line
May 7, 2024—Day 50, Morning

It's 5:55 in the morning. I'm at the other end of the main prison yard at the mess hall, waiting for breakfast at 6:00—or whenever the heck they decide to open. Today, they'll be half an hour late.

Watching the line form for the mess hall as I do some exercises to loosen up my arms and neck, I see Johnny Be Good suddenly sprint across the yard over to the adjunct medical office and bang on the door as a crowd forms around an inmate named Enrique who has just collapsed.

From a distance, I watch the spectacle as another inmate approaches me, and we start talking about the incident and a few things fall into place. I had met "Sandy" shortly after I had arrived—he had come just a few days before me.

At first blush, Sandy seemed like a very nice and affable, unflappable, and imposing fellow—early thirties, 6'2", strong and athletic, someone who should handle prison quite easily. But as we talked, he began to complain first about the nonexistent medical care and then specifically about the so-called "pill line" which is called twice a day at the medical office to dispense prescription meds.

I should say here that one of the great blessings I have at seventy-four is the lack of need for any pills or shots—no Lipitor for high cholesterol, no beta-blockers for high blood pressure, no insulin or Ozempic for diabetes, and certainly nothing for epilepsy or seizures.

The same could not be said for many of the inmates, who regularly struggled to get their prescription medicines, and in many cases, this can be deadly.

As Inmate Sandy and I talked, we speculated that our fallen comrade that morning may well have fallen for lack of medicines. Then, Sandy confided in me that it had been impossible for him to get the Prozac he needed to deal with his adjustment into prison. Instead, they had put him on an alternative that totally whacked him out and, as he put it, "made things worse."

Things did indeed fall into place for me with that confession— it stunned me, given his outward appearance—and I said candidly I had noticed a marked shift in his initial attitude when he first came into prison to what I had observed lately. Sandy had begun to always eat alone at breakfast and he appeared more and more sullen.

I also told him if he needed to talk, I'd be happy to listen and reminded him he had a beautiful wife and young child counting on him. It's always the families that suffer more—a lesson I (and my Sweet Pixie) would learn over and over.

The lesson for me about Sandy is that looks can indeed be deceiving, and sometimes mental issues have as much to do with body chemistry as physical projection. Like I say, Sandy looked a whole lot more like a marine or football quarterback who could do his eighteen-month sentence without even a bead of sweat than a head case and nutjob. But the harsh reality of losing one's freedom in a place that doesn't feed you well and can't get you the medicines you need and doesn't appear to give a shit about you can topple even the best of us.

Did I mention that when Sandy went to the piece of work otherwise known as the psychologist Torres for help getting his medicine, the bitch simply told Sandy it was not part of her job? (More about Big Nurse Torres later.)

HUCK POST 73:
Good Samaritan Prison Blues
May 7, 2024—Day 50, Evening

Each year in prison takes two years off an individual's life expectancy.
With over 2.3 million people locked up, mass incarceration has
shortened the overall U.S. life expectancy.
—Prison Policy Initiative

Enrique first grabbed my attention one late afternoon after dinner. With the sun low in the sky, the lads were mixing it up three on three on the basketball court, and this big dour dude was knocking in long-range shots bucket after bucket with a 10-knot wind raffling across the yard. Impressive, and a dude after my own heart.

This morning, this same fellow had collapsed outside the mess hall. I don't know what they did for him that day, but it sure didn't cure him.

That night, Enrique, who could crush you with one hand, came to my dorm with an interpreter and, in tears of pain, begged for my help.

Enrique's stomach was grossly distended from bloating—he looked about ten months pregnant. He had a bottle of medicine one of the physician assistant's had given him that afternoon that made me want to cry—or laugh—it was so absurd.

The medicine was none other than Tylenol—something for the pain, *nothing* for the symptoms.

As to what I might do, it was pretty obvious. The Commanding Officer for the evening had told Enrique he couldn't help him and told him to take his Tylenol.

Beyond pissed, I took Enrique and his translator back to the CO's office, explained to him that the inmate needed immediate medical attention, and raised the truthful specter of a death on his watch—appendicitis, ruptured spleen, bleeding ulcer, who knows.

I didn't even have to play the bad cop and tell the CO he'd be personally responsible if the guy died. He got the Big Picture as I painted it.

Enrique was out the door in twenty minutes to a hospital. Two weeks later, he would return with hair-raising tales of an emergency surgery for three hernias that otherwise truly might have killed him.

All I could think was *Why does it take someone like me with at least perceived power to move these people to action?* I have no idea, but that's why they call it prison.

HUCK POST 74:
A Big Swing From the Inside
May 7, 2024—Day 50

I made "the pay-pahs," as they say in my old Beantown. Just trying to advance the football in my new mission. Just a big punch in the nose to the Bureau of Prisons and its "prison industrial complex" and a wake-up call to a depressingly somnolent Congress.

Let's see if there is any blowback from my captors and jailers. Yes, I've begun to push harder on the envelope. Retaliation is never off the prison table. Gotta watch my six. . . . Here's my first op-ed from prison:

> **Bureau of Prisons thumbs its nose at Congress, taxpayers: Add "smart on crime" to political mantra of "tough on crime."**
> *Washington Times*
> By Peter Navarro—Tuesday, May 7, 2024
>
> **OPINION:**
> The failure of the Bureau of Prisons to implement two major federal laws mandating sentence reductions for nonviolent and first-time offenders costs taxpayers billions of dollars annually even as it increases recidivism risk and the crime rate—never mind the human misery such malign neglect entails. This is the most pressing of the many problems I've observed as a prisoner of conscience from inside the walls of a federal prison.
>
> In any fair and efficient criminal justice system, a prison sentence must be long enough to match the crime while sufficient to deter future criminal behavior. Based on my conversations with nearly a hundred fellow inmates and supplementary research, the United States justice system wildly over-sentences and significantly delays releases and thereby misses this mark.
>
> Here's Prisonomics 101: We must be as "smart on crime" as we are "tough on crime." Every inmate costs taxpayers $60,000 a year, and the costs of over-sentencing and the Bureau of Prisons'

failure to release inmates in a timely manner run well into the billions.

America's over-sentencing for first-time and nonviolent offenders begins with a large roster of "hanging judges" fearful of a political backlash from a citizenry rightly angry with the breakdown of law and order in our society. However, far too many of these black-robed czars have little concept of what it means to be behind bars, and it means nothing to impose sentences twice or more as long as might be needed to adequately punish and deter.

Here, the significant variance across judges in sentences for the same crimes is both well known and troubling. In my own dorm, one inmate got a soul-crushing 150 months for embezzlement while his co-defendant got a mere 30 months for a much larger role in the scam.

Second, over-sentencing has been institutionalized through outdated "mandatory minimums," which regularly put first-time, nonviolent offenders in prison for 10 to 15 years or more. Mostly, these are young men, often with wives and young children. They will go from youth to middle age in our prison system at a per capita cost to U.S. taxpayers approaching $1 million. In prison, their skills and employability will deteriorate. Tragically, their children will go from babies to teens without a male parent.

Third, there is the "RICO wing" of the Department of Justice, now exploiting and often abusing the broad powers of federal racketeering laws. Indeed, DOJ prosecutors routinely use overly broad "conspiracy" charges to threaten defendants and their family members with ridiculously long sentences if the defendants refuse to plea bargain and instead go to trial. When the inevitable plea comes, coerced defendants are often still saddled with eight-, 10- or 15-year sentences for white-collar crimes that, absent the RICO gambit, would be settled through civil rather than criminal prosecutions.

Through such coercion, DOJ prosecutors act more like racketeers than those they are prosecuting. Their goal is not justice but simply another scalp to take for their resumes and professional advancement. I have met numerous men in prison who had their lives, families, and job-creating, tax-generating businesses ruined by DOJ's RICO wing and who never should have been put behind bars.

Congress has sought to address this over-sentencing epidemic through the Trump-era 2018 First Step Act and the 2008 Bush-era Second Chance Act and its 2018 reauthorization. Yet the Bureau of Prisons has largely ignored the mandates Congress has given it. For example, during my prison stay, I have worked with dozens of first-time and nonviolent inmates. I have discovered case after case where prerelease custody into a halfway house and home confinement had been delayed for months and sometimes more than a year. I had this happen even in my own case, which has lengthened my prison stay by more than one-third.

One of the biggest reasons the Bureau of Prisons fails to release inmates in a timely manner is its failure to follow a 2022 directive mandating full forecast release credits under the First Step Act and the Second Chance Act. An equally big reason is simply bureaucratic inertia, which causes many inmates who fail to speak up to fall through the cracks.

One of the most economically perverse problems I have observed is the refusal of the Bureau of Prisons to allow inmates into prerelease custody because of the closing of some halfway houses and a lack of halfway house capacity. This is not just inhumane; it is fiscal insanity.

It costs taxpayers half as much to support an inmate in a halfway house. So when the Prisons closes halfway houses to save a few dimes and inmates have to stay in prison longer, the total cost to the Bureau of Prisons—and taxpayers—goes up.

Finally, while Congress has significantly relaxed the rules governing compassionate release, time and again, the Bureau of Prisons and wardens at prisons like mine in Miami won't approve such releases. In my prison dorm alone, there is a 66-year-old in deteriorating health in a wheelchair, an 80-year-old in even worse condition, a guy with what is likely terminal cancer, and a 40-something suffering from the aftermath of a stroke and related spinal surgery. All should have been sent home months or years ago.

This is not what Congress intended, and the Bureau of Prisons' failure to obey the laws of our land—irony noted—is needlessly costing taxpayers billions annually while increasing crime and recidivism rates. This travesty is happening on President Biden's watch. It's well past time to add "smart on crime" to the political mantra of "tough on crime."

Peter Navarro served for four years as a senior White House adviser to Donald Trump. He is currently a prisoner of conscience in a federal prison for defending the constitutional separation of powers and honoring his oath of office. He is the author of the forthcoming book The New MAGA Deal: The Unofficial Deplorables Guide to Donald Trump's 2024 Policy Platform.

[*Author's Note: Nice little plug for my new book that will come out in July, just in time for the RNC Convention. Can't ever miss a chance to pay my legal bills!*]

HUCK POST 75:
The Garage Bill Comes Due
May 8, 2024—Day 51

A week after David waxes eloquent on Zen and the Art of Prison Garaging, he dutifully drops on the breakfast table the nice little summary I asked him to do of what was needed to bring the prison garage back up to top speed.

David's list includes all the vehicles that are literally sitting idle because of a lack of spare parts—two trucks and four passenger vehicles.

This list also includes an itemized list of parts with cost estimates. For example, you've got twelve tires at $2,500, four constant velocity axles at $1,400, ten to fifteen oil filters at $2,000, and multiple front-end parts at $5,000.

Then there's a whole litany of little stuff—three carburetors and gaskets, four gas tank screws, six spark plugs, five starter assemblies, and five cam-to-carburetor hoses.

It all adds up to about $12,000—about the cost of a few bombs for Ukraine. With that outlay, you'd have everything working again and have parts to spare (pun intended).

I'm going to write it all up and take it to the warden. Let's find out just how broke they are.

HUCK POST 76:
Mad Dog and Mini-Me
May 9, 2024—Day 52

*Turns out top White House trade advisor Peter Navarro can add
General Motors and the United Auto Workers to his resume of deals
negotiated. FOX Business has learned Navarro worked with both parties
to help reach a tentative deal, which is expected to be voted on Thursday.*
—Fox Business

It's a pretty long drop from negotiating the end of a major labor strike to mediating what could well have been a bloody dispute at a Miami prison. But that's the situation I would find myself in when I came in for the Thursday 4 p.m. count.

The dispute was between two of the more difficult inmates in the dorm—the wheelchair-bound Mad Dog, who may well have shot a few folks on his way to prison, and Mini-Me, a short, extremely powerful martial artist who could easily kill guys much bigger than him.

To his credit, Mini-Me asked me to join him and Mad Dog in the utility room where they were going to talk—or duke—it out.

Of course, Mini-Me could crush Mad Dog like the bug that he was, but the danger of Mad Dog is that, as batshit crazy as he was, he might try to bludgeon Mini-Me in his bunk while he slept. So this was no laughing matter.

It was no laughing matter, especially if you knew that Mad Dog in his upright and wild and crazy youth was allegedly a "Take Down Artist" who would rob crack dealers at gun point—think of Omar in *The Wire* and you get the drift.

Of course, being a Take Down Artist on the mean streets of Miami is, as Omar has taught us, a very dangerous occupation; and one late night it had caught up to Mad Dog when one of his aggrieved victims cracked his skull, beat him within an inch of his life, and put him in a wheelchair for the rest of his life. Karma is indeed a bitch.

As for Mini-Me, his was a white-collar bid—massive overbilling of insurers by, as he described, some rogue doctors in his employ. Remember: everybody (except for the Smuggler) is innocent in the Miami prison.

At any rate, Mini-Me was a guy who at least looked normal, but he had one big problem. It was almost as if he had a low-grade case of Tourette's Syndrome, as he would just blurt out things often better left unsaid.

As is often the case, this blood feud was about territory. Mini-Me's bunk and locker were on the other side of Mad Dog's bunk, and Mini-Me, as Mad Dog had it, would sit too close to Mad Dog's bunk, bump up against, and talk too loud on his contraband phone.

Mad Dog had a point—but it was imprudent for him to go over to Mini-Me's side in the middle of the night and ransack his stuff in protest as Mad Dog had done.

After I sat and listened to the two go at it for fifteen minutes or so— each venting and popping out their chests—I came in with what was the obvious solution.

Mini-Me would agree to not bang his chair against Mad Dog's bed and not talk on his phone after 9 p.m., which was about the earliest Mad Dog might come in from watching TV.

Mad Dog would agree to leave Mini-Me's stuff alone. And that was that—we had a deal.

Except, of course, even after the handshake, Mad Dog continued to vent, and Mini-Me took the bait. Things got heated again, and that's when I earned my mediation money.

I told both of them very politely to shut the hell up, give the deal a try, and we'd check back in a couple of days.

Later, Mini-Me thanked me for reeling him and his temper back in. At least he knew he had an anger management issue.

Mad Dog didn't have a clue—I need to get that SOB out on compassionate release in the worst possible way and vowed to move that up the priority list.

Coda: A week later, Mini-Me got into it with what was his fourth inmate— no punches thrown, but damn close. He's a poster child of anger management issues and inmates struggling both with the fact of prison and the length of his sentence—even as his family was falling apart in divorce. Now, with a black belt in martial arts, he looks like a ticking time bomb. Before his time inside is over, he *will* hurt someone. That's what happens in prison.

HUCK POST 77:
Steve Mnuchin's Collateral Damage
May 10, 2024—Day 53

The Paycheck Protection Program is providing critical support to millions
of small businesses and tens of millions of hardworking Americans.
—Treasury Secretary Steve Mnuchin

After a stupefying lunch of surprisingly tasty cheeseburgers and fries and a nap resembling more of a Mad-Cow coma than the meditation I had sought, I headed out to the track for my daily three-mile walk-jog-run, one mile of jogging to kick it up a notch, and then a good brisk running mile followed by a lap around the track running backwards—don't laugh, it's good to loosen your hamstrings and back.

As I started my walk, a guy ahead of me was slowly sauntering, but as I passed him, he sped up and asked me what book of mine he should buy. I was a bit nonplussed—he was a Latino in his early forties and hardly looked like a nonfiction aficionado. But I told him maybe *In Trump Time* would be good, and I'd be happy to sign his copy.

As we walked, I asked what his story was, and it turns out the fellow was neither a drug dealer nor a pill pusher but one of the first of what looked to be a wave of folks soon to be imprisoned for scamming the Paycheck Protection Program (PPP) that Treasury Secretary Mnuchin concocted when COVID arrived.

From the minute Mnuchin had announced it on March 27, 2020, and began handing out government checks like they were popcorn, I thought the program was ill-conceived. Here we were, throwing billions at anybody with a pulse who wanted to apply, and there were plenty of folks in those fearful times who grabbed whatever they could, facing a future that at the time looked very uncertain.

Now, in the aftermath, there were plenty of true scam artists who deserved a vacation in a Federal prison. But there were also a lot of other folks like Juan who had taken some of the money and, as a CPA, had helped others apply for the funds.

When the Feds had come calling, they would both literally put a gun to his head at his arrest and figuratively put a gun to his head by threatening to put his mother, father, and brother in jail if he didn't plea to something he didn't believe he had done. At least that was Juan's story, and he may or not have really been guilty of anything other than poor judgment. But if there is anybody who also belonged in jail if for nothing more than sheer stupidity, it was Steve Mnuchin for designing such a fraud-prone program—so fraud-prone that the PPP seemed like entrapment.

The funniest part of my conversation with Juan was about his sentencing. He got a five-month bid with a year probation so I told him that under the First Step Act, he would only have to serve three months and twenty days—under FSA, you get ten days off your sentence per month in the first six months.

Why was this darkly funny? Because with his five-month sentence, Juan would be out of prison ten days before me with my four-month sentence. Remember: Because my devious Democrat of a judge, Amit Mehta, hadn't given me probation, I was *ineligible* to receive FSA credits for a quicker release. High irony for a guy who was in the West Wing the day POTUS signed the FSA.

I left Juan with some good advice to help him get out sooner and be with his wife—he had already been inside for a week, and nobody on the prison-guard side had bothered to tell him he needed to complete two surveys posted on his email account to trigger eligibility for FSA credits. He thanked me, and I got back to my run.

PIXIE POST 14:
Halfway Mark Melancholia
May 10, 2024—Day 53

Pixie here, and this past week, I have kept myself busy. Yet, even with all the beauty in Florida, and with the weather so nice—ultra blue skies, perfect sandy beach, soaring pelicans, lapping waves, lovely people, and ever-sociable neighbors—my days are mostly melancholy.

Maybe it is because we are still closer to the beginning than the end. The mid-sentence doldrums, not even yet to the halfway mark.

But I don't tell my Huck, because I am on his orders to have fun on the outside and be free for the both of us. But there is an empty space, a void. Because for three and a half years, my Huck has been my constant partner.

Maybe some weeks from now, I will truly find the joy he wants me to have, and I'll feel well and easy because it will be one less day until his release. Rain or shine, it will be sunshine and sweetness, warmth and spooning, in our hearts and souls. But not yet. Not today. Maybe tomorrow when I can hold my Ever Huck in my arms again (if the prison guards allow).

HUCK POST 78:
Walking Time Bombs, Best Laid Plans
May 11, 2024—Day 54

The best-laid schemes o' mice an' men often go awry
—Robert Burns

The day started with good news—and then went to at least semi-dung with a veritable raft of bad news items.

The good news was a summons from my favorite doc at the medical unit—Doc Chipi, the Cuban-American strongly supportive of Trump and truly concerned about her patients.

She called me over to update me on Kidney Man—fortunately, the kid with the bad kidneys was being taken better care of and was scheduled for a biopsy of the mass on his kidney. All good.

Her other news (not good) was about my own Great White Whale—the eighty-year-old, surprisingly urbane, ex-Army JAG officer and Vietnam vet waiting like Godot for the approval of his compassionate release.

Del Gowing had hit *every* mark in the process, including doctor and unit manager approval, but his paperwork was sitting in some Dilbert cubicle somewhere in the BOP diaspora, and Del and I wanted to know where it was.

Try as she might, however, Doc Chipi simply couldn't locate it. Instead, Chipi recommended that Del paper the bureaucrats in charge, including Ozuna, the assistant warden who had a rep for getting stuff done.

When I got back to the dorm, I relayed the news to Del and suggested he write letters not just to Ozuna but also Verdejo, and the woman who helped him with the application, Officer Fahie. I told Del I'd try and hand deliver them to Verdejo at the afternoon town hall.

Why is it so damn hard to send an eighty-year-old home from prison who's falling apart at the seams? Inquiring minds want to know.

HUCK POST 79:
A Princely Visit
May 11, 2024—Day 54

It was the closest thing to pulling a caper I'd come to yet at the prison—getting Donald Trump Jr. in for a visit with a horde of media locusts descending on us and a throng of fellow inmates eager to shake the Great Son's hand.

For my part, I didn't really care if all hell broke loose. But from the warden on down, they wanted to contain the chaos. So on Friday, the day before the visit, I was summoned to the building where Administrator Verdejo hung out and we agreed to quietly bring Don Jr. into the building next door to the Visitor Center.

It's not like the whole prison didn't know some bigwig was coming. The construction crew had spent the last several days painting the Visitor's Center—more lipstick on a pig—and repairing some of the seating and bathroom fixtures.

It was a replay of how they had spiffed up the prison in the several weeks before my own arrival. I'll get a laugh out of that all the way to my grave. Maybe they can polish my headstone.

At any rate, Sweet Pixie ran point on the outside—Don Jr. and Sergio Gor, the gent who ran Don Jr.'s publishing house (and who would later become a great friend) rendezvoused at the Doral before making the twenty-minute trek over to the prison.

What I love about Don Jr. is his authenticity. He's just a regular guy, albeit with a very high business and political IQ—probably the result of the Boss teaching humility at home and sending both Don Jr. and Eric out into the flyover states where they took a liking to hunting and fishing, Don more than Eric.

My mission at the meeting was twofold. First, my new book, *The New MAGA Deal*, would hit the stores on my birthday, July 15, the first day of the Republican National Convention, where DJT would accept the nomination for president.

The plan was to fly me up the morning of July 17, my release date, to Milwaukee and maybe grab a quick stage turn that night—a hard-hitting,

"If they can come for me, they can come for you" speech to rally folks around the real threat of prison for Trump himself.

My other mission was to brief Sergio and Don Jr. on the gem of a political issue that I was mining inside the prison walls. The central message: The inmates and their families love Donald Trump because he signed the First Step Act, which provides for significant sentence reduction for first-time, nonviolent offenders. And the inmates *and their families* hate Joe Biden for refusing to enforce Trump's FSA.

I wanted to get this message *exactly* right. It wasn't about going "soft on crime" but rather about being "smart on crime." The op-ed that I wrote and had Sweet Pixie get to Kelly Sadler of the *Washington Times* is an expansive rendition of this message. You read it just a few posts ago.

The point politically is that there were thousands of votes to be had in the battlegrounds if we strategically targeted the message in a "smart on crime," "save taxpayers billions" bottle.

They were intrigued. I promised there would be more to follow. And off they went with a clear lift in the spirits of both me and Pixie.

HUCK POST 80:
A Mother of a Day
May 12, 2024—Day 55

> *She's doing time with you.*
> —Inmate Ro

It's Mother's Day, and it may be the toughest day of the year for many inmates. The fact an inmate is in prison means he let down the person who brought him into this world. So there's a lot of guilt and sorrow in the air even as the mothers of inmates and mothers of the sons of the inmate pack into the Visitor Center to celebrate and mourn.

My beautiful Pixie shows up bright and early and first in line in the 8 a.m. shift as she always does, and once again, Ajemon the Terrible screws things up from the get-go by letting in the food vendors to start the morning rather than the visitors.

I see it all unfolding and go fetch the Commanding Officer to bail Ajemon out, but his screwup takes precious visiting time away from a gaggle of families and inmates on a very precious day.

My visit goes south about two hours in as my girl comes down with a bad stomachache from the bad food. We power through, and as I am running on the track later, I feel the helplessness of not being able to be at her side and comfort her, particularly if she winds up in the hospital. Prison imprisons you in more than one way.

This thought reminds me of the brief conversation I had with Ro, a thirty-something Puerto Rican father and ex-boxer in for dope dealing. As we microwaved some plastic-wrapped crap from the vending machines, we agreed prison was tougher on our women than us. He just said about my Pixie, "She's doing time with you."

On the track, I marvel at the fact that in a facility with almost two hundred inmates, I'm the only one running on the track. Only mad dogs, Englishmen, and MAGA guys go out in the noonday sun.

I bump into Ro as I'm doing my push-ups and pull-ups after my track run. He's alternating wind sprints with pull-ups.

He's candid about the life in Puerto Rico. He offers no excuses about his drug sales, but he's also not wrong that in Puerto Rico, it's either a very low paying job or making millions running drugs. It's too easy to get drawn into the life, particularly at a young age, when you're particularly not clear-eyed of the risks. He lost one brother to a gang shoot-out, his other brother went to prison as well, but he vows for his seven-year-old son that when he finally gets out in another seven years, he'll find a way to live the straight life. I wish him well, knowing full well he will be facing long odds.

Just before 3:30, I head in for the count and bump into the friend of the guy with the bloated stomach, and he tells me Enrique is back from the hospital and had—count 'em—three hernias repaired. He indeed may well have died if he hadn't gotten to the hospital.

I myself am a bit under the weather with a cold and cough that had moved through the dorm, picking us off one by one. I need to be careful— Brother Jesus can't shake his after two full weeks, and he looks like death warmed over.

Meanwhile, I'll get back to my bunk for the count and it's Salsa Sunday. "Chez Ray," the gentleman who makes extra dinner for a dozen or so inmates, has his Puerto Rican playlist at full blast, and he sings along with the tunes—a fine tenor, I might add—as he chops up sausages, slices Spam, whips up some spicy Minute Rice with beans, and, as a Sunday treat, will top off each of the dinners he will distribute with a fried egg.

The mood in the whole dorm is festive, and it strikes me how humans try to find a way to be happy and funny in their playful banter even when facing months or years more of life without freedom. My own remaining sentence of two months left seems trivial—until I remember once again Pixie and her possible illness. I'll speak with her later and try to come up with a game plan.

HUCK POST 81:
My Redd Foxx Moment
May 12, 2024—Day 55

I may not be as good as I once was, but I'm as good once as I ever was.
—Redd Foxx

I heard that joke as a high school senior back in the 1960s in the Howard Theater—Washington, DC's equivalent to Harlem's Apollo Theater in New York. It would take me until I hit my fifties to finally get it.

What's the analogy here? After more than two months in the slammer, I now know what it must feel like to go to school as a kid growing up in a ghetto, living on a substandard diet, rarely getting a good night's sleep, and sleepwalking through the fog of poverty.

A little more than halfway in, my decline in mental acuity and physical stamina, though slow and subtle, is increasingly noticeable.

I'm subsisting on a diet devoid of just about anything fresh, I'm suffering from a dearth of protein, and I'm calorie-challenged, even for a relatively small guy like me.

Through this metamorphosis, I notice that I am sleeping more, working less, and losing some of my sharpness in both memory and expression.

This is not to say I can't still work, work out, and write. I just can't do as much of anything that I otherwise would. Today was my Redd Foxx moment. And that's why they call it prison.

HUCK POST 82:
John Rawls Goes to Prison
May 13, 2024—Day 56

> *The principles of justice are chosen behind a veil of ignorance.*
> —John Rawls, *A Theory of Justice*

If I had a dime for every time I heard from an inmate, "The government destroyed my life," I'd have a lot of dimes. Collectively, the stories that I heard about abusive government overreach requires a quick meditation here on what the purpose of punishment for a crime should be.

Consider, then, a forty-three-year-old African American businessman with a wife and child who inflated the value of some assets to qualify for an SBA loan. What might be a just punishment for this indiscretion?

How about a civil suit, you might ask, which results in the recovery of the funds and a fine large enough to punish but small enough to leave the man with a future?

Not good enough for you? Then how many months or years do you want taxpayers to pay for his imprisonment while denying him the opportunity to work and contribute to the U.S. tax base? Three months? Six months? Maybe even a year?

Still not good enough? Then, suppose I told you that the government threatened the man with twenty years if he went to trial but offered "only" three years behind bars if he pled out? And suppose I told you that as part of the plea deal, this family man would have to agree to the forfeiture of all his investment properties, full restitution of the borrowed funds, and the loss of his business license—rendering restitution impossible?

Finally, suppose I told you the man's lawyer was on a fixed fee with therefore every incentive to settle the case and quickly move on rather than fight for his client?

Of course, these aren't suppositions, because that is exactly what happened to the man. As he told me his story at the mess hall over a dinner of dry shredded chicken, cold peas, and over-baked potato, he was two months into a three-year sentence and had been stripped of his assets and license. He was a broke and a broken man unable to provide for his family.

That's not justice. That is the rawest kind of an abuse of power as you'll ever see, and outcomes like that hurt us all.

As for two of the other "dime" stories I heard behind my prison walls, in each of the two cases, an entrepreneur CEO had built a very successful telemedicine practice. In one case, several doctors at the practice took illegal shortcuts and prescribed medicines without completing the requisite video call exams. In the other case, an employee fraudulently billed private insurance companies and took the skim.

In *both* cases, the CEOs were blamed for the illegal behavior even though *neither had direct knowledge of the crimes*. The way the law is written, however, they were guilty because they "should have known" what was going on.

In both cases, the government chose *criminal* over civil prosecutions. In both cases, the men were coerced into plea deals involving not just stiff prison terms but also asset forfeiture and crushing amounts of restitution. In both cases, the men lost their businesses even as hundreds of employees lost their jobs.

As they told me their stories, they did so with dignity but also as ruined men whose families would suffer.

How, then, does this type of outcome serve the American people? As I thought about this within my prison walls, I remembered studying the approach of the philosopher John Rawls to the design of justice systems.

Rawls assumes a "veil of ignorance" in which the designers of a justice system don't know their place in society with respect to their class, gender, race, skills, or talents. This veil of ignorance forces the designers to adopt an impartial perspective because they might end up as the poorest or most disadvantaged in the society they design.

The Rawlsian result is both fairness and risk aversion. By not knowing their future status, designers are incentivized to ensure that the system is just and equitable for everyone, particularly for the least advantaged. Since the designers cannot predict their future position, their design will protect against the worst results.

Of course, instead of seeing a lot of John Rawls in prison, it was more like *The Godfather* meets the Old Testament. But that's why they call it prison.

HUCK POST 83:
It's Curtains, Dicks, and Pussies
May 14, 2024—Day 57

Take that shit down or I'll take it down.
—Old-Timer Guard

I would quickly learn that prison guards are like fingerprints—no two are alike. Each one I would meet along the way would have their quirks, pet peeves, and style. Most of them were good to okay. Some of them were just dicks, and the ones *without* dicks were always the worst dicks.

In terms of pet peeves, one grizzled veteran with just a year remaining before he got his pension and was gone like greased lightning to the Florida Keys just hated when inmates put up curtains at night to ward off the wind from an industrial strength fan, the cold from our always-on air conditioner, and the noise from some of the snoring and farting, which could be loud.

I get why the guy didn't like these makeshift barriers—usually a sheet or several towels hanging from some string strung vertically between the bunk posts. It made it (slightly) harder to do the nighttime counts at midnight, 3, and 5 a.m. because it was harder to see our bodies.

Still, the only reason most inmates put the crap up in my dorm was the brutal, bitter cold—an air conditioner stuck at sixty degrees coupled with "The General's" industrial-strength fan got the wind chill into the fifties.

The General was the dorm's captain. He was a 6'6" Jamaican with a scowl that could curdle milk and he made it clear that no one was to puck with his fan.

As for the grizzled veteran guard, this prick didn't care if you were cold. He just stomped through the dorm in the middle of the night and ripped down any barrier he saw, and he did it violently enough to break the cord or strings—which were damn hard to replace.

Then, to demonstrate his ultra-prickness, the guard would trash the sheets and towels in a dumpster, get the stuff picked up at the 6 a.m. guard shift, and go home to be angry at his wife or dog. Just a sour asshole.

Sometimes, the new guards were even worse, especially the women. The women guards would often try to establish their dominance more forcefully than the men.

Sorry, National Organization of Women, I don't believe women guards belong in men's prisons any more than I believe men should be guards in womens' prisons—male guard rape is an epidemic at women's prisons.

At any rate, on Day 57, we got a new female guard—a tall Amazon lady with the meanest of glares. On her first day, midmorning, she starts out to the outer pavilion where guys are playing pool and chess and watching TV, and she just stands in their midst.

Then she starts walking to the outer track and courts and comes straight at me as I shoot hoops. Doesn't say a word. Just walks past me inches away and glares at me. Stops and stares at me for five minutes.

Then, she walks over to the racquetball area and does the same thing as guys do push-ups and burpees. It was like a poodle trying to be a pit bull marking her territory.

So unnecessary. So dehumanizing. But that's why they call it prison.

PIXIE POST 15:
My Big Sister Merri
May 14, 2024—Day 57

Pixie here, and I need and should and will dedicate more time to my sister, Merri. This is my epiphany today.

Merri—"Mares" Huck calls her—lives in NYC, but we talk all the time. She's a walking, talking news feed, absorbing everything that's printed or broadcast like a big MAGA sponge.

If I want to know what's going on in Trump Land, I don't need to put on the TV. I just call Mares.

She keeps me sane because she grounds me and is always very nurturing when hard times are there.

She calls me often because as a great big sister, she takes care of me, to the littlest details, and sometimes it can drive you nuts.

But I never take it for granted.

She is often scared for me, and she loves Peter.

She feels the same for him, which I think is so kind and sweet, and that is who she is.

I am blessed.

HUCK POST 84:
A Bootleg Milk Bust
May 15, 2024—Day 58

So we file into the mess hall for another cholesterol-killing, nitrate-infested lunch—hot dogs, for what is now four out of five days.

As we enter the mess hall, the lunch police watch us warily for any sign of a contraband food container, an errant cap, or a beltless inmate.

It's your standard cat-and-mouse game, with the cats being an OCD duty officer named Dunn who could crack every bone in your body with just one big bear hug, Torres the Shrink, who needs a shrink more than any of us except maybe Mini-Me and Mad Dog, and "Warden" Gandu, the lowly secretary.

What could go wrong here with these Gestapo on hand?

Plenty for me, as I see on my way out the door after lunch. I, the mouse in this game, have mindlessly grabbed a couple of cartons of milk that Chris had been giving out to take back to the dorm.

As I exit, about to be caught in the act, I see a pyramid of no less than fifty milk cartons stacked up kindergarten style into a pyramid that the lunch police had already seized from other inmates.

Of course, I had to surrender my cartons.

Then, channeling my inner Jack Nicholson at lunch in *Five Easy Pieces*, I thought better of it and went back and asked if I could drink mine.

Dare I say that certainly caught the guards off guard. And before they could say "no," I just grabbed back a carton from the pyramid, slowly opened it, and in front of about ten bemused inmates and perplexed guards, I slowly guzzled it down, milk mustache and all.

After I wiped the milk off my lip with my sleeve, smart-ass style, I asked Officer OCD for, as they say in military-speak, "permission to speak freely."

He said, "Sure." So I did.

I told the assembled throng that the only reason inmates take stuff like milk out of the mess hall is because they receive a starvation diet from said mess hall that lacks both the number of calories and healthy variety of food specified right in the nutritional menu. Besides, this stuff was almost rotten.

When the Psycho Psych Lady Torres explained they were trying to teach us how to prepare for the outside by getting us to follow even a "small rule" like no food taken from the mess hall, I gently pointed out that when her side of the equation fails to properly feed the inmates—and thereby breaches a very "big rule," that incentivizes inmates to break small rules.

And that, of course, is a central fact of prison life. As I have noted, limit the minutes of phone time, and inmates will get contraband cell phones. In this case, limit the food, and inmates take what they can from the mess hall. And, of course, most inmates who agree to a plea bargain for a lesser sentence are forced as part of the plea to plead guilty to at least some crimes they didn't actually commit.

With the shrink Torres, I also pointed out the hypocrisy of her own RDAP program. To be eligible for that program—*and* a full one-year reduction in sentence—you have to admit to a drug or alcohol problem. In the prison game, a not insignificant share of inmates that take RDAP don't have a drug or alcohol problem at all—they just lie to get in, and the shrink damn well knew this.

So the milk bust was indeed a petty move. I figured that maybe if I politely pointed this out, they might think twice about doing it the next time.

Nah. Probably not. And unfortunately in that moment, I didn't have a very important piece of information which would have *really* been fun to kick and stick up their keisters.

Turns out the reason there was so much excess milk coming out of the mess hall is because the guard *inside* had realized he was stuck with pallets of the stuff that was expiring that day. So that's why he had had Chris distribute it.

Boy, I would have loved to see their faces if I'd been able to drop that on them. Maybe next time I'm in prison.

HUCK POST 85:
Kitchen Patrol, Landing My Great White Whale
May 16, 2024—Day 59

It took me a month—and a little scavenging—but I finally got the coffee machine fixed in the not-so-fine dining hall—although "fixed" is a misnomer.

This was a $1,000 piece of equipment that simply needed to be plugged in to a 220-volt outlet. It was more than a year old and had never been plugged in. If there's a better metaphor for the Backwards on Purpose BOP Bureau of Prisons than that coffee machine, I'd love to see.

It was now over a month that I had waited for Verdejo to get me the parts and tools needed to hook it up. He had dutifully written it up in his little red book of reforms, but as yet, there had been no Coffee Revolution.

So, I decided this day to take matters into my own hands.

Within a matter of hours, the parts had "materialized"—don't ask me how, as some things that happen in prison must stay in prison.

And the tools were easy—don't ask me about that either.

All I needed now was the coffee. Did I mention I don't even drink the stuff? So it was not like I was feeding my own addiction.

And here was what else was funny about the whole damn thing. We had more coffee from Brazil sitting right in the warehouse because when the coffee machine had arrived last year, they started ordering both coffee and filters.

And boy, had both piled up. We could've opened a whole Starbucks.

And this was indeed a productive day. I not only got the coffee machine ready for the weekend—the only time they make coffee is on the weekends (that's why Bustelo is a huge favorite in the commissary)—but Chris also finally got me his inventory of all the *other* equipment in the kitchen that needs to be repaired *and* what kinds of foods might be cooked in a proper kitchen.

For example, the kettle has a broken water pump. Awesome mashed potatoes and soups loom on the other side.

The skillet grill—think pancakes, sunny-side up eggs, and cheeseburgers—is missing a 20-amp plug.

And let's not forget the degreaser—an awesome fire prevention tool. There are no chemicals to run it.

At one point, I'll deliver a detailed report to the warden. That's how you improve prison.

HUCK POST 86:
Sick as a Dog at Sea
May 16, 2024—Day 59

It took three weeks, but I finally got the full respiratory plague that had been systematically working its way around the dorm. Likely COVID.

It started with patient zero, Pedro. He probably got it from a family visit and off it went. Pepe went down hard. Then Jesus. Then Wally.

At night, it was a cacophony of coughs. By day, otherwise active and happy inmates walked around like zombies.

I had none of my usual defenses—fresh grapefruit, a barrage of zinc lozenges, just a decent night's sleep. It never would have got me on the outside. That's why they call it prison.

HUCK POST 87:
The Guards Fiddle While Inmates Burn
May 17, 2024—Day 60

To celebrate "Guard Appreciation Week," they handed out bagged lunches of a bologna sandwiches and potato chips and then locked us down for the day, as the guards frolicked at a picnic, grilling the fresh chicken we didn't get—and should have gotten—during the week.

I would have been as pissed as every other inmate was at the corruption and disdain for us, but I was too weak to bother—just slept most of the day.

Very hard to kick an illness that comes about from poor nutrition and overcrowded dorms. That's why people die in prison. Stay tuned.

HUCK POST 88:
Halfway Home and Fading in the Stretch on Preakness Day
May 18, 2024—Day 61

Come the stroke of midnight, I will have reached the halfway point of my incarceration. Pixie and I celebrated that thought in an overcrowded Visitors Room, but our joy was tempered by the sickness that digs ever deeper into my lungs.

I feel the strength draining from me as I'm wracked with a now constant cough. Without the endorphins of a good daily workout, I lack my usual *joie de vivre*.

I try my best to put on a happy face during our visit, but we both know it's not working. These visits are special to both of us, and they sustain my sweet girl through the lonely weekdays.

I'll try to get a good night's sleep and be better for tomorrow's visit. But it's in God's hands now, with no doctors or medicines in sight or reach.

On a happier note, Pixie and I will play our little Triple Crown game today as we love to do each year, and today, it's the Preakness.

She'll pick two horses like we did for the Kentucky Derby, and I'll pick two, and whoever is closer to the winner wins the race and our bet of the day—a choice of a restaurant when we go to Milwaukee for the Republican National Convention.

Of course one of my obvious horse choices is Catching Freedom—a loser in the Derby, but hope springs eternal.

But Shazam! Later in the day, we are delighted that Pixie picked the Preakness winner, Seize the Grey.

Wish I had been by her side watching the race. It's the little things they take away from you that can mean so much.

PIXIE POST 16:
Of Pelicans and Lucy Girl
May 18, 2024—Day 61

Pixie here, and visiting my Ever Huck Saturday was just awful, as Ajemon the Terrible made an extra special effort to make the inmates as well as the visitors feel like animals being herded around and bossed at.

It's bad enough to feel like you have absolutely no control of a situation. It's even worse when you are not being treated right at all.

It will be hard leaving my Huck on Sunday, as I have to return this week to Washington for my job and to see our ginger-colored kitty, Lucy Girl—twenty-three years old and going strong!

I have missed her—Huck calls her Gingi—and I will see her and caress and hug her.

But I will miss my Huck, my soldier man.

But I can't think of that yet. I have to be in *this* moment. *We* have to.

Yet, I can't. I know I'll be on my way home to an empty condo tonight where only the sound of nature's waves and the sight of pelicans flying high together in the sky will bring me any semblance of peace. That sustains me for now as I brace for Washington on Monday.

HUCK POST 89:
Wasting Away in DOJ-ville
May 19, 2024—Day 62

It's Sunday. Pixie is on the early morning shift and shuttling over from the Doral. Can't thank Mikail the Doral manager enough for treating my princess like a queen and for Dale the driver, so calm, kind, and competent.

Of course, the evil Ajemon is up to his old tricks, bullying the inmates, terrorizing the children, feeling up the women.

At any rate, this is a big visit because I won't see my girl for a full two weeks. She's got to go back to DC and punch the clock at her job, so she'll be alone the whole Memorial Day weekend. So I'm trying to pump up her spirits while she's trying to do the same, me still being under a tornado of weather and likely COVID variant attack.

At any rate, we're sitting in the very best seats in the Visitors Room, the back corner overlooking a little greenery with at least a modicum of privacy. For comic relief, we can gaze on the red-necked lizards and at least a few of the pussycats in the herd on the prison farm.

Directly behind me is Brother D, a new arrival to the dorm, and one of those guys who carries himself so well you just want to like him.

African-American, fifty on the nose, and a serenity about him that will get him through what I'll find out later that day, is a five-year stretch for wire fraud.

Seems that a buddy of his who claimed he was an auto dealer wanted D to sell a couple of vehicles for him on Autotrader, which doesn't allow dealers. So D registered them in his own name, sold them, took a small commission, and got busted several years later because the cars turned out to be stolen.

Given the circumstances, D figured he could beat the rap and rejected a plea deal of five years of probation that would have kept him out of prison. At trial, he got convicted—his partner in the scam vanished and couldn't be called to testify. So the judge had thrown the book at him—five years in prison.

What another monumental waste of a man's life and taxpayer money. At any rate, all D wants now is to upgrade his commercial driver's license from B to A, but he can't afford the $5,000 the prison wants to charge for the training program. So he'll waste away in BOP-ville for another few years, his wife will suffer with him, and taxpayers will foot the bill. That's why they call it prison.

HUCK POST 90:
Lunch and Lockdown Interruptus
May 20, 2024—Day 63

Put me to work. I'm Mexican. I'd rather be working and paying
taxes than sitting here doing nothing.
—Inmate JD

That piquant observation from Brother JD, one of the bluntest-speaking inmates in the camp, followed a conversation about a famous Donald Trump pledge to close all the "camps," meaning the minimum-security facilities like the one (sort of) in Miami—remember, Miami is more of a hybrid because of a surfeit of tough hombres.

Listening to JD, I first thought my old Boss was delivering a "tough on crime" message—close the camps and lock the bastards up in a *real* prison.

Turns out, as JD explained, Trump simply thought that if an inmate was safe enough to put in minimum security, it made better sense to slap on an electronic monitor and let them go, get a job or run a business, be productive for America, and pay taxes. And if they recidivated, then lock them up for a very long time.

Once again, the Boss proved himself to be smarter than the rest of us, and JD was raring to go—praying for a Trump win.

HUCK POST 91:
Sticking My Neck Out
May 21, 2024—Day 64

Today, I pushed out the envelope just a little more in terms of a public profile despite being deep inside the belly of the Biden gulag beast. I did so with an interview published this day in the upstart business publication *Semafor*.

This was not an in-person interview—the prison was blocking all of those requests despite my right to participate in such interviews. But they couldn't really stop me from doing a written interview based on some email exchanges.

I'm not surprised reporters are banned from the prison premises. A live interview would have been a high impact way of highlighting the prison reform issues I was working on.

Of course, that's exactly why the prison bureaucracy was nixing any such visits.

So an email interview was the next best thing, and below is said interview.

It is my lot in life that whenever I do anything for the business press that they have to peg me as an extremist for being the tip of Donald Trump's spear on his trade and tariff policies with comments like this:

> *His time behind bars hasn't tempered Navarro, an anti-China hard-liner who battled with more globally minded Wall Street executives who joined the Trump administration.*

Of course, I battled with Wall Street on behalf of Main Street. Such "hard-liner" policies are anathema to the Wall Street globalist elites that make money by sending our jobs to sweat shops in Asia and by importing cheap labor across the Mexican border.

So, I'm Wall Street's favorite whipping boy. But I do get my own shots in. The little playful dig at Jaime Dimon, who was auditioning for Treasury Secretary in the next Trump administration, is my favorite. Ambassador to Laos would be perfect.

SEMAFOR
Imprisoned ex-Trump aide Peter Navarro predicts Fed Chair's ouster and 'mass deportations' in a second presidential term
Gina Chon
Tue, May 21, 2024 at 5:30 AM EDT

The Scoop

Federal Reserve Chair Jerome Powell would be gone in the first 100 days of a second Donald Trump term that would also include mass deportations of undocumented immigrants and more tariffs on Chinese goods, former White House economic adviser Peter Navarro told *Semafor* from the federal prison where he is serving a four-month sentence for refusing to cooperate with a congressional probe into the Jan. 6 riots at the Capitol.

Navarro, who directed Trump's Office of Trade and Manufacturing Policy until 2021, has remained loyal to the former president. Donald Trump Jr. and other members of the candidate's inner circle have visited Navarro at the minimum-security facility in Miami where he is being held, a signal that he could have a prominent role in another Trump administration.

Navarro laid out the former president's economic priorities in an exclusive interview, writing his responses on the email system at the prison's law library, where he works.

Navarro said he hopes to speak at the Republican National Convention if he can make it out in time, with his scheduled release date of around July 17 falling in the middle of the gathering. He wants to tout Trump's economic agenda, laid out in a book he has been wrapping up in prison, *The New MAGA Deal*, which will be released the week of the convention.

His time behind bars hasn't tempered Navarro, an anti-China hardliner who battled with more globally minded Wall Street executives who joined the Trump administration. He continues to bash Gary Cohn, Trump's ex-director of the National Economic Council, and former Treasury Secretary Steven Mnuchin, both Goldman Sachs alumni.

Navarro shared his views on Trump's unfinished business,

who should lead the Fed, and what he thinks about JPMorgan CEO Jamie Dimon. The correspondence has been edited for length.

The View From Peter Navarro

Gina Chon: What are Trump's economic priorities if he wins?

Peter Navarro: Documents 100 actions in 100 days. At the top of the trade list is Trump's Reciprocal Trade Act, originally introduced by Congressman Sean Duffy in 2019. If countries refuse to lower their tariffs to our levels, the president would have the authority to raise our tariffs to theirs. It is the most common sense route to balancing our trade deficit and thereby stimulating economic growth, and strengthening the US dollar. It should appeal to protectionists and free traders alike.

Chon: What didn't get done in the last term that would be back on the table?

Navarro: One of the biggest pieces of unfinished Trump business is to solidify Buy American, Hire American government procurement and reshore our private sector supply chains and manufacturing back to US soil. We are dangerously vulnerable to foreign coercion in everything from defense applications and tech to pharmaceuticals.

Trump will also quickly seal the border and begin mass deportations. Biden has imported a wave of crime and terrorism along with an uneducated mass that drives down wages of Black, brown, and blue-collar Americans. Blacks and Hispanics, particularly males in the workforce, are flocking to Trump in droves.

Chon: What are the plans for the Fed and current Chair Jay Powell?

Navarro: Powell was Mnuchin's folly—Powell raised rates too fast under Trump and choked off growth. To keep his job, Powell then raised rates too slowly to contain inflation under Biden. My guess is that this punctilious non-economist will be gone in a hundred days one way or the other. Former Council of Economic Advisers Chair Kevin Hassett would be a logical replacement; former CEA Chair Tyler Goodspeed would be a bold choice.

Chon: Is there a place for someone like JPMorgan CEO Jamie Dimon in a Trump administration?

Navarro: I'm sure if Jamie raises $100 million for Trump 2024 and doesn't hedge his Biden bet, there may be an ambassadorship somewhere in Asia where JPMorgan helped offshore millions of American jobs.

Frankly, [Blackstone CEO] Steve Schwarzman's unforgiveable alleged unregistered foreign lobbyist activities in weakening the China trade deal has made it difficult for those of us in Trump World to trust that Wall Street denizens like Dimon, [Citadel CEO] Ken Griffin, and Schwarzman will ever represent Main Street.

Chon: What about people like Gary Cohn or Steven Mnuchin, whom you labeled as "globalists," returning in a second Trump term?

Navarro: Gary Cohn did everything he could to block Trump's trade agenda, particularly steel and aluminum tariffs. When [former Commerce Secretary] Wilbur Ross and I finally outmaneuvered him, he quit in a huff—good riddance.

Mnuchin did everything he could as well to stop or soften Trump's trade agenda and regularly clashed with Ross, Lighthizer, and myself. Together, Cohn and Mnuchin prove, as I wrote in my book, that Bad Personnel is both Bad Policy and Bad Politics.

Chon: Trump wants to ratchet up tariffs on Chinese products, which he started when he was president. Given the challenges the Fed is facing in tamping down inflation, won't tariffs make the problem worse?

Navarro: The imposition of tariffs on Communist China had ZERO impact on inflation. In a general equilibrium economic world, tariffs over time boost growth and real wages; they are not inflationary.

Chon: Nippon Steel's effort to buy US Steel is facing challenges in Washington. Should that deal go through?

Navarro: If Trump had been president, Cleveland Cliffs would have consummated its merger with US Steel and created a real

American national champion in the world market. The Nippon deal is bad for America.

Chon: Are there US companies or industries that you think are un-American or acting against American interests?

Navarro: American multinational corporations naturally want to offshore American jobs in their search for cheap, sweatshop labor and pollution havens. That's why God created tariffs.

HUCK POST 92:
Mr. Mouth Man
May 22, 2024—Day 65

One of the biggest pains in the derriere in my everyday prison life was getting a call that I had "legal mail." This happened every time some well-meaning supporter decided to send me a certified letter to make sure it arrived—it wasn't legal mail at all.

In order to receive such mail, I had to schlepp over to the low-security prison, diddle around for an hour or more until an officer decided to show up with my letter or parcel, and they always did it around lunch so you'd miss a meal that, as my body flesh dwindled away, I couldn't afford to miss. Like I said, a pain in the derriere.

The first time it happened, I asked them if I could simply reject all certified and registered letters, but they said it was an all or nothing proposition—receive ALL mail or none.

Since I was getting literally thousands of letters a week from supporters, I didn't want to cut that off—I wanted to thank them. So I kept ALL mail coming. And off I would have to go over to the low-security side.

This day I had the misfortune of traveling over to the low side with the Mouth, an inmate notorious for his inability to keep his mouth shut.

Of course, while my group waited, Mouth Man started whining to the officer on duty about God knows what. Finally, the officer told him to just shut up and sit down, but Mouth Man kept talking.

I watched this from a few feet away at the counter as I was signing for my mail, and finally said to the Mouth, "Sit down, Brother. NOW."

At least that got his attention. It's a miracle he didn't get thrown in the SHU for a few days.

Some people are their own worst enemy—that's especially dangerous in prison.

HUCK POST 93:
The Prison Spy Network
May 22, 2024—Day 65

You may recall from a prior post how the evil Special Investigation Unit (SIS) had swooped down on the camp on April 19 and left destruction in their wake. Smashed toilets. Destroyed showers. Inmate property, including mine, ransacked.

It had been an overreach, and SIS had gotten significant blowback from both the warden and Verdejo, the prison administration. But today, a month later, using its elaborate snitch network, the Evil SIS Empire had struck back. Hard.

They were clever too, because today was "chicken day." You'd get a full drumstick and thigh on your plate, the best protein of the week. So the lunch on Thursdays was always guaranteed to have maximum inmate attendance.

So here we were all cooped up in the mess hall with our chicken—get the bad pun—a captive audience. And the doors were locked around us as the SIS swooped onto the campus in what would turn out to be a precision raid.

The squad of six agents, equipped with ladders and power tools, *went like a laser beam straight to several spots*—one, an area under the roof of the Visitor Center, another, a ceiling stash in Torres' Psych building.

Bingo. Bada Boom! Struck gold.

They seized enough power tools the inmates had purloined from the machine shop or had smuggled in to equip a large construction crew. These tools were used by a few of the inmates to create hidey-holes for contraband in the walls and ceilings.

And the SIS unearthed yet another round of contraband cell phones and chargers—their largest haul to date.

Several hours later, Verdejo held a town hall in our dorm and somberly informed us that the new haul could not have been revealed without destroying tiles and ceilings and other hiding places—thereby exonerating SIS for its past sins.

The bigger story among the inmates, however, was the obvious role that one or more snitches had played in pinpointing the exact locations for the SIS to swoop down on.

In fact, prisons use a variety of tactics to constantly spy on the inmates—it's just one more variant of cops and robbers.

The most obvious method to create a snitch is to catch an inmate with contraband, then threaten that inmate with a "shot"—a written infraction—with one or more severe consequences.

Loss of phone privileges. A ban from the commissary. A reduction in First Step Act credits that could add weeks or months back to the original sentence. Did I mention there might be a week or two in the SHU—the dreaded Special Housing Unit—on top of it?

Faced with any number of such sanctions, at least some inmates will go over to the dark snitch side.

As a further source of intel, the prison staff closely monitors all phone calls and incoming mail, either or both of which may help uncover any plots to break the rules.

As a third source of snitching, there is the RDAP program—the Residential Drug and Alcohol Abuse Program, the completion of which, as I have noted, takes a full *year* off one's sentence.

The *quid pro quo*, however, is that as part of the program, inmates have to snitch on one another and others in the unit as a way of demonstrating they have been cleansed of evil intent.

Here, the whole RDAP premise is that inmates must be honest about all their indiscretions—it's secular confession—and they are encouraged to talk about all of the rules they see getting broken under the presumption that if they do so, it will help them obey the rules when they get out of prison.

Of course it's all bullshit; and the psych teachers who teach the classes ruthlessly exploit the information—with these teachers often the ones most aggressively monitoring the phone calls of their students.

Now you might think this is all fair game, but I think not. When you turn men against each other, it weakens their moral fiber on net. To save their skin, they have to harm somebody else. Dog eat dog—not exactly the New Testament. Not exactly rehabilitation. But that's why they call it prison.

BTW, in the aftermath of this latest SIS raid, the inmates uncovered the snitch. The message that went out that night in black and blue and blood red was that no matter how much pressure the SIS might put on you, the consequences of snitching will be far worse. It was not a pretty sight.

Cops and robbers it is, and cops and robbers it will always be.

HUCK POST 94:
Super Size This
May 23, 2024—Day 66

The food is absolutely atrocious, and parents have no idea. Parents are giving their kids three dollars and saying, "Okay, see you later. Go off to school and have a good lunch."
—Morgan Spurlock

In my COVID stupor, I see in a leftover *Miami Herald* in the john that Morgan Spurlock has died, and he was damn young. Just fifty-three.

I remember years ago watching his Oscar-winning documentary *Super Size Me* and thinking at the time, *This guy's a genius* and *Maybe I should short sell McDonald's*. What a takedown!

You may remember that Morgan was the star of his own film; and the conceit of the film was to track Spurlock's health parameters as he ate nothing but food from Mickey D's for thirty straight days.

Yup, by the end, Morgan was a quivering and blubbery high blood pressure heart attack waiting to happen.

Of course, Mickey D's is a powerful addiction, so the film had zero impact on McDonald's sales. But the whole episode got me to thinking: *If just thirty days of an all-McDonald's diet can nearly kill a young guy (at the time) like Spurlock, what might thirty, or sixty, or in my case 120 days of prison food do to your health?*

I found out yet again last week with my second round of COVID. This *never* would have happened—or at least hit me so hard—if I had adequate nutrition and access to immune system–building vitamins, supplements, and medicines.

I'm down twelve pounds already with thirty days to go, and I didn't need to lose a single pound when I arrived.

Super undersize that. That's why they call it prison.

Did I mention that it was hot dogs *again* for dinner? Scrawny ones at that.

HUCK POST 95:
(Almost) All Shrinks Are Crazy
May 24, 2024—Day 67

*You'd have to be crazy to work here. A psychiatrist is just a guy
who has his own problems.*
—Hunter S. Thompson

Two of my favorite guys at the prison were as different as Democrats and
Republicans.

Johnny B. Goode, as I called him, was a white guy with dreadlocks and
a quintessential type-A personality, constantly creating trouble for himself
simply because he didn't know how to stop pushing.

He was in on an arguably bogus charge. He sold advertising for time-
shares on the internet, and while it was quite legal in the state of Florida, he
had run afoul of the Feds.

All Johnny wanted to do was get the puck out and start his life back; and
one big correct way to do that in prison is to enroll in the aforementioned
five-hundred-hour Resident's Drug and Alcohol Abuse Program (RDAP).
In fact, at his sentencing, his judge had recommended RDAP, so it should
have been an easy lift.

Johnny's problem was that he first had to get an interview and approval
from the head psych lady Torres, and she was a bitch from hell.

What would transpire over six long months of torment for Johnny was
the adult, sadistic version of Lucy, a.k.a. Torres, and the football for Charlie
Brown, a.k.a. Johnny.

Of course, the more Torres delayed the interview, the more agitated
Johnny got, and the more he pushed, the more Torres pushed back. It was
just cruel because she controlled a whole *year* of a man's life of freedom, and
she seemed to revel in Johnny's torment.

Watching this soap opera—Johnny regularly sought my advice, usually
over a game of eight ball at night—I did entertain the notion that maybe
Torres was using the whole process to see if Johnny was actually suited for

RDAP. However, I rejected that idea after talking with another one of my favorite guys we've talked a little about before.

Brother Jose was also a client of my hapless and useless prison consultant, and said consultant had asked Jose to get me some stuff from the commissary for my first day at the prison.

I had gotten to know Jose pretty well, mostly at breakfast where I'd always give him whatever bananas they might hand out and he'd give me his apples as we traded stories.

What was most cool about Jose is that he is a world-class spear fisherman—he showed me his album, and the fish he's taken down in hand-to-hand combat at a hundred feet deep all over the world were bigger than I am.

Anyway, Jose had been a psychiatrist himself, in the Florida prison system no less, before getting ensnared in a scheme that dragged him into the system on the wrong side of the bars.

Yeah, I know, everyone in prison is innocent (except the guy Smuggler I identified in a previous post), but Jose did seem to qualify as an honorable man who had been falsely implicated by those who weren't.

At any rate, I told Jose a little bit about Johnny and Torres, and he was blunt in his assessment: "She's a terrible human being."

He then told me how he himself had try to enroll in RDAP, and she had not just shut him down but verbally abused him in the process.

A few months later, Jesus, a Cuban Harpo Marx lookalike I called "Genio, " had asked Jose to enquire about the Spanish version of RDAP. Because Jesus barely speaks English, Jose had sent a note off for Jesus to Torres, and the next thing he knows, Torres is all over his shit for trying to backdoor his *own* way into RDAP through the Spanish door.

When Jose explained how he was simply doing it for a friend, she called him a liar.

I told Jose my general rule: Virtually everyone in the psych profession has significant psych issues, as they say in Washington. Jose did not disagree.

Jose also told me the suicide rate for shrinks was even higher than for dentists. I was surprised—then I wasn't.

I vowed that the last thing I would do before leaving prison would be to pay a visit to Torres and plead Johnny's case.

But as I write on the eve of a long weekend, still wracked by a cough, that day seems a long way away. That's why they call it prison.

Coda: Jesus a.k.a. Harpo a.k.a Genio was a couple of bunks down, and what I loved about him was his perennial joy—as well as the cold milk he always had stashed in a makeshift cooler he was always willing to share. In exchange, every morning, I'd bring him the sugar-shit cakebread they served at breakfast which I avoided like the plague but was happy to share with Genio.

HUCK POST 96:
The *Wall Street Journal* Interview
May 24, 2024—Day 67

Here's an interview that I would do with Alex Leary of the *Wall Street Journal* by email. Like Matt Gaetz and Don Jr., they wouldn't let Leary in for a sit-down. This email interview would open the floodgates to other requests.

Note how I continue to push the envelope. So far, no retribution. So it's all good.

Jailed Trump Adviser Peter Navarro Says He Doesn't Want a Pardon: 'I Have No Regrets'
Alex Leary, The *Wall Street Journal*
Peter Navarro, a former top White House adviser to Donald Trump, isn't interested in a pardon should "the boss" return to power.

"I will not give the Supreme Court any excuse to duck what is otherwise a landmark constitutional case regarding the separation of powers and executive privilege," Navarro wrote to the *Wall Street Journal* from prison in Miami, referencing his appeal now before a federal appeals court. The 74-year-old is two months into a four-month sentence on a contempt of Congress conviction for stonewalling the House panel investigating the Jan. 6, 2021, attack on the Capitol.

Perhaps no one has demonstrated loyalty to Trump like Navarro, the polarizing, wiry former White House China hawk and pandemic troubleshooter. And no one has quite paid the same price: Navarro is the first White House official in history to be imprisoned for contempt.

"I have no regrets," said federal inmate No. 04370-510. "I didn't choose this fight, this fight chose me."

He might not want a pardon but Navarro will have a home in a new Trump administration if he wants it.

"I would absolutely have Peter back. This outrageous behavior by the Democrats should not have happened," Trump said in a statement to the *Journal*. (Navarro said he wasn't looking for a job but would consider one "if the boss needs me.")

The Jan. 6 committee was made up of seven Democrats and two Republicans, including former Rep. Liz Cheney of Wyoming, who lost a primary election in 2022 to a Trump-backed challenger. The panel wanted to speak with Navarro in part because he laid out a strategy in a book for getting then-Vice President Mike Pence to stop the certification of Joe Biden's victory.

Navarro is being held at Federal Correctional Institution Miami, which is for male inmates. Panamanian dictator Manuel Noriega spent two decades there for drug trafficking. Lou Pearlman, the boy-band impresario turned swindler, died in 2016 while serving 25 years.

Navarro is in quarters for low-security offenders. Shortly before his surrender in March, when he showed up in all black with a green bomber jacket, CNN observed that inmates could hear the roar of lions from the nearby zoo.

"This is prison, plain and simple, no country for old men," Navarro said. "Don't fall into that pastoral zoo bull—." He has various complaints, including what he says is a diet high in sugar and carbohydrates: "Protein MIA. Haven't seen a fresh orange or grapefruit in the heart of citrus country since I got here."

Navarro communicated with the *Journal* via a prison email system. A request for an in-person interview was denied. Others who have tried to interview Navarro in prison have also been rejected. Rep. Matt Gaetz (R., Fla.), who hosts a podcast, said Bureau of Prisons director Colette Peters told him Navarro is "too notorious."

Gaetz rejected that description, saying, "He's like an elderly college professor."

A BOP spokesman said the agency doesn't discuss conversations with members of Congress. The agency said it provides a variety of healthy food options, including fresh fruit daily. Navarro, though, said inmates resort to buying better food in the commissary. "I'm a hot chili ramen noodle freak," he said.

Navarro did get a recent personal visit from Donald Trump Jr. and the conservative publisher Sergio Gor as they prepare to release Navarro's forthcoming book, "The New MAGA Deal." It is billed as an unofficial guide to "Make America Great Again" policies Trump could pursue in a second term, ranging from tougher trade practices and border security to shaking up the leadership ranks at the Federal Bureau of Investigation and Justice Department, long viewed with contempt by Trump.

The book is timed for release around the GOP convention, which would already be under way when Navarro is slated to be released from prison July 17, two days after his 75th birthday.

That day he plans to fly with his fiancée to Milwaukee for a book signing.

If given a chance to speak at the convention—which would deliver the kind of dramatic moment Trump covets—Navarro plans to reflect on his plight and the various prosecutions facing Trump. "Something like, 'If they can come for me—and they surely did—they can come for you,'" he said.

He said he and Trump don't seek retribution, but added accountability is needed for those who have been investigating and prosecuting Trump. He warned that those "helping to orchestrate this mockery of our justice system should keep their emails, phone messages, and other correspondence when the Trump FBI and DOJ come a-calling."

Jailed Trump Adviser Peter Navarro Says He Doesn't Want a Pardon: 'I Have No Regrets'

A Harvard-educated economist who once ran for Congress as a Democrat, Navarro was a business professor in California when he got a call in fall 2015 from the Trump team. An aide heard him talking about China on the radio. At the time, the campaign was light on experts, and Trump wanted to make an aggressive stance on China a key message to voters.

Navarro joined the administration on Inauguration Day and quickly established himself as a polarizing figure in both style and substance, railing against "globalist" advisers Trump also brought in. Rivals, including some who weren't as hawkish on trade, blocked Navarro from key meetings, and aides were instructed to call the chief of staff whenever he got close to the Oval Office, former White House officials have said.

Navarro persisted, helping animate the tough-on-China posture that led to Trump's trade war and heavy tariffs. His role included work to boost domestic manufacturing and during the pandemic, Navarro helped marshal the government response. Trump referred to him as "my Peter" and would summon him to scratch a populist itch.

"All those people who ripped on Peter should look at what Joe Biden has done. He's trying to out-Trump Trump on tariffs," Steve Bannon, another former White House adviser, said in an interview, referring to the Democratic president's new levies on Chinese electric vehicles. Biden has largely kept in place Trump's China policies.

Bannon, too, was found guilty of contempt of Congress and sentenced to four months in prison but remains free as he appeals. He said of his jailed counterpart, "He's a bigger name now than when he went in. He's a bantam rooster that won't back down."

A typical day in prison, Navarro said, involves rising before dawn, having breakfast and walking a mile around the track to watch the sunrise before work in the law library. Lunch is followed by more work, then dinner at 4:45 p.m., and more exercise in the yard. Navarro has found ways to get his message out, penning opinion pieces for The Washington Times.

He sleeps in a dorm pod with about 50 other inmates. Covid is going around, he said, meaning a lot of coughing amid the snoring—with "no MyPillows in sight," referring to the pillow manufactured by fellow Trump loyalist Mike Lindell. When time permits, Navarro works on his appeal before the U.S. Court of Appeals for the District of Columbia Circuit.

As he logs in the days, Navarro said supporters have flooded him with mail.

"There is so much more swamp to be drained than we ever thought. Rest up!" wrote a man from Castaic, Calif., according to Navarro. Another, Navarro said, came from Three Rivers, Mich.: "We are pulling for you. Lift weights. Don't get a prison TAT . . . unless it's a MAGA."

PIXIE POST 17:
My COVID Prison Blues and Achy Breaky Heart

May 23, 2024—Day 66

Pixie here, and despite all our travails, I was sure that Huck and I were both going to stay healthy, mentally, emotionally, and physically. Prison, however, had a different plan for us.

About ten days ago, one inmate came down with a nasty strand of COVID, and in the tight dorm quarters of my Huck, it was only a matter of time before it came for my Huck, too. He was one of the last ones to fall, but fall he did, and it never would have happened on the outside, as he takes such good care of himself.

He tells me he is sure it is COVID, but no one in the prison can get tested. I ask why, and he says it's because they'd have to let us out like they let out COVID folks during the pandemic. So it's see-no-COVID evil.

And then of course, the evil got me. Fever. Fatigue. Achy now in addition to my achy breaky heart.

I so prayed that I would feel at least close to normal during our next prison date this weekend. That is what we call them now, our weekend dates.

Huck jokes I'm a cheap date, but he still can't get lucky. He's funny sometimes like that.

HUCK POST 97:
Laugh at Me, Not with Me
May 24, 2024—Day 67

Here's where the Prison Gods (and Murphy) sometimes just laugh their asses off at us. In April, you may recall that I ran out of my five-hundred-minute allotment to phone Pixie a full five days before the end of the month. It was brutal because during the week, our short morning, noon, and after-dinner calls were our precious daily lifelines.

So in May, we have been much more careful to ration minutes so we would have enough to get us through the month. But sure enough, by Murphy's Law, a week before the end of May, the phones suddenly all break down.

Or, more accurately, the software that runs the phone system for the prison breaks down. And for a full five days, I can't talk to my Sweet Pixie on the phone.

And guess what? My surplus one hundred minutes for May did not roll over into June.

You gotta laugh because if you don't, you damn well are going to cry.

And maybe I have to rethink my virtue. I'm literally the only inmate in the entire prison that doesn't either own a phone or rent some daily minutes from somebody who does.

I refuse to do either for two reasons: I'm going to follow the rules that are set because that's what I do *and* I know that if I waver even for my Sweet Pixie, it will likely become a national news story with a headline like "Even in Prison, Navarro Acts Above the Law."

PIXIE POST 18:
Just Remember I Love You and It'll Be Alright
May 24, 2024—Day 67

Pixie here, and it's 8:15 a.m., and I'm *not* in full panic mode. I'm pleasantly surprised. Huck has schooled and steeled me well by now.

He tells me every day that I might not hear from him either by phone or by email because prison stuff happens. A lockdown. Phones down. Whatever.

So, when I don't get his phone call at 8 a.m., I'm cool as the coolest of any prison moll.

Sure enough, a little before noon, Huck tells me by a long-delayed email that the phones are down and it might be a while. Some kind of software glitcheroo.

It's Friday, and the tech guys won't be around until at least Monday.

He's going into full email-three-times-a-day-until-further-notice mode.

I'm cool. But sad. Some of my greatest prison-day times have been waiting for Huck to call and then hearing his sweet voice and having him sing to me a song. Our latest, which has been a savior, is "Just Remember I Love You."

Whenever I get too blue on the phone, he sings a few bars:

> *When there's so much trouble that you wanna cry The world has crumbled, and you don't know why When your hopes are fading, and they can't be found Dreams have left you waiting, friends have let you down*
>
> *Just remember, I love you, and it'll be alright Just remember, I love you more than I can say Maybe then your blues will fade away*

I love it when my Huck sings to me. And he doesn't care if the other inmates are listening.

When we are talking on the phone, it's only us and there's no other world. That's why our calls are so precious to *us*, and we always end the same way.

I say, "love you!" He says, "Love you more!" I say, "Love you I do." And then I finish with a "Ciaobella!"

And this time, even though my Huck warned me during our weekend visit it might be days before the phones were back up, I still would take my cell phone with me every day on my morning run back in Palm Beach.

Only after I drank my coffee from Benny's at the Lake Worth Beach Pier did I allow myself to look at that phone, hoping and wishing and sometimes praying it would ring.

When it didn't, I would turn my gaze to the beautiful ocean blue, maybe see a squadron of pelicans fly gracefully along the top of the waves, take a few deep breaths, and let the surf soothe my soul—just as my Huck would want me to be from another favorite line in another one of our favorite songs:

Lady peaceful, lady happy.
That's what I long to be.

Can you guess the song?

HUCK POST 98:
Count as I Do, Not as I Say
May 25, 2024—Day 68

They want us to follow the rules and be punctual—up before 6 a.m., uniforms on by 7, at work by 8, yada yada. But it's hard to do that when they don't follow their own rules.

Breakfast is supposed to be at 6:00, lunch at 11:00, and dinner at 5:00, but they often miss by as much as a half hour, which wreaks havoc with work schedules.

As for the daily counts, the worst example is the evening count. It's supposed to happen at 10, with lights out by 10:15. As the Wise Guys in New York say, "Fuhgeddaboudit."

I asked one of the inmates to keep a log on this for a few weeks just to illustrate this point. As his log below illustrates, more than half the time, the count is a half hour late or more, and the lights don't go out until 11 or later.

So, you wind up dragging ass in the morning and taking naps you wouldn't otherwise need.

Okay, of course this is a very small bitch, and it *is* prison. But if the broken window theory works on the inside just as it does on the outside, when they break even smaller rules, we the inmates are being invited to do the same.

And if the broken window theory holds, we will wind up breaking bigger rules. Just some food for thought—but it will be served late today at the mess hall.

Inmate Port's Log for the 10 PM count

DATE:		ACTUAL COUNT:
Mon	5/6/24	10:35
Tues	5/7/24	10:37
Wed	5/8/24	10:29
Thurs	5/9/24	10:10
Fri	5/10/24	10:44

Mon	5/13/24	10:46
Tues	5/14/24	10:14
Wed	5/15/24	10:12
Thurs	5/16/24	10:30
Fri	5/17/24	10:15

HUCK POST 99:
Gang Shit Rolls Downhill
May 26, 2024—Day 69

> *The ÑETA Association (Asociación Pro-Derechos del Confinado,*
> *"Association for Prisoners' Rights", Asociación ÑETA, or simply ÑETA)*
> *is the name of a gang that began in the Puerto Rico prison system and*
> *spread to the United States mainland. . . . The Asociación Ñeta (Ñeta*
> *Association) was founded in 1979 by Carlos Torres Irriarte, also known*
> *as "La Sombra" ("The Shadow"), when several pro-independence*
> *political prisoners were incarcerated in the maximum security Oso Blanco*
> *prison located in Rio Piedras. They formed as a mutual protection group,*
> *ostensibly to improve living conditions and defend inmates from abuses*
> *committed by guards and other prisoners, as well as to fight the prison*
> *gang Grupo 27 ("Group 27"), or the "Insectos" ("Insects").*
> —Wikipedia

It's 8:30 a.m. on Sunday, I am out alone walking the track, I sure do miss my Sweet Pixie, and I'm running through our song list—singing them all out loud as I walk in the morning dew.

Bublé's "The Way You Look Tonight." Love the first lyric: "One day, when I'm awfully low, and the world is cold, I will feel a glow just thinking of you . . ." Awfully low today in prison, of course, but this lifts my spirits.

Then, Chris Stapleton's "Joy of My Life" followed by Ray Charles's "You Don't Know Me" and finishing with Ronnie Milsap's "I Wouldn't Have Missed It For The World."

It's like Pixie's right here with me, but I'm damn glad she's up in Washington, DC, rather than standing in line at the Visitor Center about to be told all visitations are canceled for the day.

Yep. That's what's going to happen today. Boy, she would've been pissed—and rightly so.

There are at least one hundred families stacked up at the center right now or en route who could have been told the night before of the cancellation. But no, wait until *after* the last minute.

Just another Backwards On Purpose prison puckup from bureaucrats who have more power than sense.

Of course, the excuse for the cancellation is a gang war that has erupted at the higher security prison across the street: A couple of shankings with some serious wounds, and an all-out *West Side Story* war between the Puerto Rican ÑETA gang and a coalition of Mexicans, Haitians, Cubans, blacks, et al.

Inside, on our side of the prison, my Puerto Rico via Spanish Harlem historian, Izzie, schools me on the history of the ÑETAs. It was a group originally organized to put an end to the rape and extortion of Puerto Ricans by prison cliques. Now, it's one of the most powerful forces within prisons across America.

Izzie fears this particular war will be prolonged and bloody. At the end of the day, there are just not enough guards in the low-security prison to keep the violence in check, so the warden will indeed face a real quandary.

The concern now among us in our facility is whether they'll also lock us down, too. Who knows?

That's why they call it prison. It's a violent place. No country for old men like me.

PIXIE POST 19:
Romeo Goes to Prison
May 26, 2024—Day 69

Pixie here, channeling my inner Shakespeare: "Parting is such sweet sorrow."

As one gets older, one understands all these clichés more. And to think that I once thought whoever thought of them was some sappy nerd (including Shakespeare).

I have indeed missed visiting my Romeo and Ever Huck this weekend because, sorrowfully, I had to go to Washington, DC, because I have to be at my job a full week a month.

It is Sunday, and it is the first Sunday in so long that I won't see my Huck. But sweetly, I am reunited with my sweet eternal cat, Lucy Girl—twenty-three years young and counting.

Lucy Girl notwithstanding, it was the wrong week for this because it was a tough week, we both admitted, just a challenging time. But he is my soldier, and as he says, I am his soldierette. And I have to be strong for him.

When I talked to Huck on the phone today, he said many of the inmates got on their nice uniforms to see their families over the weekend, but he didn't have to get dressed up either Saturday or Sunday as I would not be there, but he missed me so much. And actually, I was lucky because they cancelled visiting hours today.

So, I dodged that bullet.

Still, it was hard to have a good week or weekend in DC without my Ever Huck.

Yet, I promised him I would, as that is what he wants me to do. So, I did fun things.

Still, I was walking through them with an empty heart and soul. At least our kitty, our ginger cat Lucy, brings me peace.

HUCK POST 100:
A Memorial Day to Forget
May 27, 2024—Day 70, Memorial Day

This was one of those dog days, and it wasn't even summer—the temperature reached almost 100 degrees.

It was a somber day for me because one of my favorite sports antiheroes—basketball legend Bill Walton—died at the tender age of seventy-one of cancer.

I loved Walton for his iconoclastic and exuberant love of a game I myself had dedicated much of my youth to; and his passing was a grim reminder that I was passing some of my own precious remaining time on the planet far from my beloved Pixie and in a Democrat gulag.

This is not to say I wasn't keeping busy; and they do say if you want something done, go to a busy man. And that was what was happening now. More and more inmates were coming to me for help, and I was happy to oblige.

That's because my mission at the prison had now crystallized with the opportunity to testify before Congress—albeit in written form—about all of the abuses I was witnessing firsthand, particularly with respect to the Bureau of Prison's failure to implement both Trump's 2018 First Step Act and the 2008 Second Chance Act.

So now I was on a deadline—imagine that, on deadline in prison. I had to get my testimony written and, to do that, I had to process dozens of inmate cases (with the help of Elliot) to back up what would be explosive allegations of massive fiscal waste.

As if that weren't enough work, I also had to prepare two memos to the warden for delivery on Wednesday—both time sensitive.

One was a final request to get Dave Bossie's Citizens United film crew in for its Trump 2024 movie—we had been getting stonewalled for several months already and the deadline was soon.

In the meantime, please bow your head in prayer for Bill Walton. At least that's what I did today in prison.

HUCK POST 101:
Shave and a Haircut, Two Bits
May 28, 2024—Day 71

It's commissary day in Prison Land, and waiting around for your name to get called is as close to experiencing the old Soviet Union—or an old "Company Town Store"—as you can get. Whatever is supposed to be in stock won't be. Plus, whatever you buy will cost 30 percent to 50 percent more than at a Walmart or Publix outside the fence.

While I was waiting, I noticed that one of the biggest badasses in the prison (and only Mexican), Brother DJ, was cutting Big Mike's hair—although with Mike, I use the term loosely, since Mike had precious little of that stuff on the top of his head and barely any on the sides.

I was pleasantly surprised DJ was in gainful employment, as he seemed more of a player who would likely recidivate rather than become a hard-working, upstanding citizen again.

Curious, I struck up a conversation later that morning in the lunch line; and it was clear I had misjudged him. He had big plans, not just to be a barber or a hair stylist after prison. He wanted to open up his own salon with all the accoutrements—mani, pedi, cutting, curling, etc.

What was most interesting about the conversation is how it confirmed the glaring lack of training opportunities at the prison.

Besides learning to be a barber or getting a commercial driver's license (which you had to pony up several thousand dollars to get), that was about it. What DJ brought to that discussion was his extensive experience with the prison system.

He had entered the system in his very early twenties, and he was on one of those mind-numbing fifteen-year, mandatory minimum bids because of a dope deal plus a gun—a 924(c) in prison parlance—and he'd been to at least five different locations as he worked his way down to a minimum-security prison like Miami.

Unfortunately for DJ, Miami would turn out to be one of the worst prisons when it came to offering any kind of training programs.

I get it—prison shouldn't necessarily function as a college. That's a perverse incentive in and of itself—you want to learn a trade, go rob somebody. You see the problem?

Yet, if you want folks to live honestly, they have to know how to do honest work. And many of these inmates arrive with few skills other than dope dealing. Just some food for thought that I would chew on.

HUCK POST 102:
Pale Horse, Pale Rider
May 29, 2024—Day 72

There were a lot of jackals in the Trump White House, but hands down, the most unhinged was John Bolton. His seventeen months as National Security Advisor were marked by endless button plots and fantasies to blow shit up around the world, from Venezuela to Tehran and beyond.

So, it was a breath of very fresh air to have Robert O'Brien take over that critical White House position on September 18, 2019. From then until the end of the Trump administration, he—and we—did beautiful work, finally moving forward many of the anti-Communist Chinese initiatives I had been pushing against the headwinds of Treasury Secretary Steve the Munchkin and Larry Rose-Colored Glasses Kudlow.

At the end of the administration, Robert went off to make a ton of money advising major corporations on national security matters; but we kept in touch.

At any rate, I was so pleased that Robert was able to quietly come visit me this month for what would be two hours of what we will keep as classified info about the latest on the Trump campaign. Plus, we had a few good laughs.

What shocked and upset me, however, was how much Robert had seemed to age. This was a classic case of a now Pale Rider sacrificing his body and physical health for his broad mission to keep America safe. When he left, I urged him to get back into balance because we needed him for the long haul. Look for him in the West Wing again. And he'll do a hell of a job.

[*Author's Note: Robert ultimately chose his health over going back in, and good for him. He likely could have had his pick of jobs.*]

HUCK POST 103:
They Call It Stormy Thursday
May 30, 2024—Day 73

Con men are not just those who do shady things. They're the people who
tell you what you want to hear so they can get what they want.
—Melvin Helitzer, American author and humorist

This Stormy Thursday started when Elliot woke me from a quick nap at noon to tell me they were taking Rodrigo to the SHU—the special housing unit.

The taking of Rodrigo was a classic snitch job—the Special Investigation Unit goons had gone straight to where Rodrigo was hiding his cell phone—in his walker that he had used after an injury, no less.

SIS grabbed it, then they grabbed him, picked up every bit of his stuff, and off Rodrigo went, likely never to be seen in this prison again.

In the meantime, the other man down this day was none other than Donald John Trump. He was found guilty of thirty-four felony counts of falsifying business records allegedly linked to hush money payments made to porn comet Stormy Daniels.

The verdict was handed down by a gaggle of woke, Trump-hating jurors in Manhattan—are there any other kinds of jurors in the Big Blue Apple?

Given my own conviction by an equally woke, Trump-hating DC jury, I was not in the least surprised at the outcome. Yet, while I have taken my own imprisonment with stoicism, Trump's guilty verdict stirred my bile this day.

At the end of this postcard is the article I wrote this day and would see published next week in the *Washington Times*.

It's Old Testament stuff, and I mean every word.

It's time to kick their asses at the ballot box and then round the sons of bitches up. That's what I'm thinking in prison.

The Washington Times
Trump behind bars or the Resolute Desk? Democrats on a lawfare rampage

OPINION:
Will former President Donald Trump wind up in a New York prison rather than behind the Resolute Desk in the Oval Office? From behind my own prison walls in Miami, I can't rule that out. Indeed, the parallels between my own case and Mr. Trump's are striking.

I am the first senior White House official ever charged with contempt of Congress. This is all the more outrageous given that for more than 50 years, Department of Justice policy decreed it was my duty to do what I did—refuse to testify before Congress once Mr. Trump invoked executive privilege, which was not my privilege to waive.

Mr. Trump is the first former president ever to be charged with a felony. What's most outrageous here is how a Manhattan district attorney, Alvin Bragg, was allowed to string together minor misdemeanors into felonies with lengthy prison sentences.

Next, consider that the prosecutions of Mr. Trump and me have involved nothing but Democrats on a lawfare rampage. The House of Representatives voted on a straight Democratic Party line to hold me in contempt, a Democratic attorney general in Merrick Garland prosecuted me, a Democratic judge stripped me of any possible defense, and the kangaroo court jury itself was drawn from a District of Columbia pool in which over 90 percent voted for President Biden.

In Mr. Trump's case, Democrat-Marxist George Soros bankrolled the campaign of Mr. Bragg. Mr. Trump's inquisitor, Democratic Judge Juan Merchan, was not randomly drawn for the case. He was handpicked for the hit job despite numerous conflicts of interest.

My own judge, Amit Mehta, was similarly handpicked. Because of similarities and judicial economy, my case should have gone to the judge who presided over Steve Bannon's contempt of Congress case. Instead, I got tagged with Judge Mehta—a Democrat who put a down payment on his appointment to the bench by bundling large campaign contributions for Barack Obama.

Judge Mehta would deny my defense team critical discovery, ignore legitimate claims of selective prosecution, prevent a key witness from appearing, and make an admitted "uncharted waters" ruling about Mr. Trump's invocation of executive privilege that would take my executive privilege defense off the table and by Judge Mehta's own admission "hamstring the defense." For the kill shot, Judge Mehta let numerous jurors who openly expressed anti-Trump sentiments render my verdict.

Mr. Trump's judge, Juan Merchan, used the same Mehta playbook—and then some. Judge Merchan left on the jury some of the most blatant Trump-haters in Manhattan. Virtually every ruling Judge Merchan made on admissible evidence, witnesses, points of law and jury instructions strongly favored the prosecution.

Like mine in the District of Columbia, Mr. Trump's Manhattan jury pool was drawn from a list of voters who had favored then-candidate Joe Biden in 2020 by more than 90 percent. While wishful thinking analysts at Fox News kept floating the possibility of a hung jury—surely there must be at least one member of the jury who would see through the insanity—it was not and never to be. And guilty, on all counts, was a foregone conclusion by simple math.

Here's that math in my case: My legal team had only six preemptory challenges, and there were simply too many biased jurors to strike. On the other hand, the prosecution had more than enough challenges to strike the few potential jurors who might have gone my way. It was the same biased math with Mr. Trump as judge, jury and executioner Merchan allowed jurors who openly and loudly admitted they loathed Mr. Trump.

The next milestones in the case will involve the actual sentencing and whether Mr. Trump will be released pending his certain appeal. The big questions here, which, not coincidentally, will be answered on the eve of the Republican National Convention the week of July 15, are whether Judge Merchan (1) will give Mr. Trump prison time, and (2) release Mr. Trump pending his appeal so he can campaign for the November election—or even appear for the Republican National Convention to be nominated.

Again, my case is instructive: Given the facts in the case, my judge, Amit Mehta, should have given me, at most, a 30-day suspended sentence and put me on probation for a few months. Judge Mehta himself admitted that I had done what I had done out of an unshakable belief that I was doing what my oath of office and the Constitution required. My conviction was contrary to Justice Department policy.

Yet instead of showing respect or mercy for a public servant who had created thousands of jobs and saved countless lives during the pandemic, Judge Mehta not only threw the book at me. In his sentencing, the Machiavellian Mehta cleverly and strategically made sure I would not get any sentence reduction from the 2018 First Step Act—which, ironically, I myself had helped lobby for.

But that's not all: Unlike Steve Bannon's judge, Judge Mehta threw me in prison immediately rather than release me pending my appeal when he knew damn well that my case would almost certainly be dismissed or sent to a retrial.

Judge Merchan is likely to take these very same pages out of Mehta's lawfare playbook. My bet is that Judge Merchan will not only order prison time, like Judge Mehta, he will also send Mr. Trump to prison immediately rather than release him pending appeal.

Moreover, nothing guarantees that Mr. Trump will win his appeal despite the overwhelming evidence that he should. Again, my case is instructive.

When I appealed Judge Mehta's decision to send me to prison immediately, the DC Circuit stacked my three-judge panel with "woke," never-Trump Democratic judges rather than draw the judges randomly. These three politicians in black robes then denied my appeal in a way that, in turn, made it impossible for the Supreme Court to rule in my favor. Mr. Trump will face the same stacked deck of appeals court judges in the deep blue state of New York.

The best thing we can do right now for Mr. Trump is to work 24/7 toward his reelection, whether or not he himself is allowed sufficient time out on the campaign trail. So please send the Trump 2024 campaign a contribution. Recruit as many friends and family to register to vote and get them to the polls. Get involved with your local precinct, and make sure through peaceful citizen actions like monitoring illegal drop boxes that the Bidenites can't steal the 2024 election like they did in 2020.

Peter Navarro is the author of The New MAGA Deal *(www .newmagadeal.com), the unofficial guide to the Trump 2024 campaign platform.*

HUCK POST 104:
Pixie in Peril
May 30, 2024—Day 73

One of the hardest things about prison is making sure you have provided for your family while you're locked up and away from your bank accounts. I thought I had done a great job for my Sweet Pixie in transferring what seemed to be a large enough sum into her bank account. But unexpected expenses had popped up, she was maxing out her credit cards, and worst of all, she hadn't let me know for fear I might get upset.

Finally, my beautiful damsel in distress laid it all out for me, and I had to swing into action.

My first step was to call Stanley Woodward, give him my power of attorney, and then see if he could simply add Pixie to my own bank account with check-writing and debit-card privileges.

My second step was simply then to wait and see if Stanley could pull it off without either my driver's license or passport in his hand. Stay tuned.

HUCK POST 105:
The Gray Ghost
May 31, 2024—Day 74

The pill mills are really nothing more than storefronts for
professional drug dealers, and they are killing people.
—Senator Bill Nelson on the opioid crisis

It's a beautiful sunrise with the big red Florida ball coming up through the mist off the grass in the yard, which has been opened delightfully early for the morning walkers.

After a mile—three times around the track—I walk in and see the Gray Ghost bouncing a basketball on his way to the wall where he will perform a series of exercises with the ball that I showed him a few days ago.

I give him two thumbs up as I walk by, thinking about his plight. This ghost of a man well into his sixties is in for participating in a pill mill—fifty people likely died on his watch.

His punishment, because he had fled the country to avoid prosecution, was to languish for five long years in a detention cell where he was unable to exercise or enjoy fresh air and sunlight before he got to the Miami prison.

Now, he looks like a gray ghost, barely a skeleton with a shrunken chest and with cognitive facilities significantly impaired.

After some months, the Gray Ghost had begun to walk regularly with a group, but his upper body was, for all practical purposes, frozen and shriveled. So I showed him a routine that I myself did every morning.

For twenty minutes, I showed him how to toss a basketball against the racquetball wall from various positions. An overhead sling. A direct chest pass. Underhanded tosses like a softball pitcher with either hand. Overhead tosses like a baseball pitcher with either hand. Rinse and repeat.

I told the Gray Ghost his legs were better now with all his walking, but this would help with strength, balance, and hand-eye coordination as it built his upper body back up.

I offered this help with mixed emotions and thoughts. This guy, maybe a good guy, had done bad things. But this is the kind of shit I would do in prison.

Strictly New Testament stuff from an Old Testament guy. I can't help myself. Misery doesn't love company, and my empathy got the best of me with the Gray Ghost.

HUCK POST 106:

At the Front Lines of First Step Act Enforcement

May 31, 2024—Day 74

Today was about as good as it gets in prison.

On the personal front, I spent most of my "lawyer's call" focusing not on my appeal but rather on solving the financial problems my Sweet Pixie was dealing with as I languished in prison without access to my bank accounts.

The meeting with Wells Fargo execs in DC by Pixie and Stanley had ended with these Wells Fargo pricks refusing to honor Stanley's power of attorney, so we couldn't add Pixie to my checking account. Overnight, I had figured out if I could just get some checks mailed to our house, I could write Pixie checks for what she needed, and I could sign them on our prison visits.

Of course, she would have to smuggle the checks in for my signature, but so what? That wasn't really breaking any laws.

So, with the plan in place, Stanley was able to log into my Wells Fargo account and ordered the checks after I conjured up from memory my username and password. Problem solved.

Then Stanley and I used the rest of lawyer's call on real lawyering, namely, to discuss the status of my appeal. The big decision was whether to request an *en banc* hearing with all of the judges or simply start with the usual three-judge panel.

One of my other attorneys, John Rowley, had been worried that if we tried to go *en banc* and they said no, we might forfeit our right to the three-judge panel. But Rowley had found a case that seemed to get us off that hook—so *en banc* it would be, and Stanley would file the motion on Monday, which meant Tuesday or Wednesday with Stanley.

I had pushed for the *en banc* for two reasons. First, the DC Circuit would probably stack the deck against us with three Democrat liberals like they had with several other of my panels—like the one panel that had refused to release me from prison pending appeal. *Screw them*, I thought.

Second, for my case to be dismissed, a DC court ruling would likely have to be overturned. However, for that to happen, only the full *en banc* court and not a three-judge panel could overturn it. So why bother with the three-judge panel when it would ultimately have to go to the full court anyway?

Right after the meeting, it was the Big Show I had been preparing for the warden and Verdejo to show them how lack of enforcement of Donald Trump's 2018 First Step Act was causing long and costly delays in the release of inmates, both to halfway houses and freedom.

By this time, I had worked out a killer graph to illustrate the problem; and what was interesting was how quickly the warden understood the issue.

Seemingly, I was making good progress with the Miami bureaucracy. Not a bad day.

HUCK POST 107:
A Hat Trick of Meanness and Idiocy
June 1, 2024—Day 75

It's Saturday, and my Sweet Pixie comes back to the Visitor Center after last weekend's *timely* hiatus in which the Center had been closed on Sunday while Pixie was in DC.

Today, Ajemon the Terrible is in rare form, with a hat trick of evil idiocy.

He turns away an eighty-six-year-old father of an inmate for sweatpants and a three-year-old baby for bare arms.

In the middle of the visit, they call an emergency count, and instead of conducting it right there, Ajemon sends all the inmates back to the dorm for the count. You can't make that up, and you can't fix either mean or stupid.

As I'm writing this after dinner, Elliot informs me Ajemon was designated "Employee of the Month" for May—this after thirty-plus inmate complaints. That you can't make up either.

It's just a big middle finger to every inmate and their family, special delivery from the prison bureaucracy. But that's why they call it prison.

PIXIE POST 20:
A Wefund at the Water Park
June 1, 2024—Day 75

Pixie here, and it's another Saturday in Prison Land. As I wait for my Ever Huck—why is he not yet here???—I look around the room at what have become a lot of familiar family sights.

There's Jose the doctor/spear fisherman and his sweet wife who was so helpful in preparing me for my first visit.

There's the other Cuban Jose who looks like an impish Harpo Marx, frizzy hair and all, who gave my Huck his first drops of the Guilty perfume and who has bought all of Huck's books and has them signed for his brother.

There's big, tall Shaq and his bride who always try to sneak in early to get the best seat in the prison and spend most of their time trying to make out, children and guards be damned—hotter-than-high-school love, as my Huck describes it.

There's Elliot of course, who has become my Huck's most trusted colleague in fighting the rampant injustice within the prison. Elliot is with his wife and daughter doing his best to have a good time even though he has been inside so long that it looks like outside to him.

There's also Doc, Huck's other main colleague in taking on the prison bureaucracy. Huck puts Doc at the top of his list of inmates who don't belong in that prison. Fortunately, Doc has a big support group of his Armenian family—and it's Doc that Huck tells me helps make sure he gets what he needs from the commissary.

Then there several of the Haitians—Jean and James. Both are in for some kind of wire fraud, as Haiti seems to be a training school for that. But they are very nice fellows with big extended families, and it's really hard sometimes to match their big smiles and warmth to their crimes.

And now there's my two new boyfriends—Malik and Jamal, one eight and one nine, and both of whom seem to have a crush on little old me—and I mean little, because I'm barely 4'11".

Each week, Malik and (mostly) Jamal would tell me about their lives outside visiting their dad in prison; tell me about their school, teachers, what they loved to do. And sometimes we got a dance out of one of them, from Jamal, the younger one, who was much more forward than his older brother.

I think his older brother shows signs of anger—mostly a sad look on his face and mostly complaining, as opposed to the younger one, who his mom tells us excels at school and is the teacher's pet, and definitely a sort of pet during his prison time with his family and others, including to me and Huck.

I always try not to give the younger one, Jamal, more attention than the older one, Malik, even though he always seems too upset or angry to care about what I do. But with children, you never know what goes on in their heads.

This week it's all very charming as Jamal comes over to hug me first, and Malik shyly follows for his own hug, and then they tell me this week's big story.

They went to a water park for fun, but it rained, and they had to leave, and Jamal, the extrovert, tells me they asked for a "wefund," and it was cute. Later, Huck will tell me about how when he was their age, he went to a speech therapist because he couldn't pronounce his r's (as in refund) either.

While watching Malik and Jamal at play makes me feel happy, it's sad to see such innocence, knowing the reality of their dad being locked up.

I know that they miss their father a lot and can only see him on the weekends, and maybe it will be the case for at least a couple of more years. And who knows what's going on in their minds and how it will shape their own lives.

The same may be said of all of the other children in this big room filled with felons who sit and look bored or run around the room manic or hang out in the game room for the hours while the inmates sit with the other adults.

Is it better for these children to come and see their dad behind bars or would they be better off home? It's not for me to say, only ponder.

HUCK POST 108:
Pussy in Prison
June 2, 2024—Day 76

Comes now some comforting cognitive dissonance as I behold hardened criminals tranquilly playing with, and feeding, what seems to be a growing gaggle of pussycats in the yard.

The pussy count is up to a dozen now, with the addition this a.m. of two new ginger kittens.

These kitten gingers make me both homesick and lovesick as my beautiful Pixie has her own twenty-three-year-old ginger cat. Lucy is her name—and she has become an integral part of my new family.

I laugh as an inmate with a makeshift cat toy—a stick on a string—playfully waves it in front of a kitty like a cat fisherman.

For a moment, because of such pussy, neither one of us is in prison.

HUCK POST 109:
The Breitbart Interview
June 3, 2024—Day 77

Perhaps no one has demonstrated loyalty to Trump like Navarro, the polarizing, wiry former White House China hawk and pandemic troubleshooter. And no one has quite paid the same price: Navarro is the first White House official in history to be imprisoned for contempt.

"I have no regrets," said federal inmate No. 04370-510. "I didn't choose this fight, this fight chose me."

He might not want a pardon but Navarro will have a home in a new Trump administration if he wants it.

"I would absolutely have Peter back. This outrageous behavior by the Democrats should not have happened," Trump said in a statement to the Journal.

—*Wall Street Journal*

The *Wall Street Journal* article by Alex Leary would trigger a bundle of new requests for interviews. I got one such request via Sergio Gor, the publisher of my book, *The New MAGA Deal*. Seems that my old buddy and Bannon disciple Matt Boyle at Breitbart wanted to do one. Sergio thinks the interview will generate a ton of book sales, so I bang it right out from a set of questions from Matt I got by email.

Here it is published two days later. Note that I am cross-fertilizing material from my previous op-eds as I hone the message on my prison experience.

The mission is to elect Donald Trump as our 47th president, so every one of my responses is filtered through that prism.

Exclusive: Peter Navarro Speaks from Behind Bars in "Joe Biden Prison," Warns "Unrestrained Lawfare Designed to Interfere" in Election
MATTHEW BOYLE
5 Jun 2024. Washington, DC

Peter Navarro, the former top economic aide in former President Donald Trump's White House, who is currently languishing in federal prison serving a multi-month sentence for having stood up against subpoenas from the January 6 committee last Congress, is speaking out now from behind bars in an exclusive interview with Breitbart News.

Navarro, who was the director of Trump's White House's National Trade Council, is 74 years old and is currently incarcerated in a federal prison in Miami. He is on track to be released in mid-July, around the time of his 75th birthday.

Navarro is also publishing a book this summer, called the *The New MAGA Deal*, aimed at exploring and explaining populist nationalist philosophy on things like trade and economic policy—the core of his portfolio when he served Trump in the White House. Navarro is a true populist's populist, too, and went from being a Democrat decades ago to a top Trump adviser and Republican in recent years. This interview with Navarro focuses on his views on the weaponization of government by Democrats against Republicans like himself and Trump as well as on his views on Biden's approach versus Trump's approach to consequential American adversaries like China. Navarro also puts the stakes of the 2024 presidential election in the clearest possible terms, saying quite clearly that if Biden wins things will get worse for every American but if Trump wins the inverse is true.

The interview obviously comes after Trump himself was convicted in New York last week in his business records trial, and awaits sentencing the week before the Republican National Convention in July.

Navarro conducted this interview in writing from prison. Breitbart News sent him several questions, and he replied to them a few days later. What follows is a complete transcript of the written interview, with the full questions from Breitbart News and Navarro's full answers from behind bars.

BREITBART NEWS: What's your reaction to the Trump verdict?

PETER NAVARRO: For me, it was deja vu all over again,

and there is much for Americans—and journalists—to learn by studying the parallels between my case and President Trump's.

I'm the first senior White House official ever to be convicted of contempt of Congress. My old boss is the first president ever to be convicted of a felony.

I'm guilty of nothing more than defending the Constitutional separation of powers and George Washington's doctrine of executive privilege against a Democrat lawfare attack. President Trump isn't even guilty of the misdemeanors he was charged with while these misdemeanors were "belt and suspendered" into felonies with prison time only through prosecutorial misconduct and judicial chicanery.

In both my case and President Trump's, Democrats were involved at every step of the inquisition. A Democrat majority in Congress held me in contempt on a strict party line vote, a Democrat Attorney General prosecuted me despite a more than 50-year policy of absolute testimonial immunity for senior White House advisors, a Democrat judge stripped me of every possible defense before a jury of 12 never-Trump jurors drawn from a pool that voted over 90 percent for Biden found me guilty.

With President Trump, a George Soros-backed Marxist DA ran on a platform of putting Trump in prison, a radical Democrat judge in Juan Merchan stripped Trump of both witnesses and defenses, and a Manhattan jury drawn from a pool of voters who went 95 percent for Biden found him guilty.

In both my case and Donald Trump, this was not equal justice under law but unrestrained lawfare designed to interfere with the 2024 election. It is the likes of Merchan and Bragg and Fani Willis, and Merrick Garland and Jack Smith who belong in prison, not me or the greatest president in modern history.

BREITBART NEWS: Do you think President Trump will be sentenced to prison?

PETER NAVARRO: Again, my case is instructive. Just look at where I am writing this from—a prison in Miami.

In my case, Democrat Judge Amit Mehta freely admitted that I had refused to testify before Congress because I firmly believed that once Donald Trump invoked executive privilege, it was not my privilege to waive and I had a duty to the Constitution and my oath of office to do what I did.

Under those circumstances, Mehta should have given me no more than a thirty-day suspended sentence and sent me on my way. Instead, and ironically, he gave me the maximum possible time under the guidelines and even cleverly structured the sentence in a way to deny me any sentence reduction under the First Step Act that Donald Trump signed and I had lobbied for. It was cruel and unusual punishment right out of the Democrat lawfare game plan.

Judge Juan Merchan is likely to do exactly the same thing. I look for a prison sentence for Donald Trump. Most importantly, I also believe that Merchan will refuse to release President Trump pending an almost certain victory on appeal.

This is exactly what happened to me. Judge Amit Mehta knew damn well my case will be overturned on appeal—otherwise, the Constitutional separation of powers will be irrevocably damaged. Yet, unlike in a similar case with Steve Bannon with a different judge, Mehta refused to release me on appeal and now here I am in a Joe Biden prison. When I win my appeal, I will have already served my sentence and have been irreparably harmed.

Merchan's gambit will be even more nefarious. He will sentence Trump on the eve of the Republican National Convention in July and may even try to block Trump from traveling to Milwaukee to accept his party's nomination for president by refusing to release him pending appeal.

Wake up America. This is happening in our country and there's not a dime's worth of difference now between the courts in Communist China and Russia and the good ole U.S. of A.

BREITBART NEWS: What's it like in prison? Are people familiar with who you are? What's the reaction?

PETER NAVARRO: Miami is a particularly tough prison. It's not really "minimum security" but surrounded by razor wire with tight protocols to monitor inmates. Prescription drugs are hard to come by, the food is low in protein and calories, high in sugar and carbohydrates, and certain to worsen any conditions ranging from diabetes and hypertension to heart conditions and kidney issues. A new strain of COVID hit the facility a month ago and spread like wildfire in the cramped dorm conditions. The rec yard is littered with 30-year-old exercise bikes and other equipment that don't work while an ornery facility administrator before my time lugged off all of the strength training equipment. There's few inmate training or certification programs and little but time on most inmates' hands. It's no country for old men.

The good news is that the vast majority of inmates love Donald Trump for passing the 2018 First Step Act and hate Joe Biden for not implementing it. Same with the corrections officers—Trump and I respect the uniform and they know that while they also know Biden has been a disaster.

If I were a Bidenite, things would be a lot tougher here—and yes, they know exactly who I am and respect the fact that I stood up for a principle and didn't bow to the government.

BREITBART NEWS: Do you think if you were a Democrat or Biden supporter you would be where you are today?

PETER NAVARRO: Of course not. This is lawfare unchained, and the Democrats play it for keeps while, at least up to this point, Republicans haven't had either the balls or brains to fight back Old Testament style. Until the Democrats fear they could wind up in the same prisons they put me and are trying to put Donald Trump, Jeff Clark, Mark Meadows, John Eastman, Rudy Giuliani et al in, they will keep doing what they are doing.

If Trump wins and asks if I want to serve again, I may ask for Special Prosecutor. These lawfare bandits must be held accountable for their flagrant election interference.

BREITBART NEWS: What is your message to the broader America First conservative movement? What should they take away from your incarceration?

PETER NAVARRO: Simply, if they can come for me—and they put me first in leg irons and then in prison—they can come for you. And the only thing now standing in their way is Donald Trump.

It is paramount we win the 2024 election for many reasons—Donald Trump will crush inflation, seal our border, keep the dogs of war with Communist China, Iran, Russia and North Korea at bay, stop the Democrats from mutilating the genitals of our young boys and destroying girls' sports and dreams with a transgender nightmare, and make college graduations safe again from radicals.

But we also must put Donald Trump back behind the Resolute Desk in the Oval Office to put an end to Joe Biden's and Merrick Garland's dual system of injustice that now threatens us all—from soccer moms at school board meetings protesting the grooming and indoctrination of our children to patriots who stand at the ramparts to protect the sanctity of the ballot box.

The Biden Crime Family—Hunter, James, and Joe; The Soros-backed Inquisitors—Bragg, Willis, and Marchan; The Orwellian Demons—Garland and Smith; The America Haters—Omar, Talaib, and AOC. Guantanamo is too good for them. Accountability now for their lies and election interference!

BREITBART NEWS: How will you carry your message to the American people? What role will you play in the Trump 2024 campaign?

PETER NAVARRO: As I have been in prison these last months, my new book, *The New MAGA Deal* (www.newmaga-deal.com) has been in the printing process and is now on its way to bookstores and Amazon warehouses everywhere. *The New MAGA Deal* is published by Don Jr.'s publishing house, it's the unofficial guide to the Trump 2024 campaign platform, and my mission is to put this blueprint and battle cry for the modern MAGA movement into as many hands as possible.

In the spirit of the canon of Steve Bannon—Action! Action! Action!—*The New MAGA Deal* lays out 100 actions in the first 100 days of the Trump administration on everything from crushing inflation, securing our border and putting an end to America's endless wars to restoring equal justice under law, defending women's sports, and restoring sanity and ending wokeness in our K-12 curricula.

Importantly, *The New MAGA Deal* will help Trump supporters explain in the plainest of terms what the Trump and MAGA
agenda is—simply plain, God, Family, and Country common
sense. We must not let the radical Democrats portray us as
extremists. We must force them to look in their own mirror at
the ugliness of their ideology. That's what *The New MAGA Deal*
will help do.

BREITBART NEWS: What do you make of Joe Biden put-
ting tariffs on Communist China even as we learn more about
Hunter and how he leveraged his father's close relationship with
China's dictator Xi Jinping?

PETER NAVARRO: A lot of the salacious coverage of Hunter
focuses on the porn and the crack and the sex trafficking. But
Hunter's worst crime was to sell this country out for a few pieces
of silver, and with each new revelation, it's pretty damn clear the
"Big Guy" Joey was in on the action. That's unregistered foreign
lobbying at best and treason at worst.

Against that backdrop, it makes it all the more disingenuous
that Joe is trying to out-tariff the King of China Tariffs, Donald
Trump, in the run up to the 2024 election. The irony is that
Joe Biden created the need for tariffs on Made in China electric
vehicles through a Green Bad Deal that effectively exports our
auto industry to Shanghai.

If more of the mainstream media did their jobs—thank God
for the likes of Breitbart and Bannon's War Room—Bidenomics
would be exposed for the Chinese shell game it is.

BREITBART NEWS: If Trump doesn't win the election, what
happens to this country?

PETER NAVARRO: Double digit inflation, stagnant wages,
dog food for pensioners; a hot or cyber war with Iran, Communist
China and/or Russia; more rape, murder by fentanyl, terrorism,
downward wage pressures, and rising welfare costs from a flood
of illegal aliens; unrestrained Democrat lawfare; the end of free
speech and assembly; more conservatives and Republicans behind
bars for their patriotism; the destruction of women's sports and
more mutilation of young boys' genitals; a corporate media and

social media that will continually revise our history to match the woke ideology. Did I mention no home or car ownership or marriage and babies for much of our younger generations?

Look at what has happened to me, prosecuted and imprisoned for honoring my oath of office and defending the Constitution. It's your choice: poverty and prison or prosperity and peace. Biden or Trump.

You will decide! Please get involved in this election. Send the Trump campaign a check. Volunteer at your local Republican Party. Spread the gospel of Trump and MAGA. You are the vessel of change. Failure is not an option.

HUCK POST 110:
Pardon Me

June 4, 2024—Day 78

I got my first of what will probably be many requests to help an inmate with a pardon if my old boss gets reelected. No surprise there—and I ain't doing that.

But what did surprise me was the reason Johnny gave me. It wasn't to clear his record. It was to short-circuit the massive restitution he had been saddled with and would have to pay off for likely the rest of his life—in the millions of dollars for a guy who will be lucky to make $60,000 bucks a year.

Now, you might be thinking that if this guy swindled people or the government out of that money, he damn well should pay it back. But that's not how it works in the Alice in Wonderland world of our justice system. Enter now the raging debate over "actual loss" versus "intended loss."

In forcing restitution on convicted criminals, the government and judges don't calculate how much the criminal extracted from his victims—that's actual loss. Rather, the yardstick is how much the scheme would have made—and not just from the efforts of the criminal, but also the efforts of others in whatever organization he may have been part of.

This yardstick can lead to very weird and onerous results whereby the criminal may have gotten a relatively small amount in the scam but gets stuck with a restitution bill of $10 or $20 million.

An example here—and there were a bunch from my discussions in prison—is when a doctor might over-order lab tests and the hospital overcharges for the tests. The doctor isn't just responsible for the money lost from the lab tests he ordered. He has to pick up the tab for what the hospital *might* have made.

In Miami, there were at least a dozen inmates I talked to that would have crushing restitution burdens that they would have to make payments on for the rest of their lives—unless they hit the lottery *or*, and this is my big beef with this, went back to a life of crime.

As I write this, there is a growing movement to replace the intended loss yardstick with an actual lock loss metric, and that's likely to be a far better policy.

In the meantime, I had to be candid with Johnny that his reason for wanting a pardon wouldn't fly in any White House—nothing noble about it or his time in prison. So, I simply advised him to closely follow the ongoing debate and go back to his judge if the law changed.

Which reminds me, I've just got to tell you "Old School's" story next. It'll curl your hair.

HUCK POST 111:
Old School's Probation Blues
June 4, 2024—Day 78

"Old School" was my kind of guy. Up before dawn and on the rickety exercise bike by sunrise, just hammering it for an hour. Then a jog around the track followed by a cooldown as he read the Bible out at a table in the yard.

Old School was in his sixties, a "black conservative" and pro-Trumper; and he loved to talk politics *to* (not with) me. Yes, it was mostly a one-way conversation, as I didn't come to prison for that. But I was polite.

Anyway, the one thing I did love about Old School was his mentorship of some of the younger inmates, particularly young "J," who was lost when he arrived. He took J right under his wing and schooled him everyday both on prison life and life outside—hence the nickname, "Old School."

At any rate, when I heard Old School's story, it made my blood boil but also helped highlight the problem so many inmates have with *excessive lengths of parole*—"supervised release" in the lexicon of the BOP.

In my discussions with inmates, it was not uncommon to see three or five or more years of probation even after the prison term was over. I knew firsthand how onerous this obligation was from the weekly ritual I had to endure after I was arrested and in the many months leading up to my trial.

Every week, I had to phone in to the equivalent of my "parole officer" and let him know my whereabouts, and at any time I could be called in for a drug test. Just a pain in the ass—and an easy call to forget. (It happened twice; I'm such a bonehead sometimes.)

My theory is that these lengthy probation periods are more like full employment for prison workers. At any one time, there's about seven hundred thousand former inmates on probation and here's the kicker: If a former inmate on probation violates the terms in any way, no matter how small, BOOM, it's right back in the slammer.

Here's what happened to Old School—and the buried lead of this postcard.

After three full years on probation with only *three days* left to go before complete freedom, Old School got violated for failing to update the name of his supervisor. For that undeniably minor infraction, they immediately put him back in prison for three more months *and* reset his probation clock to three more years.

I'm sorry but that's just a waste of time and money. It's a waste of a man's life.

And how's this for a coda: Newbie Seth came into my dorm just before Old School left because of a probation violation.

Yes, he had paid his restitution every six months as his lawyer had cleared him to do. However, according to the letter of his agreement, Seth was supposed to be paying once a month rather than cumulatively every six months. For that, Seth's judge sent him back to prison for seven more months!

Seven months. That's about $30,000 in direct costs to taxpayers and another $30,000 or so from the taxes Seth won't pay because he's not working.

Put probation reform on my list of ways to clean up the judicial system's act.

HUCK POST 112:
Swish!
June 5, 2024—Day 79

*"There's a poetic simplicity to the swish of a basketball net" is
attributed to an article discussing the New York Knicks' unselfish
play and teamwork.*
—Mike Vaccaro, *New York Post*

One of the worst strategic decisions I ever made in my misspent youth was
to spend most of my time in sports playing basketball. It was a bad decision
because I was a short guy as a kid—barely 5' when I got to high school (I'm
about 5'7" now).

So it was long odds that I would play varsity in high school—I actually
did—and even longer odds that I would ever play in college, which I never
did.

In a shoulda, coulda, woulda world, I would have focused on soccer
because you don't have to be tall and the game leverages the same skill
set that made me pretty good on the hardwood court—speed, quickness,
anticipation of where the ball would go next.

But it was basketball, not soccer; and a highlight of my youth was a
couple of summers at Bob Cousy's basketball camp back in the 1960s in
New Hampshire.

(Side note: One of my best days at the White House was in the Oval
Office talking not to the Boss but rather The Cooz when he received his
presidential medal of honor.)

At any rate, from my kid days, I've always enjoyed the swish sound of
a basketball going through the net on a perfect shot. And it's always been a
bugaboo of mine when a playground court has ratty or no nets.

Case in point is the set of public courts adjacent to Eastern High School
in Washington, DC—Dave Chappelle's alma mater, by the way.

Anyway, I'd ride my bike up there from Penn Quarter where I lived
during my White House years and shoot some hoops, even in winter; and

it frosted me that the nets sucked. So I sent a bunch to the Eastern High School principal and he put them up. Swish.

Here, at my Miami prison, the balls and court were good, but the nets were ragged or nonexistent. It took me seventy-five days in the slammer, but *today* I managed to get a new set of nets installed. Don't ask me how—but it was a small victory for me and my fellow ballers. Even in prison you can have a good day.

HUCK POST 113:
Bannon in Jeopardy
June 6, 2024—Day 80

On this D-Day, the other shoe dropped on one of my best friends, Steve Bannon, when Judge Carl Nichols of the DC Circuit ordered my brother-in-arms to prison by July 1 after the DC Court of Appeals rejected Steve's appeal.

What *should* have happened next is that Steve should have remained free until his appeal was heard up the chain at the Supreme Court—or *en banc* at the DC Circuit. But Nichols was under intense pressure to toe the Never-Trump line, and he did.

And it certainly didn't help Steve that I had *already* been sent to prison prior to my own appeal—that did come up at the hearing. One wrong apparently makes two wrongs by DC Court math.

This was indeed wrong on both humanity grounds *and* the law. Now, I need to get word to Steve that he quickly must request a prison of his choice—the BOP allows you to submit a list of three.

I didn't know that before I went in. So, I wound up in my Miami hellhole—at the bottom of the list of minimum-security prisons.

I figure Pensacola would be ideal. Steve is an ex-Navy guy, and the prison is adjacent to the Navy base.

Plus, it's Brother Matt Gaetz's congressional district, and Matt would make sure Steve is treated right. Let's see what happens.

HUCK POST 114:
Joni Mitchell on KP
June 9, 2024—Day 83

For months, I had been getting one side of the "kitchen police duty sucks" story from Chris, Mark, and several other inmates working inside the beast. Just one fork-raising tale after another of rotting bananas, overcooked meat, staff indifference *and* pilferage, roaches, rats, and worse. Certainly, no shortage of reasons why the food sucked.

This a.m. I got the other side of the story from one of the guards in charge of the cafeteria—literally the kitchen police. Guard Williams had been eyeing me warily for weeks trying to decide if I might be friend or foe, but finally she decided to take the plunge and offered me a tour of her dysfunctional kitchen.

As I crossed the inmate line from food recipient to kitchen critic into the back of the kitchen, I was taken past one piece of equipment after the other that didn't work and hadn't worked for at least months and sometimes years. And this was not cheap equipment but rather high quality, commercial grade stuff.

For example, there was a huge $3,000 griddle that could have fried eggs or pancakes or hot dogs or burgers 100 at a time—all it needed to be up and griddling was a $25 plug and an upgrade of the electrical outlet costing maybe another $25 bucks.

There was also a huge deep kettle to boil eggs or vegetables or potatoes. It had been down for months because the distilled water machine that connected to it was broken.

There was an entire baking room with large ovens and massive electronic mixing machines that hadn't got a whiff of fresh bread or rolls or pizza for years. No explanation given.

There was a huge machine to clean pots and pans that would have worked perfectly if they had the chemical detergent to put into it.

There was also the biggest, most beautiful freezer in its own room that had *never* been connected. So, all of the frozen meat had to be walked over from an adjacent building on a daily basis *and* it was from a bank of temporary freezers that rented out at about $4,000 a month. Only monkeys with flamethrowers can burn cash faster.

And everywhere you looked, there were holes in the ceiling or walls where good ventilation filters were supposed to be.

Everything was just a dirty white or gray, and if you wanted to create the most depressing kitchen for Martha Stewart to work in as more punishment for her crimes, mission freaking accomplished.

So, I say to Williams, how did this happen? She didn't know. All she knew was that they just wouldn't give her the parts or repair people she needed to run an efficient kitchen.

Here was yet another case where the situation breeds guards unhappy with working conditions and inmates unhappy with the results—in this case crappy meals. And it just created more tension between the hounds and the hares, the guards and the inmates, the Hatfields and the McCoys.

The stupidest part of the whole thing is that the inmates weren't allowed to pony up the pennies needed for the parts that would have turned Hell's Kitchen into at least a McDonald's, if not Wolfgang Puck's.

I vowed to get to the bottom of this insanity for both Williams *and* the inmates, and she told me that for some reason, ever since COVID, the BOP had lost its way and things had fallen apart.

She also told me she was sorry that I had been put in prison based on what she knew, but maybe I was put here for a bigger reason. And we agreed that having somebody like me actually see things daily *from the inside* was far better than the Potemkin tours they give to gullible congressmen.

So let me see what I can do, I told her. And I damn well will try to get something done. In the meantime, billions are going to Ukraine and pennies to the BOP, and that's why they call it prison.

PIXIE POST 21:
Honk If You Love a Huck
June 9, 2024—Day 83

Pixie here, and Sunday's visit with my Ever Huck is just splendid.

We actually get some laughs, though always a bit of tears inside. I keep them tucked tightly inside, as by now I can control them.

But I hope it doesn't mean I am too hardened by all of this and vice versa for him as well. We need to work on not making ourselves harder and tougher (than we already are).

We have this new farewell routine now that my Huck figured out, and it's wonderful. After I leave the Visitor Center and walk to the parking lot where Dale is, my Huck sprints out of the Center, jogs down across the quadrangle, and slides over to the far fence; and he can then see Dale and me on our exit.

Dale stops and I get out of the car and do a little Broadway dance for Huck and then a bow. And my Huck waves and bows back.

Dale then honks his horn three times, and my Huck says it's two honks for Trump and one for Pixie. But I say no, that it's all for my Huck.

And as I get back in the car, my Ever Huck then gives me the famous Navarro TV salute that I see through the open car window.

Then I close the window, and I watch my Huck pantomiming climbing up the fence and over it to freedom as Dale pulls away and my Huck fades into the distance.

It's another Saturday night beginning with the last vision of Huck behind a razor-wired fence but with a smile on his face.

We always remember the song that goes, "Smile though your heart is breaking." Because sometimes the smile does help.

HUCK POST 115:
Am I a Racist?
June 10, 2024—Day 84

> *Golf doesn't build character. It reveals it.*
> —Sportswriter Heywood Hale Broun

So at breakfast, this white guy, call him Ron, is telling me how this other white guy snaked his lower bunk. The ritual here is that before an inmate leaves, everything he possesses—none of which he can take with him—is parceled out to other inmates, who get stuff based mostly on an informal seniority system.

In this case, an inmate had promised his lower bunk to veteran Ron, but newbie Jeff just moved in on it. It was a dick move that could have easily ended in bloodshed—Ron is a very big strong guy but Jeff is a former MMA fighter—but it got me to thinking.

Of the relatively few guys in this prison I had taken an active dislike to, every single one was a white guy. What they all had in common were court files indicating they had snitched on their colleagues to get lighter sentences. Not my kind of people, and certainly not people you can trust.

Like gold, prison doesn't build character. It reveals it.

HUCK POST 116:
Killing Time
June 11, 2024—Day 85

So just before the count, Cedric the Cook comes rushing into my dorm looking to get back his paperwork we're using to calculate when he should be released—or in this case, when he *should have been* released, which was months ago.

Seems that his case manager is hearing the footsteps of Elliot and me as we ping her with requests for data and let her know there may be a big screwup with Cedric's numbers. So, she unilaterally has decided to do what Cedric has been asking her to do for over a year, and Elliot has raised questions about Cedric's classification from a "medium" to a "low" risk prisoner.

That classification never should have been slapped on Cedric. But a notorious guard named Lua, who would have fit in well at Treblinka, had done it to Cedric out of spite.

It was yet another example of negligence at the BOP. By falsely raising Cedric's classification, Lua had cost Cedric *five* days a month of earned First Step Act credits towards an earlier prerelease to a halfway house.

Here's my beef: Everyone in this prison (except arguably me) is here because they broke the law. Yet, the BOP continuously breaks laws like the FSA and Second Chance Act itself and thereby not only inflicts misery, they also cost American taxpayers billions of dollars by keeping inmates like Cedric long past their expiration date.

There oughta be a law against such negligence.

[*Author's Note: Lua would later be promoted to Unit Manager. Talk about excrement rolling uphill.*]

HUCK POST 117:
No Good Interview Goes Unpunished
June 12, 2024—Day 86

Out of the blue, I got an invite from *The Economist* magazine to do what I thought would be a standard Q&A. Silly me.

As subtext, *The Economist* is to globalism and free trade as sweatshops are to Communist China; and during the Trump administration, I was one of the magazine's favorite tariff whipping boys.

That they wanted to interview me, however, I took as a good sign that the Boss could very well win the 2024 election. So, I answered their questions, and the result was not a Q&A as I had been promised.

Rather, my words were tightly wrapped in a snide and condescending globalist wrapper. Here's the quasi-interview. You decide who got the better of it.

Donald Trump's trade hawk is plotting behind bars: Peter Navarro's dark vision of the global economy could shape Trump 2
Ahead of America's election in November, company bosses, financiers and diplomats are busy calling on Donald Trump's allies, trying to divine the economic policies that the former president will pursue if he is re-elected.

But there is one man in Trump's orbit who holds more sway than most and who, for now, is virtually inaccessible. That is because he is inmate number 04370-510 in the Federal Correctional Institution of Miami.

Peter Navarro, a leading economic adviser in Trump's first administration, is more than halfway through a four-month sentence for contempt of Congress. He bristles with indignation at the justice system, disdains US President Joe Biden's record and longs to steer America towards hardline protectionism.

In written correspondence with *The Economist*, Navarro has laid out how he thinks Trump should approach trade—from turning up the heat on China to slapping tariffs on just about everyone else. It is a dark, angry vision for the global economy. As polls stand, it is one Navarro may shortly be able to promote from inside the White House.

Amid the chaos of the previous Trump administration, Navarro stood out as especially disruptive, acerbic and vengeful. At various points, the former economics professor was sidelined from trade negotiations, investigated for abusing colleagues and publicly castigated. But throughout it all, Navarro managed to remain in Trump's favour.

His position was only bolstered after he demonstrated complete loyalty by refusing to comply with a subpoena from the House of Representatives committee investigating the Capitol riot of January 6, 2021. It was that refusal that landed the wiry 74-year-old in prison in March.

To gauge the influence of Navarro's ideas, consider how Trump has praised his latest book. *The New Maga Deal* is due out on July 16, almost perfectly coinciding with its author's release from prison. "What he says should be highly respected," reads a dust jacket quote from Trump. "Peter Navarro is a Patriot who has been treated very badly, but he continues forward. In the end, there will be Victory!"

Back in 2016, Navarro's appeals for protectionism made him an outlier, even among Republicans. Now he is much closer to the mainstream, as shown by Biden's recent decision to slap hefty tariffs on Chinese electric vehicles (EVs), solar panels and more. It is the triumph of "the Trumpian principle that economic security is national security," says Navarro. "The debate is over."

Not that he has anything nice to say about Bidenomics. In Navarro's view, Biden messed up by making industrial policy heavy on subsidies for EVs. Not only did that "spike the federal deficit" in America, it also, perversely, encouraged China to produce more EV batteries. "If Trump had been president, this never would have happened," he says.

As with many of Navarro's claims, this is highly debatable: Biden's subsidies require battery components to be made in

America or by free trade partners, and Trump's tax cuts add even more to the deficit. But it is true that Chinese producers dominate the global EV market, and that they are investing abroad in a bid to dodge American tariffs.

Navarro's prescription is to prevent third countries from being used as conduits for Chinese goods. "Vietnam is a major shadow export platform for 'Made in China' and invites a crackdown," he says. He also warns that Mexico may imperil the free trade agreement between it, America and Canada if it accepts too much Chinese investment. "Mr. Trump simply won't tolerate a Communist Chinese beachhead on America's southern flank," he says.

America a victim

One way Biden has distinguished his trade strategy from Trump's is by trying to mend ties with allies, to form a united front against China. Some diplomats still complain that Biden's policies boil down to the same favouritism for America, albeit via subsidies rather than tariffs and couched in politer language. But Navarro's harsh analysis is a bracing reminder that the differences are substantial.

"Too many European nations are compromised by Communist Chinese influence to ever project a united front," he says. Britain? Addicted to Chinese capital. Greece and Italy? Their ports are mortgaged to China. Germany? Too dependent on China for its exports. In Navarro's Manichaean universe, Trumpian America stands alone in its righteousness.

Even leaving China aside, Navarro considers America a victim. "When it comes to steel and aluminium, the US has no allies, only competitors that cheat and dump," he says. (The suggestion is that, as president, Trump might consider reinstating his controversial steel and aluminium tariffs, rolled back by Biden.) Navarro also hopes to see passage of the Reciprocal Trade Act, which would allow the president to mirror the tariffs and non-tariff barriers of any country that refuses to lower its own to the level of America's.

He calls it common sense and a priority for Trump. As for the World Trade Organisation (WTO), rendered increasingly irrelevant by America's crippling of its appellate body, Navarro's solution is simple: boot out China, for breaking the WTO "with its ruthless economic aggression."

In practice, many of these proposals would be hard to implement and could harm America. Steel tariffs are costly for the many industries that use the metal, and so end up hurting, not helping, domestic manufacturers. Screening Chinese investments abroad would be both arduous and awkward, requiring explicit meddling in other countries' politics.

Reciprocal tariffs may sound sensible but would leave American policy looking bizarre, since each country has a blend of high and low tariffs for different sectors (which in fact allows for the compromises that make most trade deals possible). America, for instance, has hefty levies on imports of pick-up trucks and lumber. Expelling China from the WTO would be nearly impossible.

But focusing on such details may miss the point. When Trump was in the White House, Robert Lighthizer, a lawyer who served as United States Trade Representative, helped design America's new tariffs and spearheaded the investigations that formed their legal basis. "Lighthizer was more the brains of the operation, whereas Navarro was the heart and the gusto, the front-line warrior willing to get sullied and dirtied," says Dan Ikenson, a trade-policy scholar.

Navarro's main official role was to lead the Office of Trade and Manufacturing Policy in the White House, a body created by Trump with few actual staffers.

Some speculate that Lighthizer may be treasury secretary if Trump is re-elected, a perch from which he could remake American economic policy beyond just trade. Navarro, by contrast, is not much of a manager.

But his pugnaciousness appeals to Trump. In a statement to the *Wall Street Journal* last month, Trump said he would "absolutely have Peter back" in a new administration. Another sign of Navarro's good standing: Donald Trump junior, the former president's son, recently visited him in prison.

The 'world is laughing' at America

Located at the southern tip of Miami, his low-security jail sits next to the municipal zoo and not far from a safari park. That may sound pleasant as far as detentions go, but it is still prison, with a strict curfew, restrictions on movement and little privacy in a dorm-style room. In late May, there was a bloody brawl between Puerto Rican and Mexican gangs in the prison directly next to Navarro's. "It is no country for old men," he observes.

The only thing that seems to exercise Navarro more than China's mercantilism is his belief that the Democratic Party is using the legal system to persecute Trump, conspiring to prevent him from regaining power.

He describes the hush-money trial that ended last month with Trump's conviction as a ploy to exhaust his funds and keep him tied up in court instead of on the campaign trail.

"Under Joe Biden's lawfare tyranny, America is nothing more than a banana republic and the world, particularly Communist China, is laughing at us," he says. That makes for quite the contrast with Republicans' more usual depiction of Biden as a doddering fool.

Like many of Navarro's extreme views, this one has scant basis in reality. But one thing is all too clear: no one should be laughing at him, or the prospect of his ideas once more holding sway in the White House.

[*Author's Note: Got to love the cheap shot at the end—"extreme" views, like wanting to protect America from unfair trade.*]

HUCK POST 118:
The Monsoon, Lockdown, Prison Blues
June 12, 2024—Day 86

> *Desire is suffering.*
> —The Buddha

So, a huge band of pre-hurricane tropical moisture has settled over the prison and greater Miami like a sumo wrestler sitting on Peter Pan. Just a smothering monsoon.

And as they lock us out of the rec yard because of thunder and lightning and lock us into the dorms, the natives do indeed get loud and restless.

Me, I've been gripped with a bad case of speech-itis. With each passing day, I'm thinking more and more about walking out of prison on the morning of July 17, hopping on a private jet to Milwaukee for the Republican National Convention, and then hopping on stage for my five minutes of semi-fame to deliver the speech of my life.

I don't know why I'm thinking about it. It's certainly not about any hunger for fame—I couldn't give a shit at my age. But I do think I have something important to say—to add to the campaign debate. Because who else out there has gone through what I have and seen what I've seen?

At any rate, so far, I don't have a Lionel Ritchie "hook" for The Speech. But I do have a little bit of JFK "ask not" echo:

> *If we don't control our government, THEIR government will control us.*

And, of course, a little bit of Churchill:

> *We will fight them in the courts*
> *We will fight them in our schools*
> *We will fight them at the border.*
> *And above all, over the next 100 days*
> *We will fight them at the ballot box.*

But I know the odds of getting on the podium are long. I won't get out until July 17, and that evening is reserved for the heaviest of hitters—and will end with JD Vance's acceptance speech.

Not a lot of room at that inn. But a guy can dream.

Desire is indeed suffering.

HUCK POST 119:
Statement Interruptus
June 13, 2024—Day 87

Here's a draft statement I sent to Congressman Matt Gaetz in the hopes he would read it into the record at a hearing today on Capitol Hill where he intended to rake Bureau of Prisons director, Colette Peters, over the coals for all manner of incompetence.

Despite the best efforts of Matt and Congressman Andy Biggs, the statement never got in—and that kinda pissed me off because I needed it in the congressional record to advance the prison reform ball.

But welcome to my world, stuck as I am in prison. At any rate, here goes; at least it's good background to explain the mission that has come to me behind bars.

STATEMENT OF PETER NAVARRO TO THE HOUSE JUDICIARY SUBCOMMITTEE ON CRIME AND FEDERAL GOVERNMENT SURVEILLANCE
I want to thank Congressman Matt Gaetz for reading this statement into the record and I want to personally thank Matt and his wife Ginger for their unflagging support and prayers during my incarceration.

My statement today is in response to the refusal of Bureau of Prisons Director Colette Peters to testify before Congress after receiving an invitation from Judiciary Committee Chair Jim Jordan. In fact, Director Peters has much to answer for.

Here, as I sit behind prison walls and listen to my fellow inmates, the biggest beef with Peters' "Backwards on Purpose" BOP is its abject failure to fully and faithfully implement both President Trump's 2018 First Step Act and the 2008 Second Chance Act.

To augment his "tough on crime" policies with a "smart on crime" strategy, President Trump designed the First Step Act to address an epidemic of overly harsh sentences—spawned in no small part by then-Senator Joe "Mandatory Minimum" Biden. President Trump knows that when inmates remain in prison longer than necessary to impose fair punishment and deter future criminal behavior, taxpayers foot the bill—to the tune of more than $50,000 annually per inmate. In addition, with overly long sentences, family ties fray, jobs skills deteriorate, and the rates of recidivism and crime rise—never mind the human misery of the inmates and their family members.

To address this problem, the First Step Act features a system of time credits (FTC) that can be earned through good behavior, productive activity, and inmate programming designed to reduce recidivism. These FTCs are earned at the rate of 10 days per month in the first 60 days after sentencing and 15 days a month thereafter for minimum and low risk inmates. These FTCs can then be applied for both sentence reduction and the acceleration of an inmate's transfer from prison into "pre-release custody," that is, to a halfway house and/or electronically monitored home confinement.

In its latest First Step Annual Report to Congress (April, 2023), the Office of the Attorney General within the Department of Justice explained exactly how the Bureau of Prisons, by its own November 8, 2022 Program Statement (5410.10), is supposed to calculate inmate FTCs using a forecasting method rather than its antiquated "earn FTC as you go" method. According to the Attorney General's office: "[T]he policy specifies that the BOP will calculate and award time credits for the full incarceration period [including time spent in a halfway house or home confinement.]"

The First Step Act Annual Report goes on to create the FALSE impression that the Bureau of Prisons is ALREADY implementing this forecast FTCs policy when it states: "Earned time credits are now calculated at the initial stages of the individual's sentence, with the presumption that the earned credits [FTC] will accrue throughout the term of incarceration."

Here, America's Attorney General is simply lying to Congress. From behind my prison walls, through discussions with case managers and the analysis of dozens of inmate cases, I am seeing firsthand that the BOP has failed to introduce its long promised "Conditional Maximum FTC Calculator" that would forecast FTC.

Instead, foot-dragging BOP bureaucrats continue to rely on their outdated "earn FTCs as you go" algorithm, and the result is stunning: Every single FSA-eligible inmate in the BOP system will be short counted on their FTCs and each will experience significant delays both in pre-release to a halfway house or monitored home confinement and release to freedom.

To understand the critical difference between using forecast FTCs versus using the earn as you go FTC algorithm, consider a minimum or low risk FSA-eligible offender sentenced to 60 months. Using the forecast method, that inmate will earn 555 FTCs over the term of his incarceration. The first 365 of these FTCs will reduce his sentence and release date by a full year—the maximum FTC sentence reduction. The remaining 190 FTCs will then earn the inmate three months and ten days of an earlier pre-release into a halfway house.

In sharp contrast, using the BOP's "earn FTCs as you go" algorithm, the BOP will typically credit the inmate with only about 330 FTCs instead of 555. This reduction in FTCs will extend the inmate's release date by about a month, and completely wipe out the inmate's three months and ten days of prerelease to a halfway house. Cumulatively, the costs of these delays are staggering, as I shall shortly demonstrate, as there are over 60,000 First Step Act-eligible inmates in the BOP system.

The example I have offered is not a statistical abstraction. These delays involve real people with real families and real suffering.

Take Ricky Handschumacher. He's a 31-year old father who should have been back with his family last December. He didn't leave my Miami prison until a few weeks ago—at an extra cost to taxpayers of well over $20,000.

Then there's Dr. Arman Abovyan. He should have entered a halfway house four months ago; yet, he'll likely be in prison for at least another six to 12 months. That's not just tens of thousands of dollars more down the taxpayer drain. "Doc," as we call him, won't be earning a living and paying tens of thousands of dollars in income taxes as he treads water in the slammer.

As yet a third example—I've got dozens more—there's James Medard. His family is struggling financially, and he should have been sent to a halfway house last month. But like Doc Abovyan, he'll likely be in for another six to 12 more months.

Sadly, it's much the same kind of BOP neglect with the 2007 Second Chance Act, particularly when it comes to granting compassionate release. The poster child for this abomination is one bunk over from me. He's Delmer Gowing, an 80-year old distinguished Vietnam Vet in a wheelchair with a degenerative disease who should have been home at least several years ago. That's another $100,000 alone of taxpayer money down the drain, all to pay for Del's added misery.

Conspicuous in its absence is any effort of the Bureau of Prisons to estimate the extent of these costs. To the contrary, as the Office of Attorney General noted in its latest First Step Act Annual Report: "As was the case in the last report, it is too soon to assess cost savings resulting from implementation of the First Step Act."

Too soon? That's utter horse manure.

Let me do for you here from my prison dorm with a hand calculator what the BOP and Attorney General won't or can't do with their government supercomputers.

To wit, I estimate the total DIRECT cost of the BOP's failure to implement the First Step Act and associated delays to range between $1.5 to $2.5 billion for the more than 60,000 FSA eligible inmates.

I further estimate as an INDIRECT cost at least another half to one billion dollars in foregone tax revenues. This loss in tax revenues results from keeping inmates in prison past their pre-release and release dates rather than letting them out into the work force where they can help grow America's economy and pay taxes.

Finally, there's at least another half to billion dollars in indirect taxpayer costs associated with supporting the struggling wives and children of inmates who don't have their breadwinners at home because of the BOP's cruelty and incompetence. I have met some of these women and children in the Visitor's Room at the prison, and their stories are heartbreaking.

When you add up all of these direct and indirect costs, it approaches $5 billion that could be zeroed out from the Federal budget if Colette Peters and the BOP faithfully and fully implemented the First Step and Second Chance Acts.

Surely, you here in Congress will agree with me on this: If all I have told you today is accurate and true, then it is surely well past time for the Judiciary Committee to put a subpoena in Colette Peters' hand. And dare her to come testify before this committee and try to refute anything I have set forth in this statement.

And while Colette Peters is here in this House, maybe she can explain why a congressman like Matt Gaetz can't come and interview "notorious PKN"—that's what Peters has called me, Peter Kent Navarro, "notorious."

I also urge this House to immediately pass a resolution demanding that the BOP release its Conditional Maximum FTC Calculator and let case managers around the country know that the earn as you go algorithm is dead, the forecasting methodology is indeed BOP policy, and forecasting First Step Act earned time credits WILL be implemented forthwith.

In this presidential election season, make no mistake about this: The BOP's failure to fully and faithfully implement the First Step Act is a BIG political issue. From my Miami prison, I can assure you that the vast majority of inmates and their family members who vote love Donald Trump for signing the First Step Act just as they hate Joe Biden for his cruel mandatory minimum sentences and loath Colette Peters for her refusal to faithfully implement Trump's First Step Act.

Yet with Peters and the BOP now squandering billions of American tax dollars, this is ultimately a bipartisan policy issue here on Capitol Hill and I have handed you the solution on a silver platter. So get it done, and get it done now.

In closing, I would be remiss in not reminding everyone in this House why I'm in prison.

I'm in prison because the Democrats in this house led by Nancy Pelosi and Bennie Thompson voted to hold me in contempt for honoring my oath of office by defending the constitutional separation of powers and George Washington's doctrine of executive privilege against their unprecedented and abusive lawfare attack.

I'm in prison because a Democrat Attorney General, Merrick Garland, prosecuted me for upholding what has been a more than 50-year Department of Justice policy ensuring absolute testimonial immunity for Senior White House advisors and alteregos of the president.

And I'm in prison because a Democrat judge, Amit Mehta, who auditioned for his job by bundling large campaign contributions for Barack Obama, stripped me of every possible defense before I even went to trial—making my conviction by 12 Trump-hating Democrat jurors in Washington DC a foregone conclusion.

Yet, my false imprisonment may turn out to be the best thing for this nation if you here in Congress are able to use what I have learned in prison to save American taxpayers billions of dollars, lower the rate of recidivism, and end at least some of the misery my fellow inmates and their families are needlessly enduring because of Joe Biden and Collette Peters.

It's up to you now. And if you don't believe a word I've said, take this second opinion to heart from the dean of prison reform experts, Derek Gilna, when he writes in his May 6, 2024 newsletter: "There is no question the Bureau [of Prisons] is systematically depriving prisoners of their appropriate Second Chance Act (SCA) and First Step Act (FSA) sentence credits, forcing them to spend additional time in custody. It also purposely frustrates prisoners close to release from applying unused FSA credits to promised halfway houses."

Peter Navarro. Out.

HUCK POST 120:
The *Epoch Times* Blinks
June 14, 2024—Day 88

The backstory behind the interview you are about to read, which was published on this day in the *Daily Caller*, is probably more interesting than the interview itself.

This interview was originally conducted with the young journalist prodigy Adam Molon—a true patriot and keen intellect. The target was the *Epoch Times*, which Adam regularly writes for.

I, myself, had published a few op-eds with *Epoch*, and we thought it would be an easy lift. Sort of.

"Sort of" because the last several op-eds I had sent them they had declined as too political. *Huh?*

This was a newspaper founded on politics—the political destruction of the Chinese Communist Party.

Yet, beginning over a year ago, I had got the faintest whiff of a cancel culture within the *Epoch Times'* editorial ranks; and sure enough, when Adam had sent them the interview for consideration, they quickly declined.

With a little digging, we discovered that the new editorial policy was to seek a *detente* with the Biden regime. And the editors were also pissed that Donald Trump never gave them an interview. So canceled I was—along with anything remotely pro-Trump in their paper.

So, what is the *Epoch Times* now?

It may relentlessly defend the Falun Gong against Chinese Communist oppression. Yet, at the same time, it turns a blind eye to the worst kind of abuses of the Biden regime—the weaponization of our justice system and CCP-style kangaroo courts; the indoctrination, grooming, and genital mutilation of our youth; the suppression of the wages of black, brown, and blue collar Americans by an invasion of millions of illiterate illegal aliens, and so it goes.

As my old Boss might say, "Very disappointing."

At any rate, here's the interview the *Epoch Times* refused to print that would wind up in the the *Daily Caller* (and thanks, *Daily Caller*!).

EXCLUSIVE: Trump Confidant Peter Navarro Describes Life In Prison, Plans For When He's Free

Dr. Peter Navarro granted an exclusive interview to the *Daily Caller* from the Federal Correctional Institution of Miami, where he is serving out a sentence for contempt of Congress—a term he and his allies have called a political imprisonment.

"Lawfare is real. Lawfare is wrong. . . . We're not supposed to act like Communist China or a Banana Republic. But that's the growing perception of our justice system," Navarro told the Caller.

Navarro served as Director of the White House Office of Trade and Manufacturing Policy from 2017 to 2021. He is set to be released from prison on July 17, at which point he plans to debut his new book, *The New MAGA Deal*, at the RNC with Donald Trump Jr.

Navarro wrote to the *Caller* via a prison email system: "I'm in prison not for any crime but rather as a matter of honor and duty for defending the constitutional separation of powers."

Navarro invoked executive privilege when declining to comply with a subpoena from the House January 6th Committee. He was arrested in June of 2022 at Ronald Reagan National Airport by FBI agents, charged in the U.S. District Court in Washington, DC with contempt of congress and sentenced in January to four months in prison. Navarro's legal representation has noted that this case marks the first time in history that "a senior presidential advisor has been convicted of contempt of congress after asserting executive privilege over a congressional subpoena."

Navarro entered federal prison on March 19.

The following is the Caller's exclusive interview with Navarro, edited for brevity.

You're a little more than halfway through your prison term. What is prison like and how are you doing?
The Miami facility is no "Club Fed" by any stretch of CNN's imagination, but functions more like a low-security prison surrounded by razor wire with frequent lockdowns and little inmate access to the outside world.

It's a dangerous place health-wise. The low-protein, high-carb, no-fresh-vegetable diet exacerbates problems like diabetes, colon cancer, and heart disease. I'm fortunate I don't take any medicines, because prescription drugs are in short supply at the daily "pill line," and a lot of inmates needlessly suffer from symptoms that their prescription drugs would otherwise ameliorate. I'm among about 200 inmates in close dorm quarters—a new strain of COVID hit a few weeks ago and spread like wildfire.

If it doesn't kill you, it makes you stronger. So far I'm stronger, but I'm in the minority in that category within this prison. I see a lot of unnecessary misery because of mismanagement and the callous disregard of laws like the First Step Act by the Bureau of Prisons—prison can break you both mentally and physically, and it certainly doesn't prepare inmates for success and honest work in the outside world.

What's a typical prison day like?
Up before dawn, an early breakfast with dry cereal and zero protein, a mile walk around the track thinking of my beautiful fiancée and singing her our favorite song—Michael Bublé's version

of "The Way You Look Tonight." I know she can hear me—and we talk three times a day on the phone.

[*Navarro told the Caller he can speak with his fiancée Bonnie briefly at meal times, but that his phone time is heavily restricted.*]

Off to work by 8, lunch at 11, more work, exercise in the yard, dinner. At night, I work both on my appeal being prepared by my legal team and a project I'm working with inmates on to fix a massive computer error in the Bureau of Prisons that is delaying the release of inmates both to halfway houses and to freedom.

This is a huge scandal I've uncovered from behind prison walls. Incompetence at the Biden Administration's Bureau of Prisons is costing nearly $5 billion in wasted taxpayer funds, and the Democrats may rue the day they put me on the inside to see the level of incompetence and the misery among inmates and their families it is causing. Look for more op-eds on this and its emergence as an election issue.

How do you keep up on the news?
It's very difficult as there are no computers, cell phones, or internet access. Inmates prefer sports, game shows like *Family Feud*, and movies to news—although you're far more likely to see Fox News than CNN or MSNBC when news shows pop up.

I also read the Economist on a weekly basis to stay abreast of world news (albeit with a globalist spin) and at dawn I catch five minutes or so of CNBC when the rest of the inmates are sleeping so I can check the stock and bond markets—Joe Kernan, Rick Santelli, and Jim Cramer remain favorites.

Could you talk about the volume of mail you receive?
It's in the thousands and unfortunately about half of it is returned by the Bureau of Prisons for nitpicky reasons like the wrong-colored ink, colored paper, or the use of greeting cards. I've taken great inspiration from the wisdom, prayers, and support of MAGA nation—and try to respond to everyone.

The most poignant letters—always handwritten—are often from veterans who fought for our country and are appalled at the takeover of our justice system for punitive political purposes. Lawfare is real. Lawfare is wrong. They didn't fight for the right of one political party to put members of the other party in jail. We're not supposed to act like Communist China or a Banana Republic. But that's the growing perception of our justice system.

You have said you won't seek a pardon if Donald Trump is elected president. Why?

I don't need a pardon to restore my reputation. Most Americans understand now that I'm in prison not for any crime but rather as a matter of honor and duty for defending the constitutional separation of powers.

(RELATED: Trump Says He 'Would Absolutely' Rehire Peter Navarro)

Most important, a pardon might provide the Supreme Court with a reason to not hear my appeal. Yet, United States v. Peter K. Navarro is a landmark case, and I've given the court a set of perfect facts to settle good law on two key questions: Can Congress compel a senior White House advisor to testify without violating the constitutional separation of powers, and what constitutes a proper invocation of executive privilege?

If the Supreme Court refuses to take my case for any reason and fails to answer these questions, the constitutional separation of powers will be shattered and the critical role dating back to George Washington that executive privilege plays in effective presidential decision-making will forever be destroyed. That can't be the law of our land.

What are you going to do on your first day out of prison on July 17?

If all goes well, I'm going to give my fiancée the biggest hug on the planet, and then we are going to hop on a plane and go to the Republican National Convention where I'll debut my new book, *The New MAGA Deal*, alongside Don Jr. and perhaps take a brief turn on the stage—Don Jr.'s publishing house is offering *The New MAGA Deal* (www.newmagadeal.com).

You've said that *The New MAGA Deal* may well be the most important book you've ever written. Why?

The New MAGA Deal is the definitive book on, and unofficial Deplorable's guide to, the Trump 2024 campaign platform. It's important for two reasons. First, it describes 100 presidential actions my old boss will take in the first 100 days on everything from inflation, border security, and combating CCP aggression to defending women's sports, stopping the genital mutilation of young boys, and ending the relentless lawfare that has corrupted and compromised our now dual system of justice.

Second, and most important, it is the single best defense against the predictable spin of the opposition party that MAGA equals extremism. *The New MAGA Deal* illustrates that the Trump agenda and its economic populism is the most common-sense, mainstream response to the myriad crises this nation is experiencing.

Finally, what will be the approach of a new Trump administration to combating the CCP's economic aggression and containing Xi Jinping's imperialistic ventures to control the world's natural resources, markets, and sea lines of communication?

That will, of course, be up to Donald Trump if he wins what will be a very tough race. I would counsel talking softly while carrying a very big tariff stick and redirecting the mission of the Pentagon from woke madness to combat readiness. In addition, President Trump almost certainly will finish what he and I and others like Bob Lighthizer and Wilbur Ross started—reshoring American manufacturing, particularly from Communist China, and particularly in key areas like defense and pharmaceuticals. Of course, it's long past time for the CCP to be held financially and morally accountable—along with Dr. Anthony Fauci—for unleashing the COVID virus from the Wuhan lab.

Taiwan President Lai Ching-te took office on May 20, succeeding Tsai Ing-wen, even as China undertook large scale military drills to intimidate the Taiwanese. Do you think China will follow through on its plans to invade Taiwan?

I think a lot in prison about Taiwan, which has a very special place in my heart—the CCP wants to brutally imprison its people like it has done to the people of Hong Kong. My visit to the island some years ago allowed me to see firsthand the vitality and courage of the people.

Of course, I've written about the dangers to the island in my 2015 "Crouching Tiger" book—it's the crown jewel of the First Island Chain and its loss would be a loss not just for millions of Taiwan citizens but democracy itself. Strategically, it would be a huge blow to the ability of the U.S. and the world to defend itself against a growing Communist Chinese navy.

It will take only one election in Taiwan that goes wrong to allow the CCP to take the island without firing a shot. Strategically, Taiwan must become a porcupine and a master of asymmetric warfare defense—sea mines and small submarines at the vanguard to counter the massive CCP armada and missile barrages.

One clear and present danger to Taiwan right now is the drawing down of the American arsenal in support of Ukraine and countering Iran—the U.S. is simply not ready to take on a new front. Another danger is the growing boldness the CCP is taking from the inability of the West to stop Russia. It's a fraught world—when I was in the White House, the world was far more peaceful.

NOTE: The interview was conducted by Adam Molon. He is the author of New Sentry on Substack.

HUCK POST 121:
Ships Passing in the Day
June 15, 2024—Day 89

Saturday was a mini disaster. The owner and CEO of Newsmax, Chris Ruddy, came to visit me. While I sat waiting for him at my minimum-security facility, he was standing in a long—very wrong—line waiting to get into the low-security prison.

Score another screwup for my prison consultant, who had the responsibility of giving Chris the right directions. Talk about a missed opportunity.

But it gets worse. Out of nowhere, my COVID comes back with a vengeance. As the day wears on, I get more and more of a racking cough, headache, eye/light sensitivity, and malaise that comes with disease.

This is the other way prison gets you. I'm stuck in a dorm with fifty other guys, sucking in stale air and eating poorly. Very difficult for the immune system to fight Communist China's Wuhan/Fauci virus off. (Yea, Tony is as responsible as Xi Jinping for the carnage inflicted upon the world.)

On the only bright sliver of sunshine around very dark storm clouds, my second major op-ed came out on the $5 billion prison question. Once again, it's a *Daily Caller* piece.

> **PETER NAVARRO: Biden's Bureau Of Prisons Is Botching Trump's First Step Act And Costing Taxpayers Billions**
> I am in prison because I chose the defense of our constitutional separation of powers and George Washington's doctrine of executive privilege over my own personal freedom.
>
> Behind my prison walls, I have uncovered one of the great hidden scandals of the Biden administration. This is the refusal of Biden's Bureau of Prisons to implement President Donald Trump's First Step Act (FSA), signed by the president in 2018 while I was in the White House. This delay is costing American taxpayers billions, increases the rate of recidivism and crime and cruelly delays returning inmates to their families and jobs.
>
> President Trump designed the First Step Act to address an

epidemic of overly harsh sentences that was spawned in the 1990s by then-Sen. Joe "Mandatory Minimum" Biden. Its basic premise is that it is possible to be "tough on crime" while having a "smart on crime" strategy to not permanently destroy lives.

To address this excessive sentencing issue, the First Step Act features earned time credits (FTCs) that can be earned through good behavior, productive activity, and participation in inmate programming to reduce recidivism. These FTCs are earned at the rate of 10 days per month in the first six months and 15 days a month thereafter for minimum and low-risk inmates.

These FTCs are first applied for up to one year of sentence reduction–that is, earlier release. Additionally, FTCs then accelerate an inmate's transfer from prison into "pre-release" custody–to a halfway house and/or electronically monitored home confinement, both of which cost taxpayers substantially less than imprisonment.

Here's the Bureau of Prison's problem: Instead of projecting inmate FTCs as its own 2022 Program Statement requires, the BOP continues to rely on an antiquated "earn as you go" algorithm that vastly undercounts inmate FTCs. As a result, virtually every one of the more than 60,000 First Step Act eligible inmates will suffer from pre-release and release delays that range from three months to twelve months or more, depending on the length of the sentence.

These delays involve real people with real families enduring real suffering. For example, Dr. Arman Abovyan should have entered a halfway house four months ago; yet "Doc" will likely be in prison for six to twelve months more. That's not just tens of thousands of dollars down the taxpayer drain paying for Doc's "room and board." Doc won't be earning six figures and paying tens of thousands of dollars in income taxes either.

And how about the cruel and unusual punishment being meted out to the 80-year-old, wheel-chair-bound Delmer Gowing. This distinguished Vietnam War veteran, who bunks one bed down from me, should have been released 14 months ago and in a halfway house two years ago!

Conspicuous in its absence is any effort of either the "Backwards on Purpose" BOP or Department of Justice (DOJ) to estimate the costs of such delays. To the contrary. In the latest First Step Act Annual Report (April 2023), the DOJ noted: "As was the case in the last report, it is too soon to assess cost savings."

With a hand calculator in prison, I have informally estimated that the BOP's failure to implement FTCs costs the taxpayer anywhere between $1.5 billion and $3 billion for the more than 60,000 FSA-eligible inmates. Add to this as an indirect cost another one-half to one billion dollars in foregone tax revenues from keeping inmates in prison past their pre-release and release dates rather than returning them to the work force where they could otherwise have tax-paying jobs.

Finally, there is at least another one-half to one billion dollars in tax expenditures providing Food Stamps, housing subsidies, and other forms of welfare to struggling wives and children of inmates deprived of the timely return of spouses who could otherwise help support them.

House Judiciary Committee Chairman Jim Jordan invited BOP Director Colette Peters to testify before Congress on these and other matters, but she has refused. It is time, however, to put a subpoena in Peters' hands. It is also time for the House to immediately pass a resolution demanding President Joe Biden's BOP faithfully and fully implement President Donald Trump's First Step Act.

If my imprisonment winds up saving American taxpayers billions of dollars, reducing the rate of recidivism, and making inmates' families whole again, my prison journey may turn out to have been worth it–if not for me and my family, at least for this nation.

Peter Navarro served for four years in the Trump White House as manufacturing czar. His new book, The New MAGA Deal, *is the unofficial Deplorables Guide to the Trump 2024 campaign platform.* (www.newmagadeal.com)

HUCK POST 122:
His Bernie Madoff Poop Don't Stink
June 16, 2024—Day 90

Now come the ballads of Big Mike, Boris, Mr. T., Ron, and Carl . . .

So, small-hospital owner Big Mike comes into the prison on a charge of inflating lab bills to serve a couple of years' stretch. He comes in at the start of a three-month lockdown where his commissary spending is limited to $50 a month; and he needs a size 15 walking shoe. Yes, Big Mike is BIG.

The commissary actually *has* a pair of sneakers in stock in his size, but the shoes cost more than his single month allotment and they won't let him buy them. This is despite repeated requests to the warden for a waiver. So, for three long months, Big Mike is forced to walk around in a size 12 pair of sandals with toes and heels dangling over the edges and his feet on gout fire.

Meanwhile, Boris the Russian has terminal cancer and keeps everyone up half the night with his coughing. He's repeatedly been denied compassionate release, and he'll die in prison as surely as it will snow every winter in Moscow.

Then there's Mr. T. He went out for chemo for his prostate cancer and never should have come back. Yet, here he is. Why is this dude not home and off the taxpayer dole?

Ron has a PSA that has been trending up *sharply*. But he can't get a new PSA test after more than a year to see if he is getting prostate cancer because any higher PSA reading would require an expensive biopsy.

The question I keep asking myself is *Why are these people STILL here?*

In fact, I can think of only one guy in my dorm who damn well *should* die here. That's the mini Bernie Madoff a few bunks down. His greed destroyed people's lives and families; ergo, I have *zero* sympathy.

And any shred of such possible sympathy left me the day I was over at the Visitor Center with my Sweet Pixie, and the Evil Ajemon forced all the inmates to stand up for more than twenty minutes for a random count.

Instead of getting up with the rest of us, Bernie Jr. just sat there and kept talking to his wife. His message was clear: My poop don't stink. I don't belong here with you criminals.

The puck you don't. Rot here, (not) my brother, and none of your fellow inmates will care. Got that off my chest.

PIXIE POST 22:
Pale Shadows
June 16, 2024—Day 90

Pixie here, and my Huck looked a bit pale this weekend. He said he thinks the bad food is affecting him, giving him low energy. Maybe it's a COVID hangover, too.

And I am a bit sad because he says he feels brain fog due to lack of nutrition. The only fresh food he gets is an occasional apple.

He says he can think okay and still remember what he needs to, but he tells me everything is just moving a little slower.

It's bad enough they take his freedom. They shouldn't take his health.

How did we let our America get this far deep into weaponized injustice, bad decisions, bad people in high positions, and prisons that take from you more than just your freedom and time?

HUCK POST 123:
A Sharp Rebuke and Rape Reminder
June 17, 2024—Day 91

> *Half of both inmate-on-inmate and staff-on-inmate sexual*
> *victimization incidents occurred in an area not under video surveillance.*
> —Bureau of Justice Statistics

Prison is a very dangerous place. I forgot that for a moment last night, and I quickly got a friendly, funny, but sharp reminder—from an inmate who took exception to my stroll out the dorm door over to the dispenser to fill up my water bottle.

My prison sin was to do so in my boxer shorts which fall to about two inches above the knee, rather than to be fully dressed in a proper set of shorts which fall right to the knee. The quick response was, "Put some clothes on, son" from one of the veterans.

As I immediately turned back into the door, he reminded me, "It's prison."

As I thought about this incident, I thought about the risks of something far worse. Here I was in a dorm where the first rule is that there is safety in numbers. Yet, if an attack came—the all-too-common rape or, in my case, the assassination of a Trump guy in a contract hit (don't raise your eyebrows, that shit's real)—it would come in a remote area of the prison that I would stupidly venture into.

I realized in that moment that the biggest risk I was taking was in my nightly visits to the rec center where the email terminals were. The place is at a corner of the facility, it's poorly lit, and there's only one guard at night who just sits in his office, probably reading or sleeping.

It would be a simple matter for one or more guys to slip in after me, have one or more guys guard the door, and do whatever the puck they were going to do.

No witnesses. Just a dead or broken and maybe defiled body.

A sobering thought as I drifted off into sleep thinking *Be more careful*.

HUCK POST 124:
Coughing My Way to an End Game
June 18, 2024—Day 92

From various facilities in all parts of the country, medical personnel are reporting an increasing number of cases of stubborn respiratory illnesses similar to this: 'Many sick people here with respiratory and deep, deep coughs. Went out (medical procedure) and over half the staff in face masks. Fearful memories. I have been horribly sick for over a week but no worse. There will NOT be any testing here (of the upper respiratory complaints), medical states.' No tests means no reports to Central Office, another version of "nothing to see here–move along."'
—Derek Gilna, *Federal Legal News*

I became a big fan of Derek Gilna, and his newsletter, by the way, during my prison stay. He just tells it like it is.

Anyway, after three days mostly flat on my back coughing my lower back and brains out, I woke up this Tuesday morning with a very clear vision of my prison endgame. With twenty-nine days now to go, I have more to do.

As a matter of old business, I have some final chapters to draft for my book about my legal journey—to be published after my appeal finally runs it course. I had expected to finish these chapters while I was released pending appeal—but the evil Mehta had other ideas.

As the main matter of *new* business, I have to set up the protocol for the inmates here at Miami to file timely protests regarding any delays in either their release to a halfway house or final release to freedom.

This is the good First Step Act strategy I've been working on, and I finally figured out how to do it. It's a two-part strategy.

First, I've drafted a "Warden Letter" that I will personally deliver to the warden a week from Thursday. The letter provides an exhaustive compilation of BOP policies with regard to the First Step Act and then illustrates how the BOP bureaucracy is ignoring its own policy.

The letter ends with a reference to a "Warden Override." This override, which was memorialized in testimony before Congress of BOP Director

Collette Peters, should empower the warden to effect change from the local prison level up.

Of course, I doubt if he will. Yet, it's worth a try.

That said, the broader purpose of the Warden's Letter is to allow inmates to *cite it* in their complaints, and therefore cite BOP policy in support of their requests.

That's the second document that I've drafted. It's a form letter that inmates can use to submit their requests for a proper accounting of their First Step Act credits, and this form letter can be customized by each inmate for his particular case.

I harbor no illusions about the warden actually acting to use his Warden's Override to order the correct projections of FSA time credits (FTC) and then further order the timely prerelease or release of inmates. Warden Huett is nothing if not a cautious and company man.

No, I'm simply a realist who sees this strategy as opening the door to a class action suit which may spread like wildfire, not just through the Miami prison, but throughout the broader prison system.

My ace in the hole here is the aforementioned Derek Gilna, the editor of the *Federal Legal News*. If he publishes the Warden's Letter and inmate form letter and publishes the strategy, inmates at other prisons may join the cause.

This will put internal pressure on the BOP; and a win here will be the long delayed release of the BOP's conditional maximum FTC calculation, which will force a proper accounting of FTC time credits—and thereby trigger thousands of earlier releases and prereleases.

Of course, to make sure it all happens, I'm sending the Warden's Letter to both the House and Senate Judiciary Committees; and once I am free of this hellhole, I will lobby hard for the requisite charges.

That will be the best I can do. I'm pretty sure it will be good enough to resolve what is indeed a $5 billion BOP scandal.

The next postcard is a copy of the Warden's Letter. You'll see exactly what I'm up to after you've read it.

HUCK POST 125:
The Warden's Letter
June 19, 2024—Day 93

Memo to: Warden G. Huett

From: Peter Navarro, Inmate 04370-510

Re: Request Use of Warden's Override To Implement BOP FSA Policy

On December 21, 2018, former President Donald Trump signed the First Step Act (FSA). A primary goal of this landmark prison reform legislation is to reduce the rate of recidivism while lowering the taxpayer costs associated with over sentencing.

As noted in the FSA: "[A]n eligible inmate who successfully participates in Evidence-Based Recidivism Reduction (EBRR) Programs or Productive Activities (PA) that are recommended based on the inmate's risk and needs assessment may earn FSA Time Credits [FTC] to be applied toward pre-release custody or early transfer to supervised release." [Section 523.40(b)] In its November 18, 2022 Program Statement, the BOP describes how FTCs should be calculated: "[T]he Bureau will calculate an inmate's PRD [Projected Release Date] by assuming the inmate will remain in earning status through his or her sentence, including while in pre-release custody."

The Office of Attorney General's First Step Annual Report to Congress (April 2023) elaborates on the BOP's 2022 Program Statement and thereby further clarifies how FTCs should be counted over the lifecycle of incarceration and prerelease custody: "[T]he policy specifies that the BOP will calculate and award time credits for the full incarceration period [including time spent in a halfway house or home confinement.] This statement is further corroborated by a November 20, 2023, First Step Act Admission and Orientation (A&O) Addendum. Specifically, under the heading "Do FTCs change my Home Confinement Eligibility Date (HCED)" in this unpaginated document, there is a graphical depiction of the proper method of projecting FTCs.

The Attorney General's Report further asserts that the method of projecting FTCs described in the Report is already in full use by BOP personnel, including (presumably) case managers, unit teams, and the RRC/HC bureaucracy: "Earned time credits are now calculated at the initial stages of the individual's sentence with the presumption that the earned credits [FTC] will accrue throughout the term of incarceration." Regrettably, and at great cost to taxpayers and inmates alike, the Office of the Attorney General's claim is false: The BOP is not projecting and calculating FTCs as its own policy requires and as the Office of the Attorney General claims it is doing. Instead, as I have learned first hand behind these prison walls, case managers and unit teams are forced to continue to rely on an antiquated "earn FTCs as you go" algorithm that significantly undercounts FTCs.

The extraordinary result of this violation of the BOP's own policy—and FSA law—is this: Virtually every one of the more than 60,000 FSA-eligible inmates in the BOP system is facing, or will face, costly delays in both their prerelease to RRC/HC custody and/or final release to freedom or supervised release and thereby suffer irreparable harm.

The BOP's failure to properly project and count FTCs has been acknowledged in an equally extraordinary December 7, 2023, memo from two middle level bureaucracies within the Department of Justice—The Residential Reentry Management Branch and the Correctional Programs Branch. This Memorandum for Residential Reentry Managers and Correctional Programs Regional Administrators is extraordinary because it directly overrides FSA policy set at the very top by BOP Director Colette Peters even as it directly contradicts the assertions of the Office of the Attorney General's FSA Annual Report regarding FTC counting. Specifically, this Memorandum explicitly warns unit teams at the prison level "not to attempt to calculate the number of time credits not yet earned." This warning appears to be given for two reasons.

First, the Memorandum acknowledges that the rollout of the long promised but never delivered "Conditional Maximum FTC Calculator" is still "pending." I note here that this is an absurd delay; the programming for such a calculator could be done in a matter of weeks as the arithmetic involved can be done with a hand calculator.

Second, the Memorandum also acknowledges that while "RRM offices are striving to meet the requirements of the FSA . . . contract pre-release space is limited." In other words, these two middle level bureaucracies are directly overriding BOP policy and contradicting the Office of the Attorney General simply because these bureaucracies haven't properly planned for, and provided, sufficient halfway house capacity to achieve full compliance with the FSA. This is as absurd as it is costly.

Inmates and their families—as well as taxpayers—should not be forced to bear the burden of such a monumental bureaucratic failure. Indeed, the most burdensome response to "limited" pre-release space is keeping inmates in prison at a cost of $55,000 per head per year. In contrast, the least burdensome alternative for both taxpayers and inmates is to send inmates directly to electronically monitored home confinement, which costs a small fraction of incarceration and allows these inmates to work, pay taxes, and reunite with their families.

To understand the fiscal and moral implications of the BOP's failure to follow either its own policy or FSA law, consider an FSA-eligible inmate in a minimum risk category with a sentence of 60 months and no prior jail credit. Following the method of FTC calculation proscribed by BOP policy and described by the Office of the Attorney General, the inmate will earn 555 FTCs. 365 of these FTCs will be used for a one-year sentence reduction. The remainder must, by FSA law and BOP policy, be used for at least six months of RRC/HC placement.

In contrast, using the BOP's antiquated "earn as you go" algorithm (rather than the still "pending" Conditional Maximum FTC Calculator), and assuming the case manager submits the request for RRC/HC placement 90 days before the projected pre-release date under BOP policy, the inmate will earn only 330 FTCs. The inmate thereby loses a month of sentence reduction and all six months of RRC/HC placement due to the under-counting of FTCs, thereby wasting tens of thousands of taxpayer dollars—never mind the human misery involved.

Side Note: The SCA still provides for six months of home confinement, per the law. Note further that case managers routinely tell inmates at FPC Miami that as soon as they sub-mit a case, the Residential Reentry bureaucracy stops counting FTCs—another clear violation of BOP policy, and a violation that handcuffs local case managers.

Writ large, the costs of the delays from undercounting FTCs in the pre-release and/or release of inmates across the FSA-eligible prison population—as noted, a population of more than 60,000 inmates—may be as high as $5 billion while these delays inflict irreparable harm on the inmates and their families.

These billions of dollars in costs include: (1) the direct cost of incarceration past projected pre-release and release dates; (2) the indirect cost associated with foregone tax revenues from keep-ing inmates in prison past their pre-release and release dates and out of the workforce; and (3) the tax expenditures associ-ated with the provision of food stamps, housing subsidies, and other welfare programs to the families of inmates deprived of their breadwinners.

These numbers are not statistical abstractions. Here, at FPC Miami, I've reviewed the current computation sheets of dozens of inmates; and, to my shock and surprise, far too many of my fellow inmates should have ALREADY been released to a half-way house or home confinement and even to supervised release. This is irreparable harm on an unprecedented scale across the diaspora of BOP prisons housing FSA-eligible inmates. You as Warden, along with Camp Administrator Verdejo and the Unit Team, have a unique opportunity to do at the local level what the BOP's mid-level bureaucracies are refusing to do: Fully and faith-fully implement the BOP's FSA policy as it has been set forth by Director Peters in the November 2022 Program Statement and the Office of the Attorney General in the 2023 Annual FSA Report to Congress.

Clearly, you, as Warden, have the full authority to lead this innovative, grassroots effort here at FPC Miami. In her testimony of September 13, 2023, before the Senate Judiciary Committee, Director Peters gave a full-throated endorsement of the BOP's Program Statement of November 2022 and promised to "maximize an individual's ability to earn and apply [FTC] credits." To that end, Director Peters authorized a "Warden's Override" to "provide an extra layer of scrutiny." With this Warden's Override function, Director Peters has thereby empowered you and other wardens within the BOP system to take all necessary steps to ensure the BOP's FSA policy is being fully and faithfully implemented.

In the coming weeks and months, FPC inmates may be coming to you with requests to ensure their timely prerelease and release dates as determined by BOP policy and a proper projection of FTCs. I urge you to work with your case managers and the Unit Team and use your Warden's Override to promptly respond to these inmate requests. I further urge you to order inmates immediately to home confinement in cases where the Residential Reentry bureaucracy indicates "scarce" halfway house capacity rather than continue to warehouse inmates at FPC who otherwise should be out of incarceration, into prerelease custody, into the work force, and back with their families.

Finally, I urge you to send out an urgent request to the leadership of the BOP to bring the Conditional Maximum FTC Calculator immediately on line. Further delay is not an option—too many billions of dollars and too many lives are at stake.

cc. Camp Administrator Verdejo
Director Colette Peters
Members of Senate Judiciary Committee
Members of House Judiciary Committee
Congressman Matt Gaetz
Derek Gilna

HUCK POST 126:
My Lionel Ritche Convention Speech Hook
June 20, 2024—Day 94

I've got to give you the sing-along. I don't have a hook . . . it took me
probably another month of just walking around my house and everywhere
trying to find out what is the hook to "come on and sing along?"
—Lionel Ritchie on writing his hit, "All Night Long"

I've spent eight days so far working on what will be no more than an eight-minute speech at the Republican National Convention—still a big question if I will be allowed on stage.

But as Thomas Jefferson said, "I would have written you a shorter letter if I had the time."

The good news is that sometime during sunrise as I walked the track, the "hook" for the speech finally hit me. It was like a Newton's apple smack in the mouth.

It just came out like the first line and hook of every great Lionel Ritchie song—credit Lionel with the concept of the hook.

I went to prison so you won't have to.

Ka-Boom!

[*Author's Note: Little did I know that this would become the title of this book!*]

HUCK POST 127:
My Longest Day in Prison
June 21, 2024—Day 95

I will never feel more free
Than when they put those leg irons on me.
—Inmate Johnny B. Goode's Song

That's how I started my favorite day of the year—the summer solstice—
with a big laugh at breakfast. With that wisecrack, Johnny B. Goode reveled
in the prospect of getting on a bus next week for a new prison and his long-
awaited chance to take the Residential Drug Abuse Program or "RDAP."

To take RDAP, Johnny will have to get on a big bus with a gaggle of
other inmates. They will indeed strap him in with leg irons. And wherever
they will send him, it won't be in a straight line.

If it's the Pensacola, Florida, RDAP, they may route Johnny through
Tallahassee. If it's Butner in North Carolina, they may route him all the way
through Oklahoma.

Whatever hell Johnny will go through, it will be worth it because completing RDAP will get him a full year off his sentence.

What's perverse about the whole damn thing, as I previously explained,
is that only inmates with a history of drug or alcohol abuse qualify for the
program. So, if you have lived a clean and sober life, you can count on an
extra year of prison—no RDAP for you, you teetotaler.

Who thinks this stuff up?

HUCK POST 128:
Brother in Arms, Brother in Jeopardy
June 22, 2024—Day 96

If I ever had to trust one guy with my life while riding the Trump train, the guy at the very top of my list would be Dave Bossie.

I first met him at Trump Tower during the 2016 campaign. Dave was CIO and the deputy campaign manager; and over the years, we've become brothers-in-arms.

What frosted me about Dave was how he had been treated during the White House years. If Dave had been made chief of staff or chief of operations, we never would have lost the 2020 race. He would've been our North Star and never have allowed the kind of RINO trash I had had to fight in the West Wing for four long years.

At any rate, Dave came to see me this Saturday, and he had already proved invaluable in getting several of my op-eds published. The mission today was to bring me news about whether I'd be allowed to speak at the convention.

Dave was running the whole damn shebang, he was doing his best to get me on the program, the Boss kept saying yes, but there was a lot of pushback and backstabbing from nameless faces with too much power inside the Republican National Committee.

For me, this was deja vu all over again—the same kind of infighting and backstabbing I had had to deal with for years in the West Wing.

As I have told you, desire is suffering. And I'm now rethinking whether I even want to go to Milwaukee for such an anticlimax.

The other sobering aspect of the visit was news about Brother Bannon. He was to report to Danbury prison in nine short days.

Dave put the odds of the Supreme Court letting Steve out on appeal at zero, and in September, Steve would be moved to the hell of Riker's Island to be prosecuted by Trump-hater Alvin Bragg and presided over by even bigger Trump-hater Judge Juan Marchan.

The whole shebang was guaranteed to be a kangaroo court in which

Dave reckoned Steve could get at least seven years, not in a Club Fed federal prison but in the jackal-eat-jackal world of the New York state prison system.

In the worst-case scenario, in nine days, Steve's life would be effectively over. He would enter the system, do his time in Danbury, get convicted in a kangaroo court in New York City, get slapped with a ten to fifteen sentence and die in prison—or come out in his eighties a shell of a man.

Politics is a harsh mistress. Prison is a bitch.

PIXIE POST 23:
A Manilow Weekend in Johnny Cash's Miami

June 23, 2024—Day 97

Pixie here, and one of the greatest moments of this sunny Sunday, except for seeing Huck in the prison we share, is when I am in the car with Dale after my last wave goodbye, and Dale puts on the Barry Manilow classic, "Weekend In New England."

> *Last night I waved goodbye now it seems years*
> *I'm back in the city where nothing is clear*
> *But thoughts of me holding you bringing us near*
> *And tell me when will our eyes meet when can I touch you*
> *When will this strong yearning end*
> *And when will I hold you again*

Dale knows it's one of my favorites, and I start to cry; but it's a smiling cry because it reminds me of how my Huck and I used to dance to it—and will dance again to it. How he will be holding me and bringing me near.

But for now it's "Weekends in Miami." When can I touch you without angering a guard? When will I hold you again except at the start and end of each visit?

Where's Johnny Cash to write a prison love song when you need him?

HUCK POST 129:
The Prison Guard Hustle
June 23, 2024—Day 97

The thing that bothers me most about this place is that everybody's got a hustle—inmates, guards, it doesn't matter. They're all hustling.
—Inmate M

Prisonomics 101A starts with the observation that the budget of each prison depends on the number of inmates it imprisons. So, the incentive is to slow walk the release dates of prisoners as much as possible.

While this is good for the prison bureaucrats and guards, holding inmates beyond their legal "expiration date" hurts taxpayers.

Remember: it costs taxpayers $40,000 to $50,000 a year to incarcerate an inmate.

The next observation has to do with the prison guards. There are simply too few of them for at least two reasons—I'm not sure which is more important.

First, while the Biden White House and Democrat-RINO Congress might be quick to shower Ukraine with, say, a $60 billion appropriation, the BOP budget itself is woefully underfunded. So, it's difficult to hire sufficient guards at competitive salaries.

But, second, a shortage of guards leads to a lot more overtime pay for existing guards, so the guard union never pushes too, too hard for more hiring—it's classic cartel behavior.

Of course, this guard shortage further exacerbates the budget problems. Over time (pun intended), it's more expensive to pay overtime to the guards than simply use those funds to hire more guards.

Of course, too, the overworked guards eventually get burnt out and treat the inmates more like shit, and lower guard morale is part of the collateral damage.

Then there is the problem of lower pay scales for BOP guards than, say, those of competing bureaucracies like Customs and Border Patrol, the Transportation Security Administration, and, in the Holy Grail of law enforcement jobs, the FBI and Secret Service.

Because of the inability to compete in the law enforcement market, the best BOP guards are hard to hold onto in a tight labor market, so the best and the most qualified tend to move up and out quickly to greener pastures. That leaves the not so best and not so bright behind to run the place.

Meanwhile, the older guards don't want to lose any pension benefits, so they stick around. But at least some then fall prey to using their guard status to supplement their income in all manner of hustles available on the prison-guard side.

It may be as simple as turning a blind eye to the contraband trade for a small consideration. It may be an even more nefarious active role in the smuggling of phones or vapes or drugs or alcohol into the prison.

It may be what is considered among guards as the occasional rightful expropriation of fresh beef or chicken intended for the inmates so they can hold a barbecue or a holiday at the facility adjacent to the prison. Or maybe the food winds up in a trunk to take home.

Either way, it all begins with a belief based on perceived unfair wages that it's "fair" for guards to supplement their incomes in these ways.

Which begs the question: What message does this kind of small and large corruption send to inmates who are supposed to be learning how to follow the rules on the outside?

HUCK POST 130:
The Inmate Risk-Reward Calculus
June 24, 2024—Day 98

There are no rules in Changi except the ones you make for yourself.
—King Rat

The first rule of Prisonomics 101B for inmates is that most are in prison because they failed to adequately assess the risk-reward ratio when they chose a life of crime. Yes, dealing dope, bilking investors, and cheating the government can all pay a ton of money. Yet, these riches can pale in comparison to the prison price that may be paid.

Would you take a million dollars right now in exchange for a year of your life? Five years? Ten years? What's the equilibrium price in the market for crime?

In the best cases, after a jolt of prison, inmates will realize they must play the long game for the rest of their lives. Instead of a life of crime, over the longer term, they can channel their aggression and entrepreneurial skills into hard work to make even more money legally and more safely than running kilos of coke, defrauding little old ladies, or just plain robbing folks.

These are the lucky ones who have this "I ain't going back" epiphany. Back out on the street, they decide the juice from crime is not worth the squeeze of possible prison, the risk is simply not worth the reward.

And then there are the worst cases, the chronic recidivates. In my Miami prison, the head counselor, Jason Cooke, and I would talk about this all the time.

He'd say he could look at and talk with a guy for five minutes and know whether the guy would be right back in the joint shortly after he left.

I could certainly see his point, as some of the inmates seemed like they were born with "loser" on their foreheads with little or no awareness of even the concept of risk-reward.

As an aside, I saw this all the time out in the outdoor pavilion playing eight ball at night with the guys. I'm a decent player, but I could often beat guys far better than I because I would play the game *defensively* when I didn't have a good shot, effectively blocking my opponent's next shot.

Most guys I played with, however, would just let it rip. They'd either scratch on the eight ball, and I'd win outright, or they'd break the table wide open so I could run it and win. For them, the concept of managing risk and assessing odds was simply foreign to them.

What wasn't foreign, however, to the vast cadre of inmates I rubbed shoulders with was "the hustle." Inside, prison inexorably teaches you to hustle *and* lie—particularly if you don't have a dime to your name when you first walk through the barbed-wired gates.

As in James Clavell's classic *King Rat*, two types of prisoners will enter the gate—the "haves" who will have plenty of money to buy what they need at the commissary and hire a small army of servants to wash and iron their clothes and cook their food; and the "have nots" who will do this work in exchange for commissary food and who may also engage in riskier ventures like dealing cell phones, vapes, and liquor.

It is these have-not folks who are the most likely to recidivate.

These types of folks are of course engaging in exactly the same kind of risky behavior that got them into the prison to begin with. And if they get caught, they will be given "shots" that will send them either temporarily or permanently over to the low-security prison—and add months and perhaps years to their sentence.

Some people learn. Some people never learn. That's why we *have* prisons.

HUCK POST 131:
Rough Snitch Justice
June 25, 2024—Day 99

*Day by day, I struggle to maintain not only my strength
but my sanity. It's all a blur.*
—Chris Taylor (played by Charlie Sheen), *Platoon*

One of the most memorable scenes in cinema is the helicopter's eye view of the Willem Dafoe character in Oliver Stone's masterpiece, *Platoon*, being run down and cornered like a rat by the Viet Cong. And it was an alleged rat that I myself would see cornered in a chaotic morning at the prison reminiscent of that movie scene.

This chaos was dark fallout and brutal payback for the gestapo raid by the SIS the week earlier where the J-dorm, heavily populated with Puerto Rican inmates, had lost a good bit of its contraband vapes and cell phones to what was widely believed to be a snitch.

I don't know if the Puerto Rican kid who went on the run from his own kind that morning was the snitch. I do know that, while some people wear their fecklessness on their sleeves, others wear it on their face.

This kid's face was a feckless mess. He'd been a flyweight boxer in the PR for a time and had lost some of his teeth. He'd also had the stuffing beaten out of him in the low-security prison several times before coming to the camp.

That morning, he knew another beating (or worse) was coming because he had been tagged by his compatriots as the SIS snitch.

So, in a panic, the kid had run and begged the guards to move him over to the SHU in the low-security prison for extra protection.

When the guards refused, he had snapped and bolted to the exit, knowing full well he'd get what he wanted, plus more than a few bruises for his insolence.

A couple of guards did indeed run him down, the alert went out, ten more guards swarmed to the takedown, and as I had my *Platoon* flashback, the kid was roughly hauled away while we locked back up for the morning. It's your next movie, Oliver—or maybe mine.

As a coda here, the irony of all of this was that "the kid" in question was none other than Luis, who was featured in my March 20 postcard. Recall here that Luis was the young gent who said I was "okay" because I hadn't "snitched" on Trump.

Now, Luis was on the run for snitching himself—and he'd never get another good night's sleep in prison again unless he was in solitary confinement.

HUCK POST 132:
Political Prison Math
June 26, 2024—Day 100

In the morning, I'm sitting in my chair scribbling on a pad regarding my appeal, and Juan comes up to me to thank me for my help navigating his prison waters. He was getting out tomorrow, so he wanted to buy me a pint of ice cream at the commissary as thanks, but I told him, "You can thank me just by making sure you never come back."

Then I asked him to remind me how long his "bid" was. He says, "Five months." One more month than me.

Then I asked him how long he has been in and he says, "Two and a half months." So I do the math.

He got here *after* I arrived, has a *longer* sentence–it was wire fraud if you're curious—and will leave the prison, albeit for a halfway house, almost a month before I'm released.

It's just darkly funny how I'm getting so thoroughly nailed to the cross of Never-Trump politics. Don't cry for me Argentina.

HUCK POST 133:
The Chicken Calendar
June 27, 2024—Day 101

So, I'm talking to Santi last night, and he tells me that by luck of our draw, he and I are going to be released on the same day, July 17, and it's only "three chicken days" away. Huh?

Turns out Santi is not the only inmate at Miami FCI who measures time by the consensus best meal of every week—a full chicken thigh and leg every Thursday at lunch. So, by Santi's count, to get to July 17, we've only got three more chicken days. Seems like a short time when you think of it that way.

Maybe if Donald Trump gets reelected, I'll ask him to declare every Thursday National Chicken Day. Or maybe we can just move away from the Gregorian calendar to the chicken calendar. Or maybe judges should start sentencing prisoners not in years, but in chicken days.

Or maybe I'm just getting punchy from being in too long. But it tickles my funny bone. That's why they call it prison.

BTW, I wish Santi all the best. A fine, personable, and smart young man with three kids and dreams who just did something really stupid.

P.S. So I asked Santi if for some reason they don't serve chicken on Chicken Day, will we have to stay an extra week? He laughed.

HUCK POST 134:
Bannon Supremed
June 28, 2024—Day 102

*The Supreme Court on Friday rejected a bid to delay a prison sentence
for longtime Trump ally Steve Bannon as he appeals his conviction
for defying a subpoena in the congressional investigation into the
U.S. Capitol insurrection.*
—AP News

The proverbial bad day at BlackRock. As they did with my case, the Supreme Court rejected Steve Bannon's last-ditch appeal for release pending appeal.

This was surprising news because one of the judges on Steve's three-judge appeals panel at the DC Circuit had dissented over the denial of Steve's request to stay out of prison until his full appeal was heard at the Supreme court.

This Appeals Court judge indicated he thought it was highly likely that the precedential case that had played a key role in putting both Steve and I in prison—Licavoli v. U.S.—would likely be overturned by the Supreme Court.

If that happened, both Steve's case and mine would almost certainly be overturned on appeal. Yet, with this news, Steve would be forced to serve his prison term—as I was doing now.

With this news, I was almost as bummed as Steve, as my lawyers would have immediately filed a habeas petition, and I would have been home by Monday.

The next day I was to meet my erratic prison consultant at the Visitor Center to receive some legal documents, and he told me he was meeting Steve and Bernie Kerik for dinner that night and would surrender Steve to the Danbury prison on Monday.

As bad as I've had it, Danbury is going to be just as tough for Steve. And according to the consultant, they are watching Steve like a hawk already.

The consultant tells me here that he had an inmate try to buy a bunch of stuff for Steve at commissary in preparation for his visit, but the prison censors read the email and clamped right down.

It's going to be a long four months for my Brother Bannon. That's why they call it prison.

[*Author's Note: We lost Bernie to illness a few months into Trump's new term. What a loss.*]

HUCK POST 135:
Two Missions Possible
June 29, 2024—Day 103

With less than twenty days to go—two chicken days—I've got two missions to complete before I leave Lake Prisonbegon.

The first mission is to provide my attorney Stanley Woodward with a working master draft of the appeal he does not have time to write but which is due in twelve days.

I love Stanley, he does beautiful work, but he always waits to the last minute.

Not this frigging time! This appeal is for all the marbles, and the rough draft he left with me is a pale shadow of what must be our future self.

So, with all the time I have here, I've proposed that I write the master draft using the bones from his rough draft, that my deadline is Wednesday, and that I will damn well will hit that mark.

Then Stanley will visit on July 8 or 9, we'll go over the final, and that will be that.

But I wouldn't bet on it. Let's see what happens.

My other mission is to leave the guys here with all the ammunition they will need to press their cases forward so they are released on a timely basis. To that end, my prison consultant came for a visit and dropped off sixty copies of the Warden's Letter, along with sixty form letters that can be customized for each inmate.

We'll start submitting requests to the warden, build a record, and then hit them with a class action suit that should spread like wildfire through the BOP system—there are over sixty thousand First Step Act eligible inmates that might be interested.

All systems on this are a go.

PIXIE POST 24:
As the Prison World Turns
June 30, 2024—Day 104

Pixie here, and this week's Sunday visit provided the added bonus of a soap opera episode. It's going right into the movie if they ever make one based on the scribbling of Pixie and Huck going to prison.

It starts out in the morning right at the top of the visit with me noticing that the *father* of my prison boyfriends, young nine-year old Malik and eight-year old Jamal, is sitting with *another* woman who is holding a young baby daughter no more than three in her arms. Malik and Jamal—as well as their own Baby Mama—are nowhere in sight. Until an hour later.

When Malik and Jamal do arrive on scene with their mother, hijinks ensue.

Pretty soon, the two mamas are going at it like cats in a cage— just heated words so far, no hair pulling. Daddy is standing off to the side sheepishly trying to figure out how his best laid plans of seeing his two apparent families secretly and separately got merged into one. And Fredericks the Guard—a sub for Ajemon that day—is surprisingly cool in light of the heat.

Eventually, things calm down and they all sit together like one big family. Daddy, the two mamas, Malik, Jamal, and baby daughter. More stuff you can't make up, but it was quite a show there for a while.

The tragedy, of course, is that the father, no more than twenty-five years old, already has three kids that he won't be able to support for at least another five years. That's going to be a whole lot of visits and by then the boys will be in high school and all sorts of stuff may go wrong.

As I am leaving at the end of the visit and Huck is walking with me over to the exit, Malik comes over and tugs on my sleeve and says, "Come meet my little sister." The innocence of the boy's voice not really knowing or caring about how and what is really going on, just wanting to give love and receive it too, and share it with me, is touching.

So, Huck and I go say hi to one and all, and it looks like, out of the love for the children (all three) even though from different moms, they were all going to find some peace, at least temporarily on this June day.

We leave with hugs from both Malik and Jamal. And off I skip out the door to Dale's chariot, with a goodbye salute from my Ever Huck.

HUCK POST 136:
Jail, Not Yale
June 30, 2024—Day 104

It's 8 a.m. Sunday morning, and I'm waiting outside the Visitor Center door for Ajemon the Hun to open up so I can see my Sweet Pixie, and there's a young man on crutches, and we strike up a conversation. Yet again, here in Prison Land, I'm aghast at his story.

He's an American-born son of Cuban immigrants, and his good old madre and padre had operated a health-care center that over-billed private insurers like Blue Cross. They were quintessential white-collar criminals, and each deserved the twenty-nine months sentence they had received. But what about this kid?

He freely admitted he had known about the fraud when he worked there. But he was only eighteen years old at the time, and I wonder why he had gotten six months in prison for it when probation seemed far more appropriate—even the prosecutor told him that, but unfortunately, Anthony had a son of a bitch of a hanging judge.

I had to wonder even more about the sentence after Anthony told me he had to withdraw from college to report to the prison—jail, not Yale (or even a community college), for him.

Once again, it all stirred up that "nature vs. nurture" debate in my head. In this debate, it was pretty clear that "nurture," or the lack thereof from his parents, had put Anthony in the slammer—hell, it was his own parents who had turned him out.

While I felt bad for the kid, his situation was also darkly comical to me in at least in one regard. While his sentence was six months and mine only four, he would also get out earlier than I would. That's because, unlike me, he was eligible for First Step Act early release credits because he had probation. Just one more case of just too funny prison math.

With that, the Visitor Center door opened, and he and I piled in to see our honeys. But the first thing I saw was not my Sweet Pixie but rather Ajemon shaking down a double-amputee old man in a wheelchair.

The guy was the uncle of one of the inmates and well into his seventies, maybe even eighties. He was probably a diabetic and he had two artificial legs under a set of baggy sweatpants that Ajemon thought the guy might be smuggling contraband in with.

So up went the sweats to expose the prosthetics and off went the artificial legs from their knee insertions. Grim sight indeed, enough to knot my stomach.

The only thing Ajemon found inside the prosthetics was yet another way he could humiliate someone. Ajemon, Ajemon, Ajemon.

BTW, did I mention that the day before, Ajemon had inserted himself between one of the strongest inmates in the camp and the guy's wife because the guy had gotten too close? Ajemon literally stepped on the inmate's toes in the process.

It's a common guard tactic—trying to provoke an inmate to an incident he can write up. This inmate didn't blink. But he did roll his eyes.

But that's why they call it prison.

HUCK POST 137:
Sisyphus or Peyton Manning
July 1, 2024—Day 105

So, I'm just at the end of my daily run, a leisurely three miles, I'm sweating like I got trapped in a steam room, and my entire body is covered in black specks that are gnats that died a horrible death drowning in my sweat, and I hear the guard on duty call my name over the loudspeaker—"Navarro, report to the office."

So, I hustle in dripping wet and the guard says to me that the warden and Verdejo want to see me. Finally, it's the long-delayed meet on the First Step Act delays that had been postponed twice last week.

I ask the guard to get back on the loudspeakers and order my partners in this mission, Doc and Eliot, to immediately report to the Visitor Room where the meeting will be held. And then I go towel off and get into a dry uniform.

We had done our homework, and I'm pleased with how my team is now able to do the FSA calculation for any inmate and is primed to start moving complaints through the system. Will we be Sisyphus rolling a ball uphill or Peyton Manning scoring inside the red zone?

The first thing we show the warden and Verdejo is a list of eleven inmates, each with a precise calculation of their prerelease to halfway house and release dates. Half of the poor schlepps should have been out months ago. The other half should be going to a halfway house in the next month or two, but that *won't* happen because the request hasn't even been made.

The next thing we hit them with is the Warden's Letter that summarizes the Bureau of Prisons policy on counting time credits, shows how much it is costing not to follow that policy, and describes a "Warden Override," which would allow the warden to break this logjam.

To the warden's credit, he totally understands the problem—he was a former case manager familiar with the calculations. But he faces the reality of a top-down bureaucracy which is really difficult to push upon.

My pitch is that I—meaning the team—am going to start flooding the system with requests for expedited release according to policy, and maybe that pressure will help him lobby the system above him. That's the best we can hope for at this point.

Of course, once I get out, I can then go up to Capitol Hill and lobby the members of the Judiciary Committee to push on BOP leadership to fix this $5 billion problem. The Holy Grail is forcing the BOP to finally release its update calculation that will accurately project prerelease and release dates *and* issue a new policy that if an inmate can't get into a halfway house because of capacity constraints, he must be sent into home confinement under electronic monitoring.

Once these two steps are taken, the floodgates should open. If I can pull that off, prison will have (almost) been worth it.

Spoiler Alert: I managed to actually get this done when I got out. Pretty damn good work if I do say so myself. DOGE fixed the calculator. The new BOP director fixed the policy.

HUCK POST 138:
Richie to the SHU
July 2, 2024—Day 106

Sad news today at dinner. One of the happiest and hardest-working inmates in the prison was whisked away to the punishment Special Housing Unit (SHU), likely never to be seen again. I had noticed Richie a few days earlier on his daily laps around the track, and he looked uncharacteristically down—I thought it was his shoulder acting up again.

He was a Colombian-Italian, an exotic mix, and he'd gotten into trouble running some Cali coke out of Colombia under family pressure. As a first-time offender, he seemed to have learned his lesson in prison and just wanted out, and he was a model inmate.

Besides serving as the prison photographer for inmate family visits, Richie had also completely renovated the softball field, which now, after years of dust, weeds, and neglect, regularly hosted evening softball games —Team Puerto Rico vs. Everyone Else.

Turns out Richie's kryptonite was a hot, bipolar, and vengeful wife who had filed fake spousal abuse reports on him. Because of one of her complaints, Richie had a pending charge against him, his lawyer had missed the court date which would have gotten the charge dismissed, a warrant had gone out for his arrest, and by the rules of the prison road, they had to scoop Richie up and put him in a higher security prison until it all got sorted out.

Just messy *and* tragic. Richie, we hardly knew ya.

HUCK POST 139:
I Prefer Ping-Pong to Beethoven
July 3, 2024—Day 107

So, if there is one guy in our dorm who makes everyone's skin crawl, it's got to be, let's call him "Abe the Jew." Please don't construe this as anti-Semitic. That's what everybody calls Abe because he wears his Jewness on his sleeve, as well as his head (yarmulke) and belt (the stringy things known as Tzitzit) and food (Kosher bags from the kitchen) . . . and never eats with anyone, even fellow Jews.

Every morning, as close to dawn as the opening of the track allows, Abe is out by the track in his prayer shawl with a coal miner's headlight on his head, reading the Torah aloud and rocking back and forth in whatever kind of rapture he can conjure up.

Then in the middle of the night, he does the same thing at a little table by the showers—at night, he silently mouths the scripture so no one beats the crap out of him for waking them up.

Watching his rituals, you get the idea that the guy just takes his faith very seriously. But really, you have to wonder what really goes on in this guy's head.

For starters, he's in prison for allegedly making millions bilking drug addicts and the government. Got a bit of his Old Testament justice, I guess.

But how does this man of deep faith square that faith with his criminal behavior? Ripping the government off. Messing people up on oxy. Bilking private health-care insurance. It's an enigma and a conundrum.

Anyway, what I found amusing about Abe is that when he's not rapturing through the Torah, he's up on his bed reading one ultraviolent Greg Iles novel after another.

I guess it makes sense. The whole thriller genre is Torah-Old Testament—good guys taking an eye for an eye, and a head for a head, rinse and repeat.

I can't read that violent crap anymore or watch violent movies—too much of that in the real world as it is.

At any rate, the thing that annoyed me most about Abe wasn't any of this. It was his two-hour evening interludes at the prison's piano, which happens to be in the same frigging room as the email computers.

If he were tickling out some jazz on the ivories or maybe a mellow rendition of "Blackbird," it would not affect my concentration. But with his Beethoven sheet music, Abe bangs those concertos out like a jackhammer tearing up asphalt. Jack Nicholson in *The Shining* comes to mind.

The only thing that came close to this noise and nonsense was the ping-pong played in the computer room. The table is set up right in the room not twenty paddle lengths away from the piano. If the ping-pong players are really good, the noise can be deafening. Plus, every once in a while, they'll bounce an errant ping-pong ball smash shot off your back or head.

But God bless those ping-pongers last night. I started doing some emails, and Abe comes in and starts banging away. I groan.

Then, ping-pongers come in a few minutes later and start banging away. But I don't groan.

Instead, it's music to my ears because the ping-pong symphony drowns out Abe's crappy Beethoven coming from an out-of-tune piano. The whole cacophony between the two competing noise orgies blends into a blissful white noise; and I can get back to work.

Did I mention that most of the white-collar Jewish inmates in my dorm got reduced sentences by snitching on each other and everyone else they could implicate? Reconcile that with the Torah, too, please. I don't get it.

HUCK POST 140:
Irony and Independence
July 4, 2024—Day 108

Spending Independence Day in prison has a touch of irony to it. Indeed, the only reason I'm *in* prison is because I sought to defend the Constitution which is the fountainhead of America's most sacred political holiday.

I alternate my day between various forms of exercise—basketball in the a.m., running in the afternoon, weights and push-ups/pull-ups in the early evening—with time in the computer room.

The first laugh of the day I got was at lunch. After months of the usual zero-star-rated starvation diet devoid of anything fresh, they hit us with the July 4th Lollapalooza—two cheeseburgers, a hot dog, French fries, and—drumroll please—two gigantic slices of watermelon.

Most of the guys devoured this prison feast in one sitting and then went to the dorm and into a sleep coma for the rest of the day. Me, I nibbled and then took the rest back to the barracks to eat for dinner—can't run around a track with that much food in ya.

The best part of the day turned out to be the night. It was balmy, with a slight breeze, and as I did my nightly stretches on a yoga mat beneath the stars, I was treated and feted to four different fireworks shows in four different directions—east over Miami Beach, northeast over the nearby zoo, and two other directions, locations unknown.

Incredibly, I was literally the only inmate actually outside watching this beautiful and inspiring spectacle. And I don't know why.

Maybe it really is a sad irony that each of the inmates feels even more their own loss of freedom on Independence Day.

HUCK POST 141:
On the Back Nine
July 5, 2025—Day 109

Once you're on the back nine, you start to think about the end of the round.
—Jim Nantz

Ah yes. The "back nine" as a metaphor for the coming end.

I'll be out of this hellhole in fourteen days, but who's counting? I'm on the glide path—the back nine as they say in golf metaphors—and I'll spend the rest of my bid tidying up loose ends.

That's my plan—unless some inmate sticks a shiv in me or some other prison catastrophe befalls. Hey, shit happens. That's why they call it prison.

At any rate, I had my last meeting and exit interview with my case manager. Good guy, good heart, but a company man who, at the end of the day, never bucks the system.

How else do you explain the fact that I should have been out of this place and put into home confinement almost a month ago if these bastards had simply followed the law? That's why they call it weaponized politics.

At any rate, in the category of "no good deed goes unpunished," my case manager tells me I can't walk out the door on July 17 in a T-shirt and gym shorts but will need to find some sweatpants.

This is really too damn funny. It's funny because just yesterday, I gave away my one pair of sweatpants, along with a big bag of excess winter clothing. Yep, no good deed goes unpunished.

Between now and July 17, my mission is clear. I need to work with my inmate team—Elliot, Doc, Josh, Gil, among others—on pushing complaints about delayed release into the system.

On that note, I came up with what may turn out to be a stroke of genius. The backstory here is that an inmate in Leavenworth, Kansas, filed a handwritten *pro se* habeas motion requesting emergency release because prison officials told him he had to stay in prison, even though under the First Step Act, he should be released *because* they didn't have any halfway house capacity—THE binding constraint now in the BOP system.

The judge, however, ruled in the inmate's favor and ordered him to be immediatey released. If they didn't have halfway house capacity, they had to send him to home confinement. As Steve Bannon loves to say, "KABOOM!"

So, I'm teaming up with Del Gowing, the eighty-year-old in a wheelchair, who is a damn fine lawyer, and we're going to write up a habeas petition using Doc as the perfect test—he should have been out two months ago to a halfway house.

Florida's 11th Circuit will be a tough nut to crack—we're not in Kansas anymore. But the other genius part of my idea is to use the just dropped "Chevron" decision by SCOTUS—the Supreme Court.

This Chevron decision will prevent agencies like the BOP from making up their own rules to subvert the intent of laws made by Congress—with the "makeup" here by the BOP being "keep 'em in prison if there's no halfway house capacity." So, let's see what happens.

Finally, in the wind down, I have to get the appeal of my own case in, due July 11. Stanley Woodward is supposed to show up on July 10 with a redline edit of the draft I sent him.

In the meantime, I hope I "par in" on the back nine, with maybe a birdie or two, if you get my golfing drift. We'll see.

HUCK POST 142:
The Tyranny of Forfeiture and Restitution
July 6, 2024—Day 110

The masses were burdened with such vast reparations that, like beasts
of burden, they collapsed under the load.
—Adolf Hitler, *Mein Kampf*

The [Versailles] treaty by overstepping the limits of the possible, has
in practice defeated its own ends. Nothing can then delay for long
that final civil war between the forces of Reaction and the despairing
convulsions of Revolution, before which the horrors of the late German
war will fade into nothing.
—John Maynard Keynes in *The Economic Consequences*
of the Peace (1919)

It's not often that you have two polar-opposite figures like Adolph Hitler and John Maynard Keynes agreeing. But the postcard I'm about to share has a grim analogy. To wit:

Just as the crushing reparations payments the victors imposed on Germany after World War I led to World War II, the often-crushing asset forfeiture and restitution payments that courts impose on inmates often ensure these inmates will return to a life of crime and thereby spike the rate of recidivism. As cases in point, many of the inmates I met had grim tales about the indentured servitude that arises from the onerous restitution burdens placed on them.

Under our asset forfeiture laws, the federal government has broad powers to seize assets at the time of an *arrest*—so much for "innocent until proven guilty." Then, upon conviction, the assets can be auctioned off, with the proceeds going to the government under the theory that these assets have been purchased using the monies raised from illegal activities. So far, so good—crime should not pay.

As a practical matter, however, asset forfeiture has become a license for the federal government to steal—even assets purchased with *legally* earned monies. More than one inmate shared instances of the Feds seizing jewelry, expensive handbags, even cars belonging to family members which never make it onto the inventory lists—and which would disappear into thin air. In such cases, the Feds act like pirates and treat assets like plunder.

One inmate described how much of his wife's jewelry and clothes simply disappeared. A second inmate described a nighttime raid in which his young children and wife were brutally pinned to the ground by FBI agents while he was being hauled away in handcuffs and his automobiles and other valuables were being siezed.

The worst part of this inmate's story was the plea bargain he had been coerced into under threat of a crushing sentence if he went to trial. As soon as he pled, his assets were sold, and his wife and kids are now living in government-subsidized housing and using food stamps to survive.

By the way, the man, a prominent doctor, swears he was an innocent victim. In his rendition, the real criminal was an employee who over-billed private insurance companies, skimmed the money, and then falsely pointed the finger at said doctor in exchange for a green card—she even went missing as a witness before what would have been his trial, so he wound up pleading.

You can believe this doctor or not—as Red said in *The Shawshank Redemption*, "Everyone in here is innocent." But you'd be surprised to see how many top-ranking executives wind up in the slammer for the sins of their employees. Out of the forty-two guys in my dorm, at least four may fit that profile.

As for *restitution*, about 15 percent of all inmates are saddled with this. Again, in theory, it sounds like a good idea—criminals should be required to compensate their victims as a matter of both fairness and deterrence.

Yet, in the real world, overly burdensome restitution can truly be the Weimar Republic ball and chain, at least for those inmates who are poor or have only moderate earnings potential.

Once outside, even in the best of circumstances, most inmates face a hostile job market—as soon as they check that "I'm a felon" box, it's adios. And in today's world, even with a decent job, paychecks don't go far enough for many inmates to provide for themselves and their families, much less use after tax dollars to pay restitution.

The Hitlerian Treaty of Versailles problem here is that many inmates will turn to crime just to make ends meet. This is not speculation on my part.

Numerous studies of both juveniles and adults have found that the higher the reparations imposed, the higher the likelihood of recidivism. [For any nerds, check out, for example, Harris, Evans, and Beckett (2010), Piquero and Jennings (2017), or Martin, Sykes, and Shannon (2018).]

As for the retribution imposed upon the wealthier of inmates, the big beef here is how it is calculated. More than one inmate told me the retribution is *not* based on the direct impact on a victim or victims. Rather, as we have discussed, it is on the *total* value associated with whatever scam was operating.

The difference here can be in the millions—and millions enough to spur an otherwise well-off ex-con to do it all over again, too.

HUCK POST 143:
Pimps and Hoes
July 7, 2024—Day 111

Sunday with my Pixie at the Visitor Center was joyous, if for no other reason than this would be the last time we'd ever have to sit six feet apart, me facing the guard's desk, and the guard watching every inmate to make sure nobody stole a kiss, exceeded their hug quota, or passed along any contraband.

But contraband was the watchword of this day. After weeks of us talking about how risky it might be for Pixie to smuggle in an Egg McMuffin so I wouldn't starve during our visits, I was able to drag her even deeper into my pimp seduction to break the law by bringing in said McMuffin.

I have to say, that Egg McMuffin was like ambrosia in my mouth. I hadn't had a real fresh egg in four months, and it sent my body into palpitations of pure pleasure.

Okay. I'm getting a little carried away here. But it tasted a whole lot better than the junk food they mostly forgot to load the vending machines with.

The next morning at breakfast, I sat down with Johnny B. Goode, and I told him about my smuggling adventure with Pixie. He is always looking for vignettes for his *Orange is the New Black*-type knockoff comedy he's trying to sell to an agent.

Naturally, the conversation turned to how prison turns just about everyone into a criminal, prisoners and guards alike.

On the prisoner and family side, leave the vending machines empty in the Visitor Center and pretty soon, family members are smuggling in everything from Egg McMuffins to Cuban sandwiches and whole chickens.

Serve small, ladylike portions of bad food to grown men, and some get a job in the kitchen and start stealing onions and peppers and eventually milk and meat and loaves of bread. Or, you get a job in the commissary and steal there. Just to survive, mind you. I'm *not* judging.

Then there's the whole phone scam we've talked about. Restrict an inmate's minutes, and pretty soon, a guy is sporting a cheap burner phone if you're a lowly, small-time drug dealer with little means or a new iPhone if you're a Captain of Industry who got caught bilking the government or a private insurer.

Of course, the lack of a reliable source of prescription meds spawns a black market in said meds—pass the Xanax please at ten bucks a pop.

Pretty soon, it's like an episode out of *The Wire*, with platoons of scouts and watchmen to make sure nobody gets caught by a guard with something you could otherwise buy at a 7-Eleven, like a vape or a pack of cigarettes.

So, yes, the criminal mind thrives in prison, and that's why, again, they call it prison.

PIXIE POST 25:
Away We Go!
July 7, 2024—Day 111

Pixie here, and today is my last visit to the prison. I won't go next weekend because I will travel up from Palm Beach on Tuesday to pick up my Huck, and Dale will whisk us to the airport for our trip to the Republican National Convention in Milwaukee.

It's still up in the air whether my Huck will speak. President Trump has given it his thumbs up, but forces within the campaign are trying to keep my Ever Huck off the stage for reasons unfathomable to both of us.

When I arrive at the prison and stand in line, some of the inmate families know that it is winding down for me and Huck, and they say they will miss me.

I will miss them too as I realize I have had my own prison family of these visitors. Together, we would wait every weekend in a long line with each other, often in the sweltering sun and sometimes in the driving rain.

We from all over the globe wait to get in to see our loved ones, many of us with not much in common. Yet still, we chat about our loved ones and our situations.

And I still remember when I first saw my Ever Huck in his green uniform with the other inmates. It broke my heart to know that many committed crimes and took too many risks and that caused them to not be able to live with their families and loved ones for a really long time.

As I stand in line today waiting, I think about how human beings naturally form bonds, and especially out of necessity in hard situations, to cope together. It's better than alone.

I will want to forget these past four months as quickly as possible, but I will always keep these families and children in line at the Visitor Center engrained in my mind forever. That is the human condition.

And what better day to be my last than today. Not just because I will never have to go back. It's also because everyone inside the Visitor Center is in a festive mood, as Ajemon the Terrible has been rotated out of this duty in favor of a very nice and funny man named Frederick.

In this new regime, crowded today though it is, Huck and I manage to dance a bit, hold hands, kiss, hug, and sing as if there were no barbed-wire fences between us.

And when it is time to go, my Ever Huck and I say our *Love you*s, and then I skip away in the playful fashion he loves to see. Then I stop and look back, and even with the glare from the glass and sun, I see Huck clearly.

For the first time, my heart doesn't break, and I don't feel at all like crying. In just ten more days, we *both* will be out of this prison.

I get to the car now, and Dale is there. We drive midway down the parking lot where Dale and I will say our last goodbye to Huck.

There my Huck is behind the barbed-wire fence, and we blow each other kisses, and Dale honks the horn his signature three times.

Then Navarro salutes, and we salute him. And as Jackie Gleason and my sweet and funny father, Harold, used to say, "Away we go!"

HUCK POST 144:
From Guerilla Warfare to Frontal Assault
July 8, 2024—Day 112

If this were a novel, you'd probably accuse me at this point of bringing in a *deus ex machina* to wrap up the plot and story. On the other hand, sometimes truth is stranger than fiction; and the truth is that the wife of my own lawyer Stanley Woodward may turn out to be that *deus ex machina* to take my adopted prison mission to both the next level and denouement.

You could have knocked me over with a roll of prison toilet paper—probably knocked me out, that shit is so hard—when Stanley told me that his wife had seen my *Washington Times* articles blasting the Bureau of Prisons for keeping inmates in prison for longer than the law (the First Step Act and Second Chance Act) required. At a cost, mind you, of as much as $5 billion as I had estimated and a whole lot of human misery.

Stanley's wife, Kristin McGough, had seen that article and immediately thought this might be an issue for the nonprofit organization she worked for, the Washington Lawyers' Committee for Civil Rights and Urban Affairs.

Wow, under the same roof as my lawyer, another lawyer who might turn what had been my guerilla warfare on the issue into a full-scale frontal assault.

So, we had set up a call for today as a legal call in Officer Cooke's office, and over the course of the hour, I not only explained the issue to her and a colleague, Clare. I brought Elliot and Doc onto the call at the end to introduce themselves and assure Kristin she'd have full support and access to literally dozens of inmates and potential plaintiffs suing the BOP for relief.

Doc and Elliot were perfect as possibly the first two test cases, each for different reasons. On the one hand, as I have noted in earlier posts, Doc *should* have been prereleased to a halfway house months ago. But the gap between the "bid" and the "ask" was huge. By our math, Elliot's prerelease date should be in November. By BOP math, however, wrongly computed, Elliot was looking at a prerelease date more like twelve months than four.

In his case, we'd have time to exhaust all administrative remedies, and a judge couldn't use that as an excuse to deny Elliot's claim.

So, the big question was, what would be our strategy and best line or lines of attack? One option would be a case-by-case, rifle-shot approach: Win one habeas petition at a time, such as the one for Doc that Del and I drafted.

The other possibility was the mother of all class action suits—there are over sixty thousand FSA-eligible inmates in the class; and almost every single one will be released later than they should be.

I don't know which strategy Kristin will choose, or even whether her organization will take the project on—and off my shoulders—but in the best case scenario (pun intended), we'll quickly back the BOP into a corner and force them to take the two steps that would immediately solve the problem.

One: The BOP immediately releases the long-promised but long-delayed "Conditional Maximum FTC Calculation" so First Step Act earned time credits (FTC) are projected, correctly calculated, and factored into accurate forecasts of inmate prerelease and release dates.

Two: The BOP Director, now Colette Peters, orders bureaucrats down the chain to send inmates ready for prerelease immediately to home confinement *if* halfway house capacity is not available.

If this is the result of all my efforts during my four months in prison, somebody ought to give me a damn medal—or at least a pat on the back. That's because saving $5 billion in taxpayer monies and improving the lives of over sixty thousand inmates and their families is a very big deal. You have to admit, it would be pretty cool.

As the Boss says, "Let's see what happens."

[*Author's Note: As I told you earlier, I did indeed get this done.*]

HUCK POST 145:
Smooth as Silk—Nature/Nurture
July 11, 2024—Day 115

For months I've been pondering the nature/nurture theory as I listen to story after story from inmates as to how they wound up in prison.

TK should have gone to college on a football scholarship as a star tight end but had to drop out of school at thirteen to survive after his family disintegrated.

Josh should have gone to MIT or the Harvard Business School, but he's on his second bid for dealing dope after growing up poor in a broken household.

Zach reads more books than anyone in the prison, is sharp as a tack, grew up as proverbial "white trash," but would likely be a captain of industry on Wall Street if Daddy had been a corporate executive in Manhattan with a commute from Scarsdale.

And just Puerto Rican after Puerto Rican who grew up on the mean streets of San Juan with a choice between a $5 an hour job at a tourist trap or some high-risk drug running with a million dollars in Miami or Tampa or Nuevo York.

Still, Silk's story was so unexpected that it floored me. He's a light-skinned African American—I mention skin color because it's part of the plot.

In his forties, Silk's perfectly chiseled, right out of a men's fitness magazine. Impeccably groomed, smart, soft-spoken.

We had struck up a bit of a friendship, as we were two of the few "loners" in the workout regime folks in the yard.

Silk did his thing. I did mine. But a lot of the other guys worked out in groups.

Zach, for example, ran his daily "killer workout" for a whole platoon of inmates—200 burpees, 500 push-ups, 100 pull-ups—just crazy-ass stuff that was too much. Not my thing. Not Silk's.

Silk and I separately focused on fitness for the long haul, and it was interesting to talk about that. Working out to being able to work out another day—and doing some part of the routine every day.

This day, as I was doing my three-mile daily run, Silk uncharacteristically asked if he could join me for the last mile, and off we went.

In three laps, I found out that his love of school and baseball had been interrupted when he was fourteen years old. Four ebony-skinned and older kids had jumped him to rob "Whitie," as they derisively called him for his lighter brown skin. Silk had pried a knife away from one of them and sliced up a few of them up pretty good.

It was a clear case of self-defense, but they put him in juvenile hall for the next five years anyway. Just stupid, brutal, and inhumane.

So instead of playing ball and learning, reading, writing, and arithmetic, Silk spent most of his time just fighting to survive. When he got out at eighteen, they wouldn't let him join the military, he had zero job or life skills, and at some point, he succumbed to the temptation of easy money and was back in prison.

There's no moral to his story. Only sadness.

I wish Silk the best. He's still got *years* on his bid to go. But I hope that when he finally gets out, the third time will be his charm.

And put this one squarely in the "nurture" column, because this man wasn't a born criminal. He just had the bad luck of a very bad draw.

HUCK POST 146:
Bingo with the Boss
July 12, 2024—Day 116

After several weeks of wrangling to get on the stage to give my speech in Milwaukee and being told a few days ago by Susie Wiles via Sergio Gor that I did not make the cut, I decided to call the Boss directly and make the pitch.

And that's exactly what I did—a quintessential Hollywood TV pitch.

I call Donald Trump's private line from Cookie's office, POTUS answers, we have a brief, very warm exchange, and I get down to business.

> **Navarro**: Imagine a senior presidential advisor who goes to a Joe Biden prison for defending the Constitution, walks out of that prison in Miami on Wednesday morning, and then gets on the stage in Milwaukee at the convention that night and delivers a PERFECT speech on the weaponization of our justice system and why we need Donald John Trump back in the White House.
>
> **The Boss**: I love it. It's perfect. Susie [*to Susie Wiles*]. Let's get Peter on stage Wednesday night for fifteen minutes. He's got a great speech on the weaponization of our justice system.

Bingo! And so it was done. Weeks of back-and-forth B.S. with the underlings brushed aside in ninety seconds with the Boss.

It should not have been that hard to get on that RNC stage. The optics of the whole speech *are* perfect—and I shouldn't have had to even call the Boss.

But now, it's done. At least probably done. You never know in Trump Land.

I head off to the mess hall for a hot, Italian sausage dinner to celebrate. Sometimes prison ain't so bad.

[*Author's Note: The speech, which this memoir ends with, would turn out to be the most popular of the whole convention, other than those of the Boss himself and JD Vance. It just brought the house down, particularly after a surprise cameo from Pixie herself, who stole the show. No one was more surprised than me at the thunderous reception.*

A big thanks to prison counselor Jason Cooke who let me make the call. It almost didn't happen. When I decided to call the Boss, it was a last-ditch whim just after I had finished running three miles on the track and doing my weight routine after.

After the bad news from Sergio, I had resigned myself to a no-go on the speech and me being a no-show at the convention despite having a private jet waiting to take me. If I wasn't going on stage, I wouldn't be going. It would just be too hollow and a stupid missed opportunity, not for me, but for the campaign.

So I thought Why *not give it one last shot?*

Cookie was in his office and the Boss answered the phone. Lady Luck was on my side that day.

It would—and wouldn't—be on the Boss's side the very next day, the worst day of my incarceration, as this same man I just had a beautiful conversation with would both be shot (the bad luck) and dodge the bullet of death (the good luck).]

HUCK POST 147:
Shots Fired
July 13, 2024—Day 117

I'm not supposed to be here tonight.
—Donald Trump, RNC Convention, 2024

Right now, at 8:40 p.m., I want out of this Democrat gulag.

A little more than twenty-four hours ago, I had a perfect call with a man who wants nothing more than the best for Americans—a funny and warm and incredibly smart and caring man.

And an assassin's bullet missed taking him from us and this world by mere millimeters.

And all I can do is helplessly watch this spectacle on TV behind bars and in a lockdown triggered by that very shooting.

Let's be clear here. They don't just want Donald Trump and his advisors like me in prison. They—the radical left whipped up into a frenzy for more than eight years now by the CNNs, MSNBCs, and *New York Times* of this world—they want to kill Donald Trump and a whole lot of the rest of us. And they almost got Donald John Trump tonight.

It's time for some Old Testament justice.

No more free passes for anarchists like Antifa and BLM.

No more masks on protesters shouting river to the sea.

No more no bail for serial offenders.

No more illegal immigrants flooding across our borders, many with mal intent.

No more bullshit propaganda from the *Morning Joe*s and *Rachel Maddow*s and *Joy Reid*s and Stephen Colberts and Bill Mahers and Jon Stewarts and SNLs and Whoopi Goldbergs of this woke legacy media world, with their violent, hate-filled rhetoric.

No more sustained assaults on Trump and his supporters from rags like the *New York Times* and *Washington Post* without accountability.

No more America-hate and Trump-hate from the Talibs and Omars of this world without exposure to charges of treason.

No more lies without prosecution from intelligence community spooks like John Brennan, James Clapper, Michael Hayden, and Leon Panetta.

The assassin shot the gun. These haters loaded it.

I've had it with these jackals on the Left. They took my freedom. They tried to kill Trump.

Enough. I'm ready to get the puck out of here and go do the work of campaigning. Trump24 for Trump47.

And I haven't even mentioned the fact that the Secret Service allowed my old Boss to rise up and pump his "fight, fight, fight" fist at the crowd not once but *twice*—once on stage and once by the limo.

Sure, it was *great* TV and yielded iconic images both for the 2024 campaign and the history books. *But* if the shooter hadn't been killed—the Secret Service agents guarding the Boss didn't know that—or if there had been a second flanking position shooter, the target the Boss presented was a can't-miss proposition, and he'd be dead.

So, what am I saying? Consider here:

1. The FBI and intelligence communists see Donald Trump as a dangerous threat to their agencies who, if elected, will investigate them for everything from their collusion in the Russian Hoax to the "it's a Russian disinformation campaign" to cover up the Hunter Biden laptop scandal.
2. First rule: Clear and occupy *any* rooftops with the access to a target. Rule broken!
3. Second rule: Shut an event down if you receive information about a possible shooter. Rule broken!!
4. Third rule: Secure the target immediately. Rule broken!!!

I feared the Butler, Pennsylvania, venue from my first look at it on television—a band box doubling as a shooting gallery.

My first thought after the shots were fired was that the shooter was probably in the stand of tall trees overlooking the stage. Too damn dangerous for the Boss to be so damn close to a tall stand of trees. Who does that?

The Boss was lucky. That was a one-in-a-billion miss—a headshot at a short distance that drew blood in the most minimally invasive way.

One millimeter to the right or left, and Donald Trump would be in the ground.

For me, the rallies—and I have been to plenty—have always been like riding a motorcycle. The question of a possible crash—or in this case, an attempted political assassination—is only a matter of *when* not *if.*

We have to manage the risk better. And the FBI and Secret Service simply can't be trusted.

The lines getting into the RNC Convention which I will head to Wednesday morning suddenly got longer.

Last take: The guys in my prison who get caught with contraband like a cell phone or vape machine invariably get caught because they get too comfortable. Next thing they know, SIS is on and up their ass, they're on their way to the Special Housing Unit (SHU), and they're about to get docked for phone, commissary, and visitor privileges.

We got too comfortable running the rallies, and we let our guard down. And the guards themselves were either asleep at the wheel or part of the whole damn plot.

Yes, it's time to release all the JFK files to the public, and I hope the Boss will do that if and when he gets the opportunity.

HUCK POST 148:
No Conspiracies, No Coincidences
July 14, 2024—Day 118

There are no conspiracies, but there are no coincidences.
—Steve Bannon

The morning after the shot heard round the world, I'm still stuck in prison. I'm still thinking about what, and what might have, happened. And I'm having flashbacks of the first dark days of the pandemic in April of 2020.

I'm on Maria Bartiromo's Sunday morning Fox News show, and I conjure up Occam's Razor—the simplest explanation of something is usually the right explanation.

I use that scientific axiom to say on national TV as a senior White House official that the COVID virus almost certainly was genetically engineered and came from the Wuhan Institute of Virology.

Of course, I sustain withering attacks across the media.

Of course, years later, I am proven right. Not only was the virus from the Wuhan lab, none other than Tony Fauci enabled that Chinese bioweapons lab to design the virus using gain-of-function research tools.

I was right not because I'm some genius, but simply because it was so damn obvious.

A deadly virus presenting as a possible bioweapon pops up within a few kilometers of a Chinese bioweapons lab. Can't be from the lab. Must be from a wet market. Right? Wrong!

Comes now an assassination attempt by a lone gunman who somehow moves freely into a kill zone less than two hundred yards from the Trump stage.

The gunman is sighted by several observers who frantically warn the Secret Service agents who do nothing.

The counter-sniper who shoots the rooftop gunman dead hesitates long enough after he sees and sights the gunman to allow enough time for that first kill shot—always the most accurate before recoil and adrenaline make the next shots less precise.

By Occam's Razor, either (1) this was a hit the Secret Service/FBI tacitly condoned through lax security and late actions OR (2) the FBI and Secret Service are totally incompetent.

As they say at the Harvard Business School, "You decide."

HUCK POST 149:
Happy Prison Birthday!
July 15, 2024—Day 119

If you are of the school who believes there are no coincidences, you may find it at least curious that when the BOP scheduled my March 19 entry into their prison system in Miami, they made sure, with a four-month sentence and an exit date of July 17, that I would spend my July 15 seventy-fifth birthday *inside* prison.

These prison officials also likely knew that I might miss my chance to appear at the Republican National Convention which would begin on July 15 and end on July 18.

To be honest, I didn't really mind having to spend my birthday in prison—I'm not a sentimental guy.

But it did piss me off that my late exit would indeed make it much more difficult to get to the RNC Convention not just to possibly speak but to also launch my latest book, *The New MAGA Deal*.

So, for months, I had submitted multiple requests for an early release of no more than a few days—or even a furlough where I could come back and finish out the sentence after the Convention.

It speaks volumes to both the depravity and politics of how those requests were repeatedly rejected by my Judge Amit Mehta and separately by the BOP bureaucracy—either could have granted me relief.

I gave my woke sadist judge, Amit Mehta, every possible reason to give me a two-day early release. At the top of the list of said reasons was that I should have already been out of prison and to a halfway house some forty days ago based on the sentence reductions *mandated* by both the First Step Act and Second Chance—mandates which the BOP callously ignored.

Then there was the birthday factor—you only hit seventy-five once, and most folks don't make it that far. By the BOP standards for "compassionate release," it should have been a no-brainer.

Then there was the convention itself. The honor of speaking on the stage of a presidential election convention that only happens once every four years falls to a small handful of people. Denying me that honor—and the ability to speak to the entire nation—was just cruel and unusual punishment.

Here's what I want to say to Amit Mehta's children: your daddy is a callous scumbag who used me as a political steppingstone to what he hopes will be his next step up the judicial ladder to the Supreme Court.

Once you hit eighteen kids, you should disown the jackal quicker than Angelina's kids disowned Brad.

As to why I pick on the kids, it's something that I would *never* have done before prison. But I'm not going to be the "bigger man" here.

When Mehta went after me, he also went after my family and my Sweet Pixie.

So, fair in this case is foul. Mehta's family, along with the rest of America, needs to know what a partisan, woke, weaponized prick Amit Mehta is.

You think that's beyond harsh? Just remember it was Democrat elites with names like Mehta and Garland and Smith and Bragg and Willis and Millett and Pillard and Pelosi and Schiff and Raskin and Thompson who declared lawfare war on folks like me and Bannon and Jeff Clark and John Easton and Mark Meadows and Rudy Giuliani and of course the Boss.

They put me and Steve in prison. They took the bar cards of Jeff and John. They drained Meadows dry and bankrupted Rudy. And they almost got the Boss killed—*twice*.

Every one of these woke partisan lawfare jackals deserves to be outed both to their families and the world. And they all belong in prison. Just sayin'.

And Mehta. That particular petite little pompous jackal kept me in prison on my seventy-fifth birthday, two days shy of my release.

Mehta did it because he could, and he did it even after he fully acknowledged I firmly believed I was doing my duty in defending executive privilege and the constitutional separation of powers—*not* committing any crime.

So, Mehta kids: go ask your Daddy first why he put me in prison in the first place when he should have released me pending an appeal he knows I have a very good chance of winning.

Then, kids, ask your Daddy why he wouldn't let me out two days early so I could first celebrate my seventy-fifthth birthday and then go to the RNC to celebrate democracy on national TV.

Yea, I'm just a little pissed sitting here. Can you tell?

At least I got that off my chest.

And the birthday here behind bars and razor wire was fine.

Pixie wrote me a sweet letter and we talked on the phone, morning, noon, and dusk.

Dinner was even pretty good.

And I'm out at midnight tomorrow.

Praise the Lord.

HUCK POST 150:
My Birthday Present—The Speech Is Really On
July 15, 2024—Night 119

> *If WE don't control OUR government, THEIR government*
> *will control US.*
> —RNC Speech Draft

The good news is that it looks like the speech is on. Sergio sent me an "edited" draft of what I sent them, cut down for time. Of course, the edit butchered much of the language and beautiful cadences I had built into the speech. But the speech at least is on!

[Author's Note: Once I got to the convention, by luck, the guy running the speech copy was my old compatriot Cliff Sims from the 2016 campaign and first Trump term. So I was able to restore the speech to its original version, with a few cuts for time.]

PIXIE POST 26:
Pixie Says Happy Birthday to Huck on His Substack

July 15, 2024—Day 119

[*Huck's Note: My sweetheart surprised me in prison on my birthday with this beautiful note on my Substack at www.peternavarro.substack.com. My kind of girl.*]

Before I continue with my dedication note, I would like to send my heartfelt condolences to the family whose loved one was taken from them during President Trump's recent rally. I wish them sometime soon to find peace and strength. I am so sorry for those injured as well, and that a hero, Donald J. Trump, had to go through this, when he only wants to save America and do good.

Today, July 15, is Peter's birthday. On this special day, I want to dedicate it not only to my dearest fiancé, Peter, but as he would do and want—to dedicate this day to all of you, to celebrate a birthday, but mostly to celebrate all of you—to thank you for your support for him during these months while he has been in prison. And importantly, a huge dedication and celebration for all those who managed his messaging and carried on his mission during his time behind bars. I celebrate all of you today. You know who you are.

I refuse, honestly, to be sad on this day; that injustice has taken me away from Peter and I cannot celebrate his special birthday with him and for him. As he rightfully says, if we do put our heads down, if I shed more tears on this day, then they win. So, let's all find the joy in this day to make us even more positive and give us strength on this journey towards more justice in our most beautiful country we are so proud of. Please, on Peter's and my behalf, go dance with your loved ones, go sing, go laugh, go find joy for me and him today. Promise this.

I have suffered the heartache of my fiancé being away for so long. Peter, throughout our three-year relationship, has always taken care of me in many ways, and he didn't stop while in prison. He not only called me three times a day and sends me love notes all the time, but he wanted to take care of all of you and carry the burden of being in prison to make all of our lives better, more free, and more joyful.

He worked for our country every day he was in prison and will continue to, because that is Peter. He is relentless in his love for me, for you, and for our country. Today we celebrate all of you and this warrior still behind barbed-wire fencing. I thank you all because you have helped me with your support for him so much and thus, my heartache has been, for the four months, just a little less painful.

Thank you, my dear Peter, for your relentless fight and the inspiration you bring inside prison and out.

Happy Birthday, Dr. Navarro. Love you I do.

Bonnie

HUCK POST 151:
She Got Tired of Waiting
July 16, 2024—Day 120

James Medard (06771-104) - James should have been released to RRC/
HC. Yet, no paperwork has been put in to receive a date to go to a
RRC/HC. [Halfway house or home confinement]
—Team Navarro Inmate Notes

Tomorrow, it's adios; and I'm saying my goodbyes today to a lot of folks, and a lot more are saying goodbyes to me. They all want assurances that I won't forget about them and that I'll continue to press the case forward.

I tell each and every one of them, "Of course I will"—and I damn well will.

At noon, I see James Medard taking a break from his domino game at the icemaker. James is a Haitian in for one variation or another on the fraud-type beefs that for some reason the Haitians seem to have a market corner on, at least here in the Miami prison.

James has been one of my case studies as I worked with Elliot and Doc and Josh analyzing the records of scores of inmates, and James is one of the worst examples I found of an inmate being detained in prison *long* past his expiration date.

When I see James, I offer him my condolences. I had heard his mother had died—and of course, the warden wouldn't grant a temporary leave for James to go to the funeral.

James just says to me, "She got tired of waiting."

I can think of no better example of the toll that prison can take on one's family.

James should have been home long ago. He should have been able to see and comfort his mother. His Mom might even have been alive today if he had had that freedom.

She did get tired of waiting. But that's why they call it prison.

HUCK POST 152:
I Unwittingly Outsmart a Psychopath
July 16, 2024—Day 120

How do you like them apples?
—Matt Damon, *Good Will Hunting*

For weeks, my fellow inmates had dreaded the arrival of the new Unit Manager at the prison. For far too many of these inmates, there was nothing new about Oscar Lua at all.

Lua had previously served as a case manager, and he was notorious for his aggression and abusive behavior with the inmates. Against all rules, he regularly put hands on inmates with rough, unannounced, legs-spread searches.

As a case manager, Lua eagerly and regularly did everything he could to delay the exit of inmates—the exact opposite of his job description. And he was also constantly harassing inmates.

In fact, one of the jailhouse lawyer inmates had filed a lawsuit against Lua for such abuse with what were reportedly more than thirty affidavits from inmates documenting the abuse. Of course, the BOP's countermeasure was to quickly transfer said inmate to Kentucky after an extended dose of diesel therapy and simply move Lua over to the low-security side of the prison.

Now, Lua was back; and his first act was to lock the small utility room in our dorm where some folks prayed, others like me liked to do some stretching or sit-ups, and still others played chess.

It was a signature prick Lua move, but up until today, Lua had left me otherwise alone.

I made the mistake of leaving my locker half open when he made a pass through the dorm, and when he saw I had some fresh apples the guys had given me from the mess hall—that's legal—Lua pounced on those apples like a grizzly bear on a picnic basket.

Lua threw all six of my precious apples—the only fresh thing in my diet—in the trash. And then to make sure nobody dumpster-dived, Lua even ordered the trash removed.

I thought the whole thing was pretty funny when Del reported the news to me—he had watched it firsthand in his next door bunk. It was particularly funny because all I really needed was just one more apple for my last breakfast in prison the next morning.

And while I did have the half dozen apples Lua grabbed on a shelf on the right side of my locker, he *missed* the seventh apple I had tucked back on a shelf on the left side.

In this way, I unwittingly outsmarted a psychopath. That apple would taste even sweeter tomorrow morning.

BTW, Lua is on my checklist of BOP abuses to air in the press. Sadists like Lua should not be in control of other human beings.

But that's why they call it prison.

[*Author's Note: Press, please do your frigging job now. Investigate the guy!*]

HUCK POST 153:
Exit Strategy
July 16, 2024—Day 120

Pride goeth before destruction, and a haughty spirit before a fall.
—Proverbs 16:18

I'm not generally a prideful man eager for a compliment or pat on the back. I'm more of an introvert who, increasingly, at my age, doesn't care a whit about what people say or think of me.

Part of that is taking so many slings and arrows in the political arena. Remember here—if you've seen those who attack in the press:

- I'm a "crackpot economist" for thinking tariffs are an appropriate defensive response to Communist Chinese aggression.
- I'm an "extremist" because I think manufacturing on home soil is good for America.
- I'm a "convicted criminal" because I stood up for the Constitution.

They can twist it any way they want, but I know who I am.

After 120 days in a weaponized Democrat prison, I now know even better who I am.

I like what I have seen.

I wasn't sure how this prison thing would go at the age of seventy-four, set in my ways, decades from any environment where I had to regularly interact with scores of people and, yes, there's that pesky loss-of-freedom thing.

But today, I'm pleased, if not prideful, with how I quickly adapted and wound up turning a big bag of lemons into some lemonade.

You have to remember here that as a young man, I joined the Peace Corps for a reason. And I have spent all of my professional life in service to others, first as a professor at the University of California and then in White House service to this country.

So. I am afflicted with the "do gooder" impulse.

And that's what I tried to do here in prison—some good, not just for my fellow inmates but for the broader prison system, which needs as much help as it can get. Here, I can safely say this—and it will please Pixie to no end:

Prison didn't change me. I changed prison.

Pixie will be happy about this because she told me outright going in that she didn't want me to come out of prison playing that old predictable "I'm a changed man" prison song like you hear from real criminals.

That list includes everyone from Chuck Colson, Robert Downey Jr., and Martha Stewart to Oscar Wilde, Nelson Algren, and the despicable Michael Dirty Deeds Cohen.

The big "good" I did—and it's still a long way from the finish line—was to identify a $5 billion problem inflicting untold misery on tens of thousands of inmates and their families.

You've read about it enough in these pages, but it boils down to a Bureau of Prisons grossly violating both the 2018 First Step Act and the 2008 Second Chance. The net result is the systematic delay of the release of inmates back into society at great financial and human costs.

Fortunately, it is an easy fix. All the BOP has to do is introduce its revised "Maximum Conditional FTC Calculation," start counting inmate time credits as they should be, and then, if they don't have adequate halfway house capacity to prerelease a prisoner to, that inmate *must* be sent straight to an electronically monitored home confinement. Problem solved.

To push the BOP to do this, I've left behind a solid team of inmates who are pushing complaints through the system. This will set up the possibility of a class action suit with a potential class of tens of thousands of FSA eligible inmates.

To assist, I've recruited a main nonprofit law firm, and, as I write this, I hope they will take the project on.

Of course, when I get out, I intend to take this egregious public policy failure straight to Capitol Hill where the issue should get very wide bipartisan support.

I think I can get the result we need in less than a year. As the Boss says, "We'll see what happens."

As for the smaller do-gooder stuff, my most fun achievement was to get the White Whale of a brand new coffee machine fixed after it had sat without electricity for more than a year.

My most humane acts were to get one inmate an emergency operation, possibly saving his life, and another inmate some kidney work that was long overdue—and possibly saving his life, too.

In this small-stuff category, I also got nets on all of the basketball court baskets, although I confess here I benefitted as much as the rest of the inmates.

There were other things as well. Acting as a mediator several times to avoid ugly confrontations. Free legal advice which actually may make a difference in a few appeals.

Other advice to "newbies," like if you are stupid enough to get a contraband cell phone that could land you in the SHU, don't be even stupider by walking around the track talking on it where both inmates and guards can see you.

The help went very much in the other direction as well. Extra food and clothing—particularly running shoes—came my way not because I was somewhat of a celebrity but because inmates, at least at this facility, have a strong culture of helping others.

Of the roughly two hundred inmates at the facility, I got to know over 90 percent of them pretty well; and I only had trouble with one of them—the consensus asshole in the prison who had trouble with everyone.

At the end of the day, I want to reiterate that I won't say prison "made me better," because it didn't, and my fiancée would punch me if I said such stupid shit.

But I do indeed believe I made the prison better. And if I am ultimately successful in being a catalyst for solving the BOP problem I've shone a bright spotlight on, it'll be a public policy home run and *almost* worth going to prison.

So tonight, after the count at 10:30 p.m., if all goes well, they'll come get me, take me over to processing, and by 12:01 a.m., I'll be back in the arms of my Pixie heading over to the Trump Doral (courtesy of Eric) for a quick night's sleep and then an early morning flight to Milwaukee for the Republican National Convention.

As Voltaire once said in a difficult context: "Once it's an experience. Twice it's perversion."

So, I hope I don't "recidivate," because I sure do not want any more of prison.

But if it ever comes down again to standing up for principles and going to prison versus groveling on my knees before the woke Democrat elite gods, prison will see me again.

Navarro. Out.

HUCK POST 154:
I Went to Prison So You Won't Have To
July 17, 2024—Day 121

There's no shortage of loyalty to former President Donald Trump on display at this week's Republican National Convention. But perhaps none demonstrated it more fervently or dramatically than Peter Navarro, who arrived on the convention hall stage Wednesday evening just hours after finishing a four-month prison sentence for contempt of Congress. Navarro was greeted with a thunderous applause and a standing ovation—the longest of any speaker so far since the convention began on Monday.

"Yes, this morning I did walk out of a federal prison in Miami," he said. "Joe Biden and his Department of In-Justice put me there."

His remarks were met with chants of "Fight, fight, fight!" from the audience. . . .

"They did not break me," he added. "And they will never break Donald Trump."

—Time Magazine

In the end, the warden and Verdejo wanted to get me out of prison as quickly as I wanted out on my release day. By scheduling that release a minute after midnight instead of at 10 a.m. that morning as per custom, they avoided a press conference and circus in the morning—and all the negative attention that might have drawn.

For me, I had no intention of speaking to the press until after my speech that night. So, get me the Hades out of here, thank you very much.

My Sweet Pixie was waiting for me for the outtake with Dale, the driver who had so kindly taken care of her during her many trips to visit me.

It was a surreal joy to have her back in my arms as we floated in the SUV over to the Doral for a quick night of sleep before a 9 a.m, jet departure for Milwaukee and the RNC.

I had no idea what to expect when I walked on that stage that night. I did know that I wanted my Sweet Pixie to take the stage with me.

And she did, towards the end of the speech.

> *I'm going to leave you with the last three words my beautiful fiancée*
> *said when I left that morning for prison.*
> *They weren't "I love you." That was a given.*
> *She simply said, "We got this. We got this."*
> [cheers, applause, crowd starts chanting, "We got this! We got this!"]
> *Bring my girl out now.*
> *That's what these lawfare jackals don't understand.*
> *When they put people like me in prison and fire figurative and now*
> *literal bullets at Donald Trump and us, they also assault our families.*
> [cheers for the fiancée as she comes onstage]

Then, we kissed and we danced in a beautiful display of love and affection that came to be known in Trump lore as "the kiss" and "the twirl."

The greeting from the crowd was indeed thunderous for me—and even more thunderous for Sweet Pixie. In my seventy-five years on the planet, I have never felt such warmth and support.

At the beginning of the speech—you can read the transcript below—I improvised with a little quip about getting a MAGA prison tat.

Then I got right into it on the teleprompter—which I didn't really need, since my words were straight from my soul.

At the end of the speech, as I called my Sweet Pixie on stage decked out in her MAGA hat for the kiss and the twirl, I finally felt what that mythical Cloud Nine must be like.

The next morning, we flew back home to Florida and got down to the joy of love and the business of helping the Boss get elected.

And of course, on November 5, Donald John Trump became our 47th president.

As the Lee Greenwood song says, "God bless the USA."

Peter Navarro
Speech Before the Republican National Convention
Milwaukee, Wisconsin, July 17, 2024
Ladies and Gentlemen, please welcome former Director of the Office of
Trade and Manufacturing Policy to the stage, Peter Navarro.

[*Walks on stage to thunderous applause. Navarro raises fist. Crowd chants "fight, fight, fight."*]

This is a beautiful thing.

I think you folks just wanna know if you can see my MAGA tattoo I got there [in prison]. [*Laughter*]

This morning, I did walk out of a federal prison—a federal prison in Miami.

Joe Biden and his Department of INjustice put me there.

But tonight I'm here with you in this beautiful city of Milwaukee, and I've got a very simple message for you.

If they can come for me. If they can come for Donald Trump. Be careful, they will come for you.

If we don't control our government, their government will control us.

If we don't control all three branches of our government—legislative, executive, and judicial—their government will put some of us like me and Steve Bannon in prison and control the rest of us. [*boos*]

Here's how it went. Here's how I got in prison.

The legislative branch [Congress] came for me first.

Your favorite Democrat, Nancy Pelosi, [*boos*] created your favorite committee, the sham January 6 committee, which demanded that I violate executive privilege.

What did I do? I refused. [*cheers*]

The January 6 Committee demanded that I betray Donald J. Trump to save my own skin. I refused. [*cheers*]

Here's the thing about the Constitution.

They demanded that I break the law because they have no respect for it. I refused.

And a Democrat majority in the house then voted to hold me in contempt. What happened next?

The next jackboot to drop was the executive branch. Another one of your favorite Democrats, the Democrat Attorney General Merrick Garland [*boos*]—there's a winner—he and Jack Smith indicted and prosecuted me for criminal contempt of congress. [*boos*]

Here's what's weird about it. [Prosecuting] is something the Democratic prosecutors refused to do against one of their own, including two guys with blood on their hands, [former Attorney General] Eric Holder and [DHS Secretary] Alejandro Mayorkas, the great border czar. [*boos*]

Both Holder and Mayorkas actually got people killed.

For decades, the Department of Justice policy stated—hear me out on this—if Congress slaps a subpoena on a senior white house advisor like me, the advisor's duty is to politely tell them to go pound sand. [*cheers*] That's exactly what I did. [*cheers*]

So far we have two branches, legislative and executive. The judicial branch delivered the final blow.

Just as—here's another favorite of yours—just as Democrat judge Juan Marchan [*boos*]—You know this guy?—[*boos*] did to Donald John Trump in his Manhattan kangaroo court, another Democrat judge, a guy named Amit Mehta—keep your eye on this guy, an Obama appointee—he stripped me of every possible defense.

And then what? Just like in Manhattan with Donald Trump, they threw me to the wolves of an anti-Trump jury in where? The DC Swamp.

They convicted me. They jailed me.

Guess what? They did not break me. [*cheers, chants of "fight, fight, fight"*]

And they will never break Donald Trump. They will never break Donald Trump. [*cheers*]

That is the most important thing I'm going to tell you. You are maybe thinking this cannot happen to you.

Make no mistake. They are already coming for you. Joe and Kamala.

They threw out the blue carpet across the Rio Grande and opened our borders to what? Murderers and rapists.

When Donald Trump said it in 2016. When Donald Trump said murderers and rapists, they said he's a racist.

Guess what. We read the papers. It's murderers and rapists!

Murderers and rapists. Drug cartels. Human traffickers.

Terrorists. Chinese spies. And a whole army of illiterate illegal aliens stealing the jobs of black, brown, and blue collar Americans.

They [the Democrats] have put them right on your front doorstep.

Here's another thing Joe Biden did. And you gotta love this.

The Green New Scam. [*boos*]

We are in the heart here of Milwaukee. Around all this, this is where the auto industry is.

That Green New Scam is destroying our auto industry and leaving us at the mercy of the battery factories in Shanghai and slave labor in the Congo.

Biden inflation. You're going to hear a lot of this because it's so frigging true.

Biden inflation is coming after what is left of your savings and eating your wages.

Here's the thing. I'm sitting in prison thinking about this. It just eats at me.

The Democrats come for your kids. They are indoctrinating them with poisonous attitudes on race and gender.

And here's the thing. When politics fails, the investigations and prosecutions begin.

They did it to me. They're going to do it to Donald Trump. But hear me out.

They've also done it to Catholics, pro-life activists and parents who are just standing up for the kids at school board meetings. [*boos*]

It's a tale of two Americas. And you know it wasn't this way when Donald Trump was president.

I remember the days I was there in the White House. In Trump's America, you were safe and our borders were secure.

In Trump's America, you were more prosperous and you didn't have to choose what? Between food on the table, medicine in the cabinet, and a roof over your head. [*cheers, applause*]

And in Trump's America, you didn't have to worry about being locked up for disagreeing with the government. [*cheers, applause*]

I went to prison so you don't have to! [*cheers, applause, audience stands*]

I am your wake-up call. [*cheers*]

This is where I'm going to have fun now.

I'm going to leave you with the last three words my beautiful fiancée said when I left that morning for prison.

They weren't "I love you." That was a given.

She simply said, "We got this. We got this." [*cheers, applause, crowd starts chanting "We got this! We got this!"*]

Bring my girl out now.

That's what these lawfare jackals don't understand.

When they put people like me in prison and fire figurative and now literal bullets at Donald Trump and us, they also assault our families. [*cheers for the fiancée as she comes onstage*]

On Election Day, America will hold these lawfare jackals accountable. [*cheers*]

And here's the sweetest thing that will come off my lips: "Vote Trump-Vance 24 for Trump 47." [*cheers*]

I'm Peter Navarro. I went to prison so you won't have to. This is my beautiful girl. She did the time with me. That's what these frigging Democrats don't understand. They do this to our families.

[*Navarro kisses his fiancée to cheers*]

She's my girl.

I love you. Let's win!

Do not let up! Do not let up!

Pedal to the metal to November!!

[*Huck and Pixie leave the stage with a dance twirl and cheers*]

PIXIE POST 27:
Epilogue

Pixie here, and after the RNC soiree, Huck and I hit the campaign trail on the Trump Bus and Trump Force One. In a whirlwind, we helped barnstorm Pennsylvania, Pennsylvania, and Pennsylvania—with a little Georgia, North Carolina, and Michigan in between.

The last day of the campaign was a peach: we were on Trump Force One and sat in the audience watching the Boss at 3 a.m. in Grand Rapids leaving it all on the table.

It was a beautiful time for us. It was a beautiful time for MAGA. Donald Trump won the election in a landslide.

Huck returned to the White House on Inauguration Day in January of 2025 as the Senior Counselor for Trade and Manufacturing.

Huck's lawyer Stanley Woodward also came to serve, first in the White House and then as the #3 lawyer at the Department of Justice.

Huck's prosecutors were demoted to processing misdemeanors—karma's a bitch. Merrick Garland and Liz Cheney are in hiding. Joe Biden isn't sure where he is. Steve Bannon is a free man.

The Department of Justice is now supporting Huck's appeal of his conviction—we can't get our time back from the jailing, but Huck wants to make sure that, as he says it, "good law is settled" that will protect the constitutional separation of powers and the doctrine of executive privilege.

It will likely be up to the Supreme Court to settle that law. Huck often wonders aloud if they will have the courage to do what assuredly should be done. Otherwise, it will be open season on anyone who dares serve in any White House.

In April of 2025, Huck and I attended the swearing in of the new Bureau of Prisons Director—the old one who treated Huck so badly had been fired right after Trump took office.

The new guy is already fully enforcing the First Step Act, and Huck even helped the BOP get their calculator updated by the DOGE team so that it accurately projects release times for inmates. Huck promised himself he would make this happen, and in Trump Land, promises made are promises kept.

All in all, it has been a great way for us to close the book on what was one of the most difficult periods of our lives.

We are blessed by the support we have gotten and wish all of you well who have been so kind to us. We will never take our freedom for granted again. Huck and Pixie, out!

Check out Peter's Substack for the latest: http://peternavarro.substack.com.